ZULU
BEADWORK

Detail from a beaded panel worn by a married
woman living in the Valley of a Thousand Hills,
near Durban. Early to mid 1970s.

First published in South Africa in 2014
by Print Matters
an imprint of Publishing Print Matters (Pty) Ltd
6 Opal Way, San Michel, Noordhoek 7979
Western Cape, South Africa

www.printmatters.co.za
info@printmatters.co.za

ISBN: 978-0-9870293-0-0

Editorial Panel: Elisabeth Anderson, Luke Arnold, Robin Stuart-Clark
Series Design: Robin Stuart-Clark

Key to photographers:
VG – Vivienne Garside
MH – Mike Hall
DH – Debbie Heustice
HAC – Hillcrest AIDS Centre
BH – Bruce Hopwood
MF – Mike McFaydean
AN – Amica Newman
RO – Robin Opperman
EP – Elizabeth Perrill
MP-W – Mark Preston-Whyte
RP-W – Robert Preston-Whyte
KW – Kate Wells

Formatting: The Design Drawer, Johannesburg
Printing: Creda, Cape Town

Right: A dancing cap for a smart young buck, *circa* 1950.
Note the peak and streamers hanging down from the back
of the cap. (The Campbell Collections)

PUBLISHER'S NOTE
Whilst every effort has been made to trace and acknowledge copyright holders of images featured in *Zulu Beadwork*,
regrettably some have proved impossible to trace. The publisher welcomes any information regarding these sources
and will redress any omissions in the event of a second edition.

Some of the images reproduced in *Zulu Beadwork* were scanned from photographic prints or transparencies
and despite their quality were essential to the text.

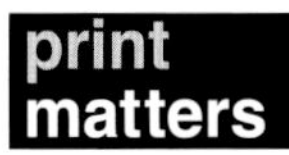

ZULU BEADWORK

Eleanor Preston-Whyte

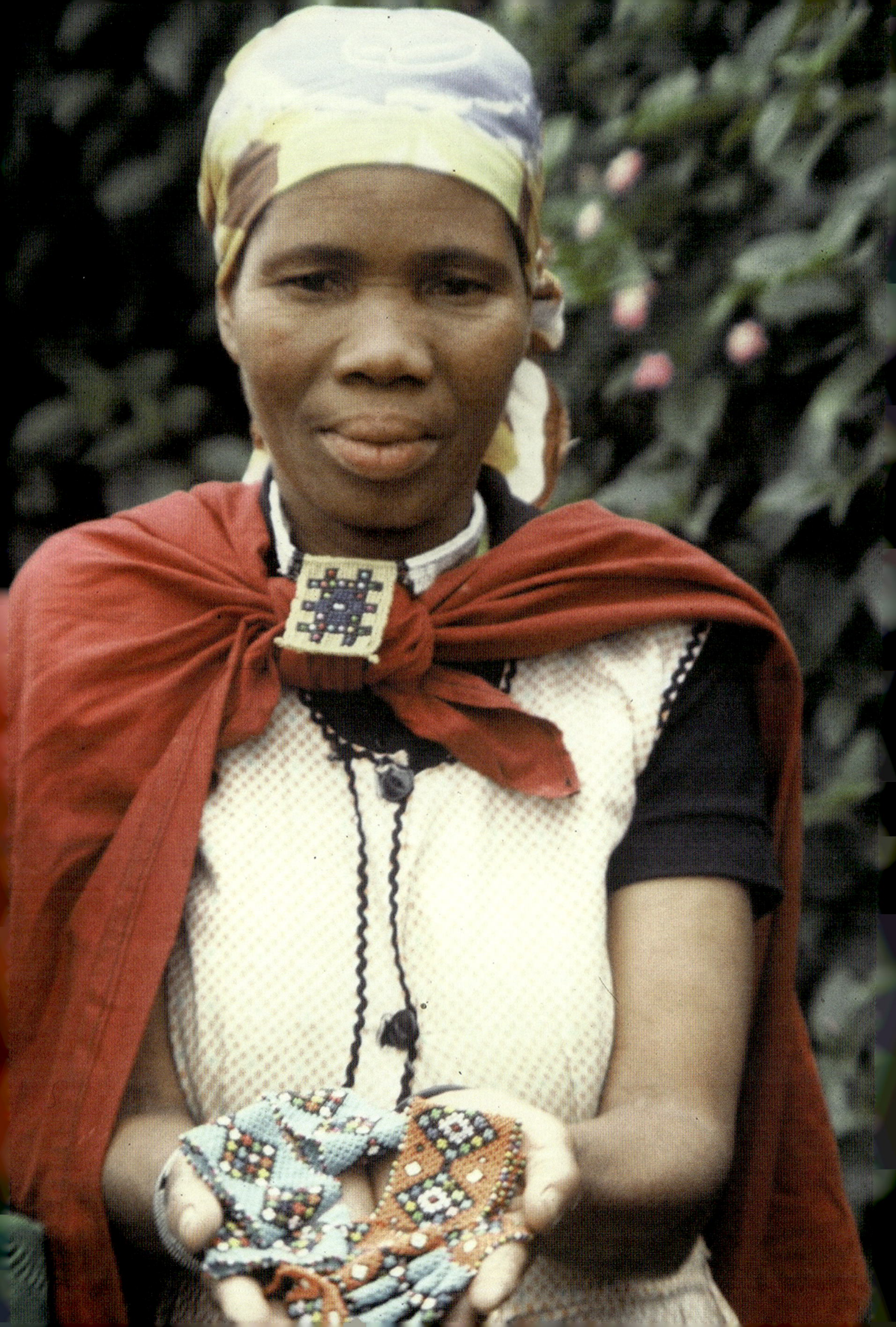

acknowledgements

Love letters in profusion: a handful of beaded love letters catering to the growing external demand for portable and cheap Zulu curios in the 1960s.

MY HEARTFELT THANKS are due to the many people who assisted in both the research for, and subsequently, in the writing of this book. These include, first and foremost, the beadmakers who welcomed me to their homes and answered my endless questions with smiling goodwill. In similar vein, I thank the traders and middlewomen, project leaders and senior government officials who made valuable suggestions related to the planning of my work both during the initial research undertaken in the 1960s and 70s and during the early years of the new millennium when I was writing this book. I wish that I could mention them all by name but they will know who they are and I trust that they will remember our discussions with something of the pleasure that I experienced myself.

A number of people deserve special mention, both in terms of the contribution they made to my understanding of the challenges facing both craftspeople and the leaders of the craft development projects I encountered, both during my fieldwork in KwaZulu-Natal in the 1960s and 70s, and more recently, as I was planning this book. The first is Debbie Heustice, the director of info4africa, and the second is Vivienne Garside, who is the curator of the Vukani Cultural Museum in Eshowe. I have called upon them constantly, and even mercilessly, as my thinking has developed and led to new and more complex questions. Both have also either taken or procured pictures of many of the most important and beautiful images that grace the book. My thanks are also due to Yovonne Williamson and Emily Krige of the Killie Campbell Africana Library and Museum in Durban, both of whom assisted and advised me in the finding and reproduction of material from the Campbell Collections which immeasurably enhanced the impact of this book.

I am indebted to a number of people who were responsible for many of the beautiful photographs which grace the pages of this book. Among those are Robert and Mark Preston-Whyte, Debbie Heustice, Taryn Millar, Kate Wells, Vivienne Garside and Bruce Hopwood.

Sadly two of the people with whom I shared many adventures in the early days of the research, are no longer with us. They are photographer, Jean Morris, and Jo Thorpe, who was the director of the Durban African Art Centre. I have greatly missed their sage advice in the writing of this book and I salute them not only for their insight which was well before its time, but from which I was fortunate to benefit.

Finally, but by no means least, my thanks are due to Ronald Miller for his support and assistance throughout the writing and compilation of this book and to Robin Stuart-Clark for inviting me to write the book and for his patience and guiding hand throughout the process of its production.

Eleanor Preston-Whyte
July 2014
Johannesburg

contents

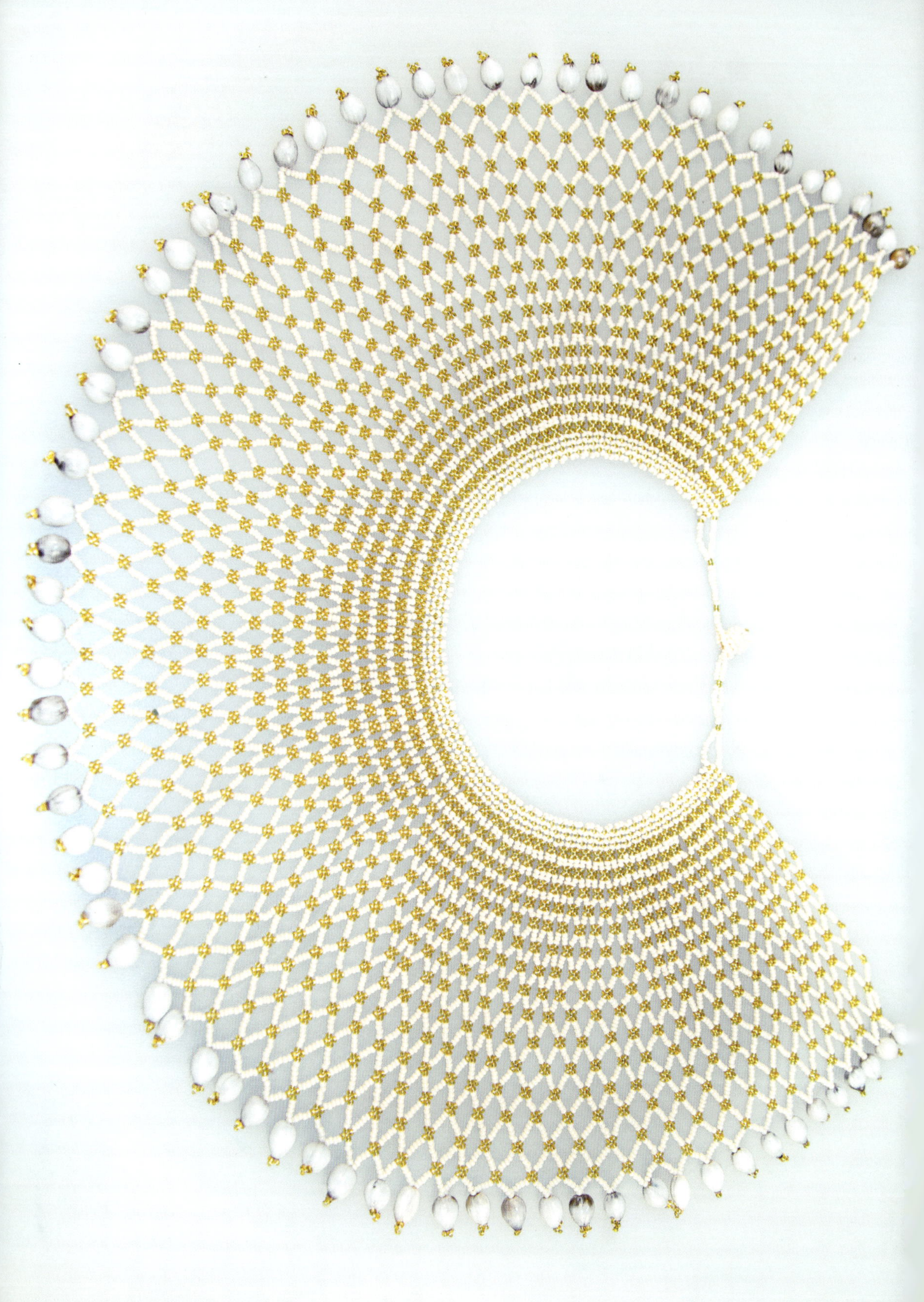

foreword

An unusual Vukani choker in white and yellow beads decorated with seeds, bought from the African Art Centre, Durban. (AN) (Preston-Whyte Collection)

THE INTRODUCTION of brass, glass and later plastic beads into South Africa gave Zulu women three enormous opportunities. The first was an exciting new medium for creating adornment; an artistic expression that satisfies every woman's love of beautiful apparel. A beautiful pot or platter is admired – but beadwork enhances personal attractiveness.

The second was the opportunity for communication, where beads could be used to indicate messages secret to the sender and recipient, or could announce status and region to the whole world. And in due course, the third opportunity developed – that of self-employment. As husbands went to work in the mines or big cities, sometimes never to re-appear, many a wife had to raise her children on what she could earn with her nimble fingers.

An innovative Vukani necklace.

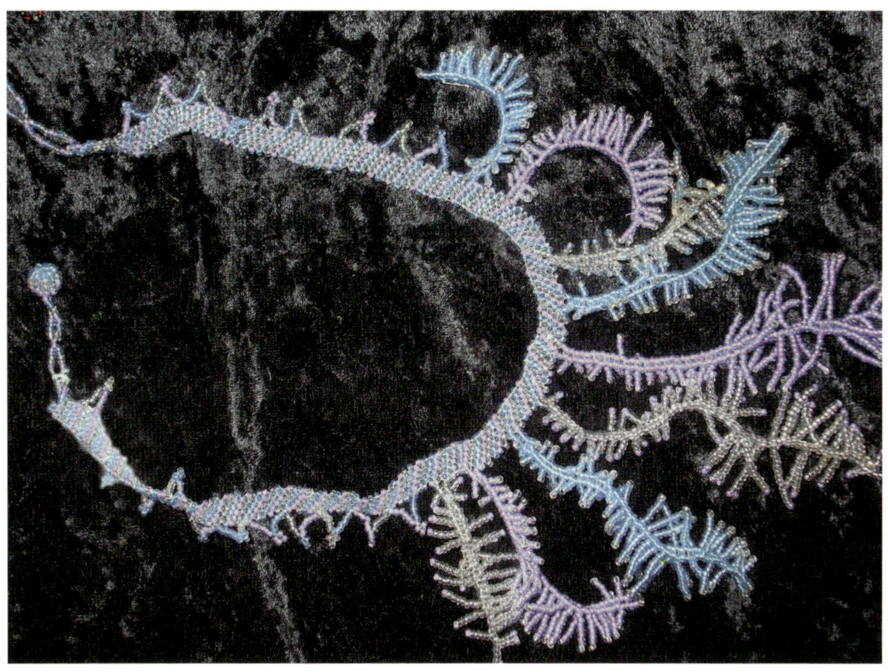

After meeting Eleanor Preston-Whyte at the Borneo
International Beads Conference in 2011, and realizing that she
was the co-author of my favourite reference on Zulu beadwork,
she had to be the first choice when looking for an author for
the third book in this excellent series on Zulu craft. Eleanor's
love for beads breathes through every page and she has done
a marvelous job in bringing alive the exciting changes that
are taking place as contemporary beaders explore the widest
possibilities of this medium.

I congratulate the author and Print Matters on another valuable
reference work.

Vivienne Garside
Curator: Vukani Zulu Cultural Museum

preface

ZULU BEADWORK draws on anthropological research begun in the early 1960s in the burgeoning craft markets that were then beginning to line the highways to the north and south of Durban, KwaZulu-Natal. As these markets grew in size and number, the research came to include both the craft makers who supplied the markets and the trading networks along which craft travelled from often far-flung rural areas to the marketplace. My thanks are due to the many craftspeople, traders and facilitators who answered my seemingly endless questions and cheerfully accompanied me to places I would otherwise never have visited.

In order to do justice to both the beauty and the complexity of different beadwork genres, it is often necessary to anticipate future events and re-examine some events discussed previously but from different perspectives. In this sense the stories told here are often as interwoven as the most complex and intricate items of beadwork themselves.

Zulu beadwork is best appreciated when viewed through the lens of the past. The reason for this lies in the many different meanings beadwork holds, both for those who wear the beads and for their various audiences. Although in the past bead making and the wearing of beaded clothing had deep traditional meaning Zulu beadwork today has many meanings, so that its messages differ from situation to situation. In some contexts the meaning is much the same as in the past, while in others it is different. Sometimes beadwork is, however, purely decorative and designed to attract potential buyers. Today Zulu beadwork provides a welcome source of income for a growing number of people, and particularly for women.

Eleanor Preston-Whyte
Johannesburg, January 2014

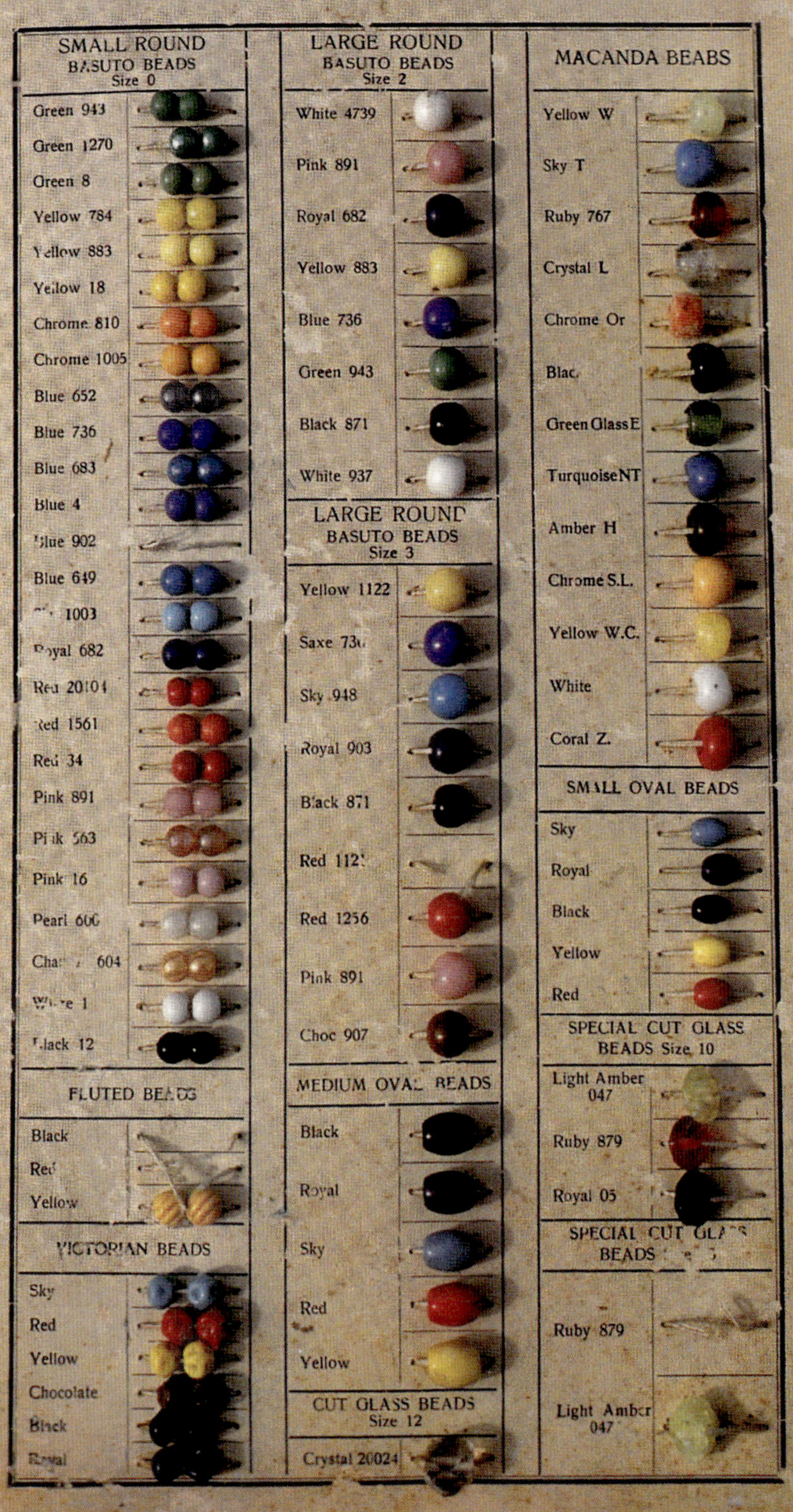

NATAL

SMALL ROUND
BASUTO BEADS
Size 0
Green 943
Green 1270
Green 8
Yellow 784
Yellow 883
Yellow 18
Chrome 810
Chrome 1005
Blue 652
Blue 736
Blue 683
Blue 4
Blue 902
Blue 649
1003
Royal 682
Red 20104
Red 1561
Red 34
Pink 891
Pink 563
Pink 16
Pearl 606
Cham 604
White 1
Black 12

FLUTED BEADS
Black
Red
Yellow

VICTORIAN BEADS
Sky
Red
Yellow
Chocolate
Black
Royal

LARGE ROUND
BASUTO BEADS
Size 2
White 4739
Pink 891
Royal 682
Yellow 883
Blue 736
Green 943
Black 871
White 937

LARGE ROUND
BASUTO BEADS
Size 3
Yellow 1122
Saxe 730
Sky 948
Royal 903
Black 871
Red 112
Red 1256
Pink 891
Choc 907

MEDIUM OVAL BEADS
Black
Royal
Sky
Red
Yellow

CUT GLASS BEADS
Size 12
Crystal 20024

MACANDA BEABS
Yellow W
Sky T
Ruby 767
Crystal L
Chrome Or
Black
Green Glass E
Turquoise NT
Amber H
Chrome S.L.
Yellow W.C.
White
Coral Z.

SMALL OVAL BEADS
Sky
Royal
Black
Yellow
Red

SPECIAL CUT GLASS
BEADS Size 10
Light Amber
047
Ruby 879
Royal 05

SPECIAL CUT GLASS
BEADS Size 5
Ruby 879
Light Amber
047

continuity and change in
Zulu beadwork

CONTEMPORARY ZULU BEADWORK is a heady mix of tradition and modernity. With one foot in the marketplace and the other dancing in celebration of the richness of African culture, bead makers and those who purchase and wear Zulu beadwork are at one in reading into it a message about the relevance of the past for the present.

This book seeks to capture the beauty and complexity of Zulu beadwork by telling a number of parallel, but intersecting, stories. The first recalls the grandeur of the dress and beaded finery worn by the men and women encountered by the first white travellers journeying through pre-colonial Zululand. Moving to the recent past and the present, the second story recounts how from as early as the 1950s bead making in KwaZulu-Natal was transformed, from a predominantly local skill employed mainly for personal adornment into a rapidly diversifying source of external monetary income. Not only bead makers benefited from this trade. So did the plethora of traders and middlemen who penetrated deep rural areas in search of local craft to satisfy the demand for 'African curios' from the growing number of holiday makers descending upon Kwa-Zulu Natal's North and South coasts.

The third story explores the impact of philanthropic development agencies, many of them internationally based and funded, intent on preserving and diversifying local Zulu craft skills – including beading – in order to generate income for local people, and particularly for women, in KwaZulu-Natal. The intervention of these agencies has been rewarded by the proliferation of novel bead jewellery and later beaded clothing which, from the mid-1960s, took both local and international fashion markets by storm and continues to enchant prospective buyers today.

Subsequent developments have included the appearance
of beaded animals, figurines and sometimes small beaded
tableaux sold in upmarket curio shops and even in large
department stores both in South Africa and overseas.
In addition, an increasing and ever-changing array of birds and
animals, both large and small, are peddled on street corners
in many South African towns and cities, holiday resorts and
popular tourist destinations. As a result, the sale of beadwork
now constitutes an important income source for those
employed in both the formal and informal sectors of the South
African economy.

The wearing of bead work items, and on certain occasions
the donning of the full traditional beaded regalia in order to
give symbolic expression to Zulu identity appear to have little
to do with the harnessing of beading skills, of creativity and
innovation, in order to make money. Yet these two strands
illustrate the complex interaction of continuity and change in
the making and use of Zulu beadwork over the last sixty years.

Echoes from the past

*They danced in parties of eight, arranged in four, each
party wearing different coloured beads, which were crossed
from the shoulder to the knees. Each wore a headdress of
black feathers, and four brass collars, fitting closely to the
neck.*   Henry Francis Fynn

This vivid description of how beads and beadwork were used
to complement and enhance the dress of the Zulu people was
left to us by Henry Francis Fynn, who, accompanied by Francis
Farewell, a local trader, visited the Zulu capital to report his
arrival to the great King Shaka. While there, Fynn and Farewell
witnessed massed dancing by both men and women whose
dancing regalia included a profusion of multi-coloured glass
beads.

G F Angas
(1849 Plate xix).
A dramatic portrait
of King Shaka's
nephew, Utimuni,
which echoes Fynn's
general comment:
"The (Zulu) chiefs
and principal people
wear a profusion of
beads, with heavy
brass bangles from
wrist to the elbow".
(The Campbell
Collections)

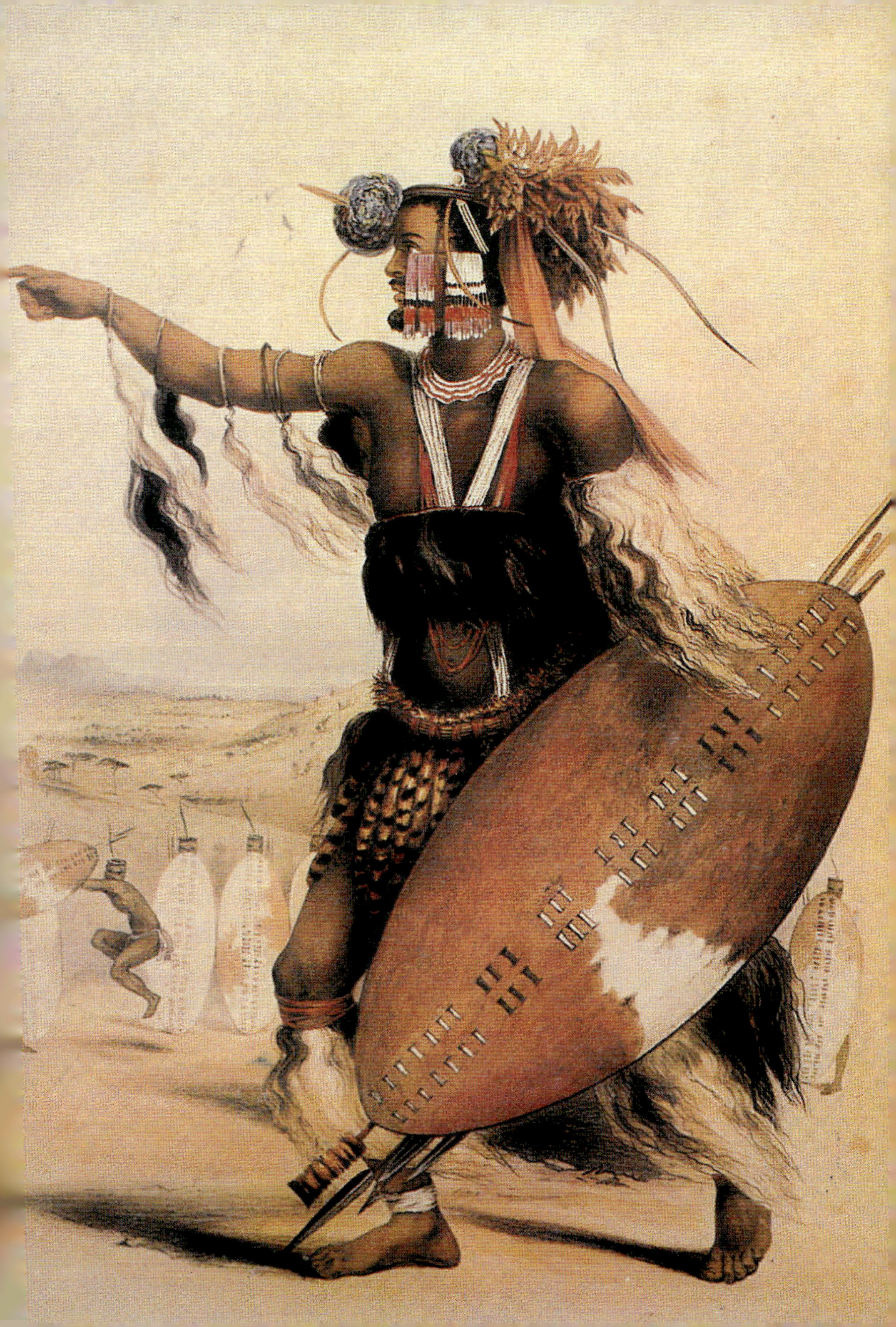

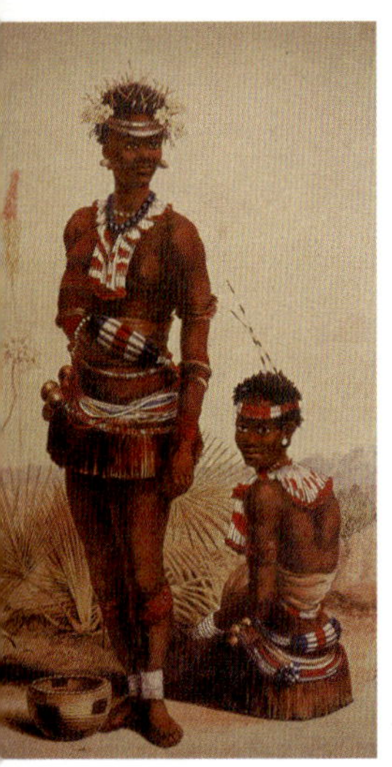

G F Angas (1849 Plate xix). *The Kaffirs Illustrated – Two of Umpanda's Dancing Girls*. Note the small beaded basket in the left hand corner. (The Campbell Collections)

Prior to the widespread availability of these imported glass beads, wood, shell, seeds, animal teeth and possibly also clay were used to make local beads. Brass beads were manufactured by local smiths and were highly valued not only for their beauty, but for their relative rarity. Alongside locally made beads, a variety of beads made from glass, cowrie shells and other materials had long been imported by Arab traders from as far afield as India, Persia, Arabia and the Far East. In the early sixteenth century, however, Portuguese explorers opened the way for increasing European penetration of parts of Southern Africa; as time passed, imported glass beads had spread across the countryside because white travellers and settlers used them to pay for food and services. In time, glass beads were also imported via the Cape, and later through Port Natal.

By the time Fynn and Farewell visited the Zulu capital, these glass beads had become a highly valued part not only of the ceremonial dress of the wealthy and influential, but in the exchange of items of value that marked the celebration of important life changes in Zulu society.

By the end of the nineteenth century some varieties of imported beads were so common that preferences in colour and bead size had developed among both wearers and beaders. This led eventually to the appearance of distinct local styles and colour combinations, many of which are still widely used and recognised. Beads were stocked by the ubiquitous trading stores along with imported cloth and other staples of the Zulu rural economy. In time plastic beads became available and had the advantage of being both cheaper and considerably lighter to wear although they lacked the vibrancy of glass beads.

It is clear from the written record, as well as from illustrations accompanying many accounts of early travellers to South Africa, that much of the dramatic effect of early Zulu beadwork lay in its skilful combination with other decorative items such as the black feathers and brass collars mentioned in Fynn's description. For an outsider witnessing massed Zulu dancing for the first time the overall effect must have been strange and exotic, even overwhelming. For at least some early observers, however, the dancing and particularly the performers' dress was both enthralling and alluring, as is indicated by the exquisite and sensitive treatment of local dress in the paintings, and subsequently the lithographs by G. F. Angas in the late 1840s. Modern Zulu beadwork is reminiscent of the exquisite beadwork captured in paint by Angas and described by Fynn and other early travellers in Zululand.

Evidence from the historical record

A similar continuity in beadwork style and regional differences can be seen in the early Zulu beadwork on display in a number of South African and international museums. Of particular interest is the bead collection housed in the Robert Hull Flemming Museum at the University of Vermont in New England in the United States. This consists of a number of bequests made by or on behalf of locals who spent long periods of time in nineteenth- and early twentieth-century South Africa. These included the Reverend Louis Grout, a missionary who lived and worked in the Umsunduzi area from 1847 to 1862, and Mrs Robert Catlin, the wife of the General Manager of Consolidated Gold Mines, who lived in Johannesburg between 1895 and 1906. The collections are well documented by Brotten and Lang (1973) and the text and photographs of many of their major items allow for detailed comparison with illustrations of Zulu beadwork from earlier and later historical periods.

Of interest also is the recently published description by Jolles (2012) of the highly specialised collection of Zulu dolls dating from the late twentieth century in the Dugler-Collection, now housed in the State Museum of Ethnology in Munich. Another source of information on Zulu beadwork is in the standard monograph on the Zulu by Eileen Krige (1936), which was compiled largely from the literature available in the 1930s and published under the title of *The Social System of the Zulus.*

The wearing of beaded finery by sections of Zulu society is implicit in a number of the monographs by Vilikazi, Berglund and Ngubane dating roughly from the 1950s onwards. Because these were field-based studies of a general anthropological nature and did not particularly focus on beadwork, they are of limited use to readers interested specifically in Zulu beadwork. Fortunately, however, useful material on Zulu beadwork dating from the late 1960s to the present is available in a number of articles, such as those by Schoeman (1968) and Twala (1958).

Three other sources provide descriptions, detailed drawings and photographs indicating how Zulu beadwork was integrated into both everyday and ceremonial wear at different stages in the lives of both men and women from the late 1950s to the late 1960s. The work of Grossert and Tyrrell although aimed at different audiences, made important contributions to the history of Zulu beadwork. Grossert's slim volume, *Zulu Beadwork* (1978), remains the authoritative text on beadwork styles and functions dating from those years, when, as the provincial educational organiser for arts and crafts he undertook extensive rural research, which informed the teaching of Zulu crafts in black schools.

When first published, Grossert's work was criticised in liberal political circles on the grounds that because African craft was part of the syllabus in black but not in white schools, it constituted yet another example of racially biased and discriminatory legislation. In retrospect, however, beadwork lessons provided black women, who did not learn beading at home, with a money-making skill, which would stand them in good stead in later life.

In contrast to Grossert's workmanlike approach to beadwork, Tyrrell's volume entitled *Tribal Peoples of Southern Africa* consists of exquisite colour drawings made during her travels around South Africa, when she documented a wide range of black rural lifestyles. Although when first published the volume enjoyed

Items of Zulu beadwork typical of the 1950s and 1960s as recorded by Grossert (1978).

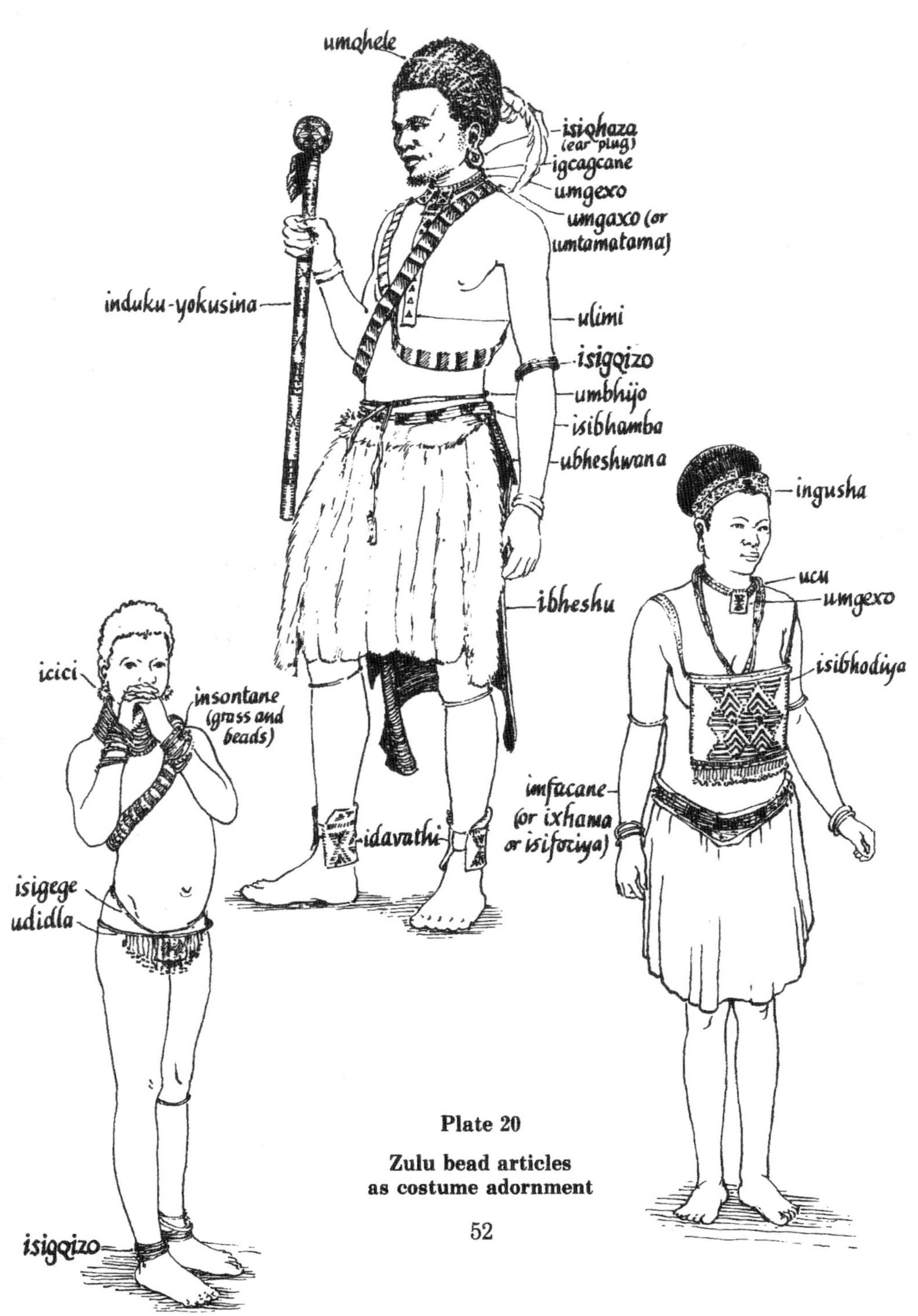

Plate 20

**Zulu bead articles
as costume adornment**

52

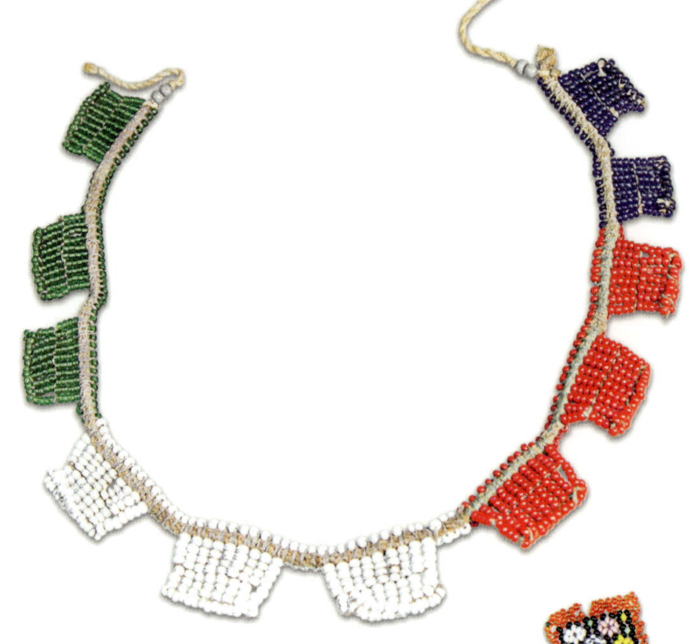

Two examples of traditional Zulu beadwork threaded on string and cotton. The underside of the circular necklet is shown in order to indicate the string used to hold the small decorative panels together. Date unknown. (AN) (Preston-Whyte Collection)

a predominantly white, and particularly an international readership, the section on Zulu dress highlighted the integral role played by beadwork, not only in ceremonial, but in everyday life. With the end of apartheid, when an increasing number of black South Africans became interested in the heritage of their past, the readership of her book broadened sufficiently to warrant the mounting of an exhibition of her work in a prestigious Cape Town gallery.

The work of photographer Jean Morris, who travelled extensively in the mid 1970s is an impressive record of how Zulu beaded clothing enhanced the ceremonial and the daily working lives of ordinary people. A representative selection of her photographs was published under the title *Speaking with Beads (1994)*. Taken together with the studies discussed above, these photographs allow useful comparisons to be made between older and contemporary Zulu beadwork. They assist in dating beadwork, as well in assessing the sources of the major changes in beading style and usage that have shaped what is now an extremely diverse range, serving both the internal and, increasingly, external markets associated with the tourist trade.

Until recently, the wearing of beadwork was typical of only the section of the Zulu community that had resisted conversion to Christianity. We need, therefore, to return to history in order to understand the magnitude of the social division that not only split Zulu society as a result of the advent of Christianity, but which, until fairly recently, influenced both the day-to-day and ceremonial wearing of beadwork.

A community divided

The appreciation for local dress and custom shown by early travellers to Zululand such as Fynn and Angas was not shared by subsequent waves of white settlers and traders, and particularly not by the large numbers of Christian missionaries

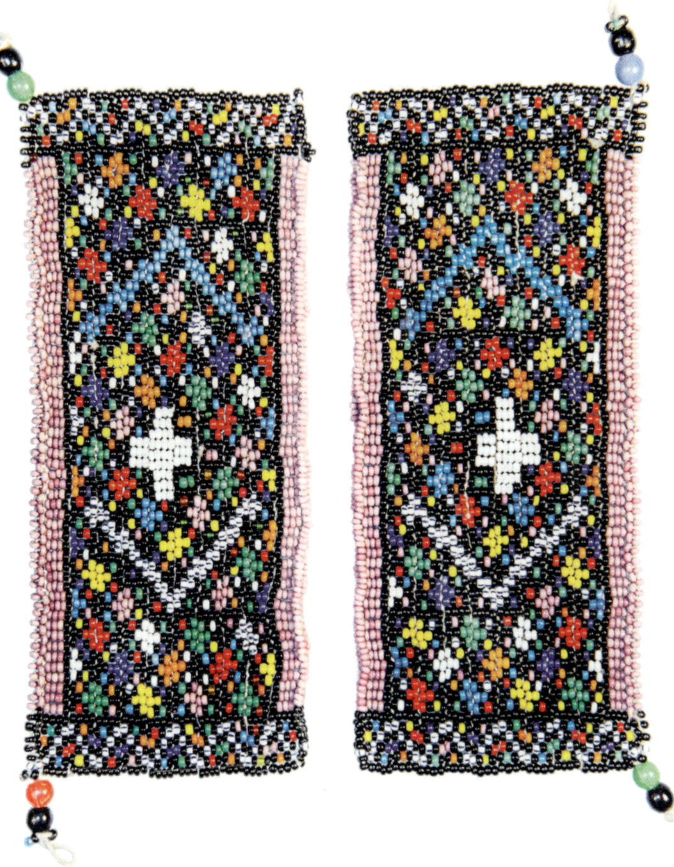

Traditional beaded anklets. (AN) (Preston-Whyte Collection)

entering Zululand. One of the first actions of many missionaries was to require their converts to replace what they regarded as the blatant and ungodly nudity of local dress, which included the wearing of beaded ornaments, feathers and skins, with far more prosaic western clothing made from cloth imported specifically for the purpose. In many cases, particularly in the early days of white penetration into the interior of Zululand, converts were also prevailed upon to move from their homes and local communities and to settle on mission stations.

Neither beads and beadwork, nor other flamboyant forms of traditional ornamentation and dress had a place in the lives the new Christians forged with other converts. These converts did gain, however, the opportunity to learn the language of the conqueror, and their children soon began attending mission schools, which together with the mission church formed the focal point of daily mission life. These early Zulu Christians became the backbone of a new generation who, in some areas, were known as 'School People' in contrast to the unconverted, often referred to as 'Red People' because of the widespread custom of decorating their bodies with local clay. It was in this latter section of the community that beadwork continued to play an important part in both the everyday dress of young men and women before marriage, and in the elaborate dress worn by Zulu adults on ceremonial occasions. Babies and toddlers were given simple beaded decorations, some of which were designed to contain protective herbs. Later they wore beaded loin coverings.

In traditional families adolescent girls began to learn beading skills in preparation for courting. Bead bands as tokens of their interest and even affection were presented by lovers or prospective brides to particular young men. For their part, the young men wore these tokens proudly entwined about their upper bodies. Married and unmarried women were easily distinguished, not only by the overall style of dress, but by the style of the beaded finery they wore, and particularly in the case

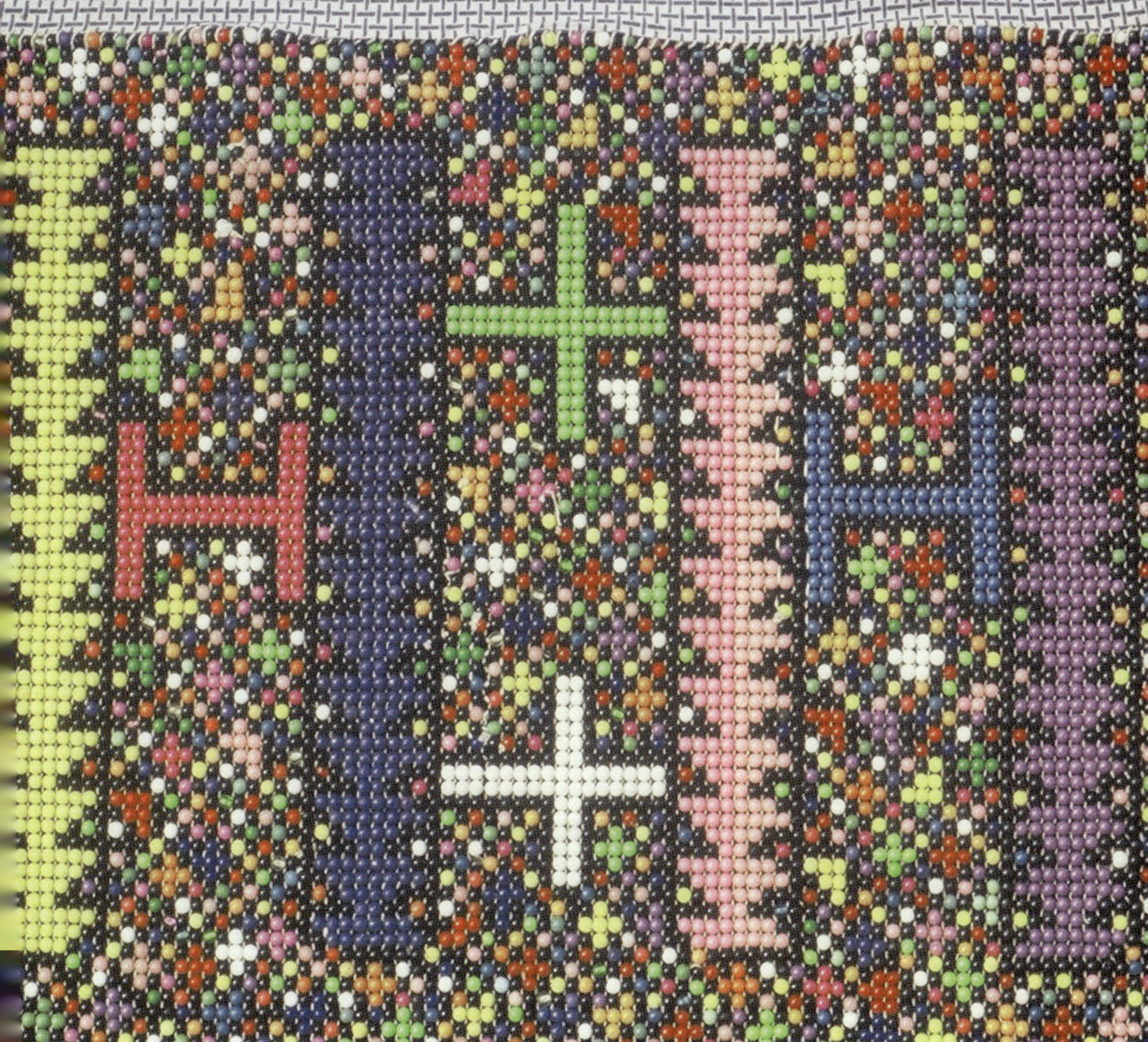

of recently married women, by the profusion of their beadwork.
Young warriors dressed with flair and panache, as did King
Shaka's nephew, Utumini, who as we saw above, was painted
by G.F. Angas in the mid 1800s. Older married men and elders
wore beaded ornaments too, although their senior status was
indicated also by skin cloaks and feathered headdresses. Here
again beadwork complemented other indicators of position and
status, and its colours and patterns often indicated the region
from which the wearer hailed.

Full panel of Nyuswa beadwork dating from the 1970s. Note the material on which it is made visible at the top of the panel. (Preston-Whyte Collection)

The divisions recede

In time the rigid divide between traditionalists and
Christians lessened. It was not possible for all converts to be
accommodated on mission land, and increasing numbers
of Christians began to live adjacent to, or even surrounded
by, traditional communities. As time passed, the separation
between them lessened as they attended the same local courts,
clinics, hospitals and, on occasion, the same traditional healers.

Because of the important and highly visible part played by
beadwork in the dress of many traditional healers and the
continued use made of their ministrations not only in rural
areas, but in towns and cities throughout KwaZulu-Natal, it is
useful to provide a brief outline of their areas of competence
and of how they are called to their profession.

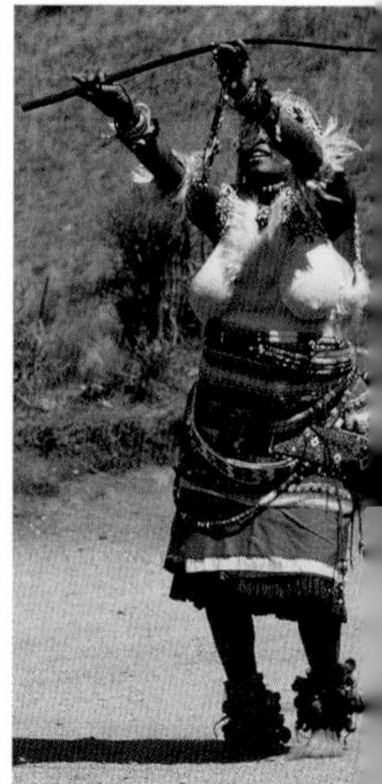

An isangoma dancing
in full beaded regalia.
(RP-W)

Indeed much of this personal history can be read in their
beaded headdresses and the strips of animal skin which
criss-cross their chests. *Izinyanga*, for example, rely on herbal
medicines to cure their patients and do not wear the elaborate
dress of the *Izangoma*. These diviners are called to their
profession by their ancestors.

When assisted by their ancestors, *Izangoma* not only diagnose
serious and lingering illnesses, but they can find lost or hidden
objects. They are also believed to be able to identify potential
enemies who may be using witchcraft to call down illness on
individuals, or a long run of misfortune that may have beset
them or their families. In this, diviners are regarded not only
as the protectors of society, but as a potent force in the fight
against evil in the community.

It is not surprising, therefore, that the *Izangoma* should continue
to be distinguished from ordinary people by their dress and their
characteristic demeanours of power and importance. The prolific
use of beadwork in their dress and particularly in their elaborate

headdresses, sends an important visual message: the power
which has been conferred on them by their ancestors, with
whom they are in continual contact and whom they appease and
please by wearing dry gall bladders in their headdresses. White
beads often predominate the profusion of beadwork worn about
their persons, not only on special occasions, but also as they go
about the routine of their daily lives.

Over time large extended families often contained both
Christian and traditional branches, with members meeting
at important family events such as marriages and funerals.
While it was largely traditionalists who continued to practise
the old crafts and who wore traditional beaded finery for
family celebrations and important political events, the social
boundaries and differences between the two groups lessened
as Christians began to look on traditional wear not as a sign of
backwardness, but as part of a past that was not only shared,
but also increasingly valued.

Although it was largely traditional women who maintained
and elaborated the skills of beading, the product itself could be
donned on appropriate occasions by Christians, and later by
members of the educated and politically sensitive elite. Indeed,
replicas of the 'traditional' married woman's headdress can now
be bought in trading stores and craft shops.

Traditional style
beadwork made
with plastic beads
threaded on string.
Note the method
of fastening using
larger beads than in
the panel itself. (AN)
(Preston-Whyte
Collection)

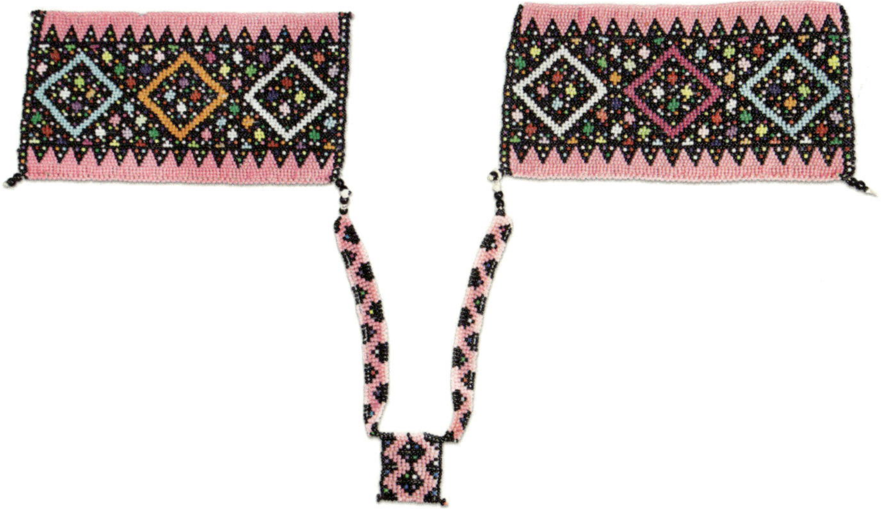

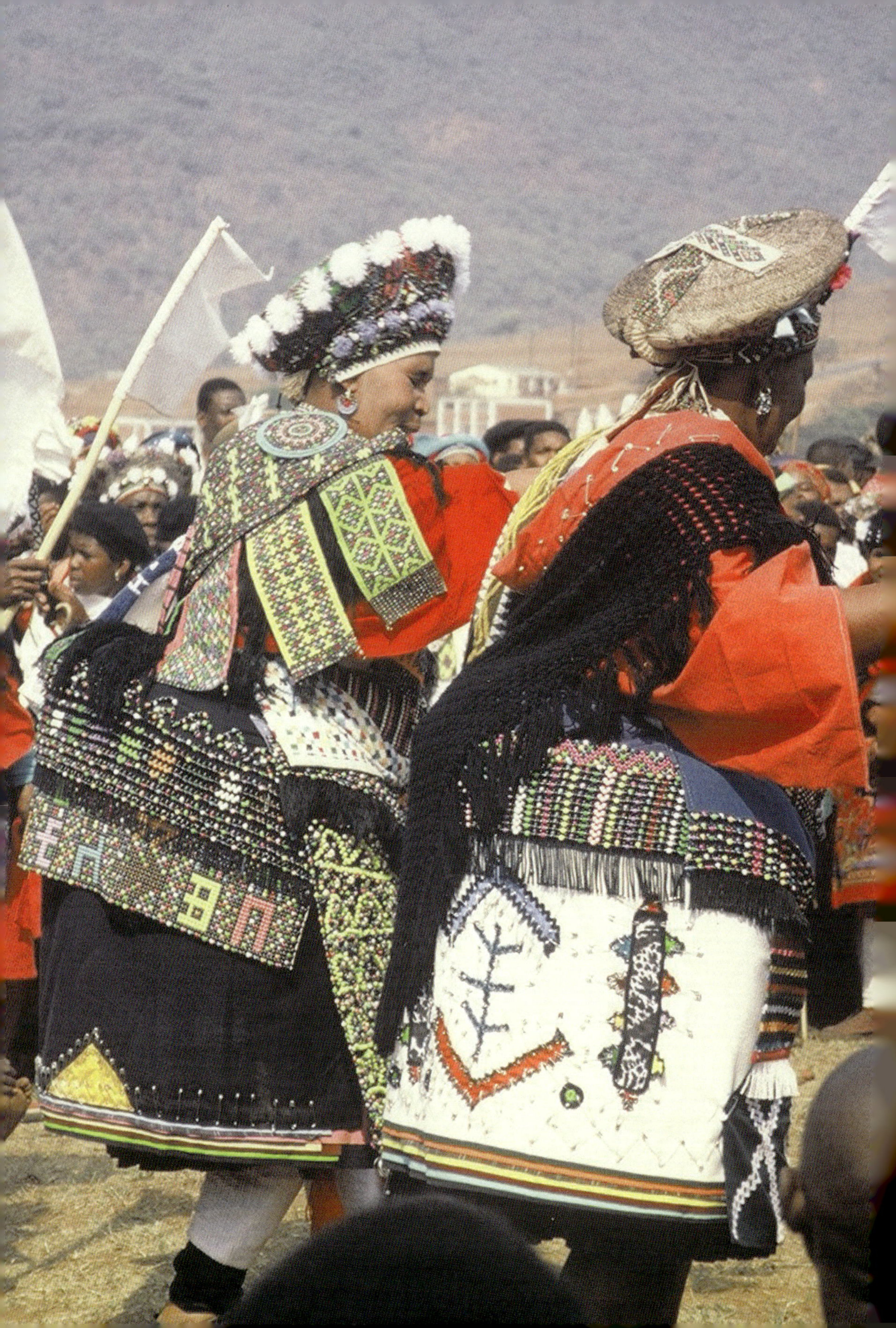

2

in praise of the Lord:
new wine in old wineskins

Dancing women in traditional dress. (RP-W)

IT IS AGAINST the brief historical background provided in Chapter 1 that we now consider the many and varied arenas in which Zulu beadwork flourishes today. The title of this chapter is borrowed from the study of early separatist religious movements in Southern Africa undertaken by Sundkler in the 1940s. One of these is the Nazareth Baptist Church, which combines traditional Zulu ancestral and Christian beliefs – a synergy that is elegantly captured by Sundkler's phrase, 'new wine in old wineskins' (1961).

The Nazareth Baptist Church, founded in about 1910 in Ekuphakameni, part of the mountainous area of Inanda near Durban, is one of the largest separatist churches in KwaZulu-Natal. It is often referred to simply as the Shembe Church after its founder, Isaiah Shembe. Although Shembe died in 1935, the Church continues to draw thousands of adherents, not only from within KwaZulu-Natal, but also from outside the borders of South Africa.

It is not only in theology that the Church draws on Zulu tradition. Zulu beadwork is one of the major defining features of the spectacular and elaborate dancing regalia worn by members of the Church during the massed dancing, which takes place in July during the annual pilgrimages to one of the church's holy places. The wearing of distinctive Church uniforms of which complex and ornate beadwork is an integral feature, is an eloquent reminder to participants and onlookers alike of the past glories of the Zulu kingdom and of the relevance of the past for the present. It also provides a striking example of both continuity and change in contemporary Zulu beadwork. The Shembe Church remains not only one of the largest and most active in the region, but also one of the most visible.

It is important to stress that participation in massed dancing and the wearing of beaded dancing regalia is a visible marker of personal piety. In July the beaded costumes of women – and to a lesser extent men – together with the massed dancing, draw crowds of spectators and, these days, an increasing number of tourists and professional photographers.

The scene is breathtaking. Ordered groups of men and women come and go as they take turns to dance and to sing the hymns of the Church. The idiom is military. Each dancing group has its distinctive uniform, and is referred to as a regiment in the fight against evil. The regiments are organised on the basis of gender, age and marital status. Mature women are dressed in the heavy cowhide skirts and the tall bead-decorated headdresses worn by Zulu matrons in the past, but also by married women in contemporary traditional Zulu communities. Cascades of looped beadwork are attached to the headdresses and hang down to cover the women's shoulders and the wide lacy white beaded necklaces they wear around their necks. Each woman carries a small replica of a Zulu shield and also a large black furled umbrella similar to those used by early Christian missionaries to protect themselves from the scorching African sun. Today the shield and the umbrella, the one drawn from Zulu tradition and the other from the world of the earthly conqueror, are symbolic reminders of the potent weapons available within the Church to pursue the fight against evil.

Long flowing dark purple or black cloaks that are often decorated with brightly-coloured woollen and beaded roundels, hang from the dancers' shoulders. Heavy beaded belts and intricate beaded bands encircle their waists and hips and decorate the stiff black leather skirts, which reach below their calves. Beaded bracelets and ankle bands complete the dancing costume and are worn above bare feet because the dancing arena is holy ground.

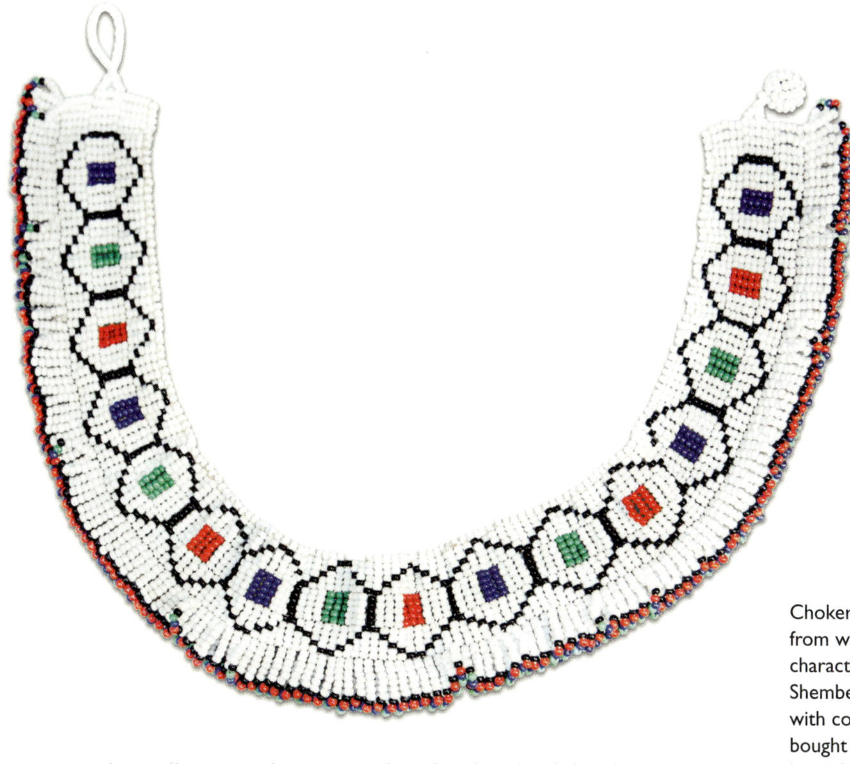

The uniforms and, in particular, the details of the dancing costume of the women conform to a common basic design. This is immediately recognisable, not only to other members of the Church, but also to non-members from all over the region. Differences occur also in the details of the uniforms worn by the regiments of older and younger married women, and particularly in the uniforms of women from different local areas. Dancers themselves may also introduce minor stylistic changes, which please their aesthetic sense, but which may or may not lead to widespread innovations in the future.

Perhaps the most striking feature of the dancing regalia of married women lies in the number and variety of the individual pieces of intricate beadwork worn by each dancer. Another lies in the glowing colours of the beadwork, which are in stark contrast to the sombre tones of their leather skirts and the brown or ochre of their elaborate headdresses. The latter vary from round and flared to elongated, depending once again, on the geographical area from which the dancer comes and, to some extent, on the nature of the occasion on which they are worn. For the massed ceremonial dancing the choice is in keeping with the religious importance and public nature of the occasion. It may also be motivated, however, by the personal pleasure that wearing a particular headdress brings to the dancers, who have chosen their costumes with care in anticipation of the dancing. Around their ankles they wear ropes of white beads above patterned anklets which may, but do not always, have small white crosses picked out against a background of coloured beads and enclosed by a white border. Similar oblongs of patterned beadwork may be used to decorate the front of the matrons' uniforms.

In contrast to the married women and matrons, unmarried women and girls dance bare breasted, save for bands of intricate beadwork that encircle their chests, to which small oblongs of colourful beadwork are attached and decorate the upper part of their breasts. The young women wear short dancing skirts covered by wide round bands and ropes of beadwork in which white beads symbolising purity

Typical Nazarite beadwork in which the design incorporates cross-like motifs on a white background. (AN) (Preston-Whyte Collection)

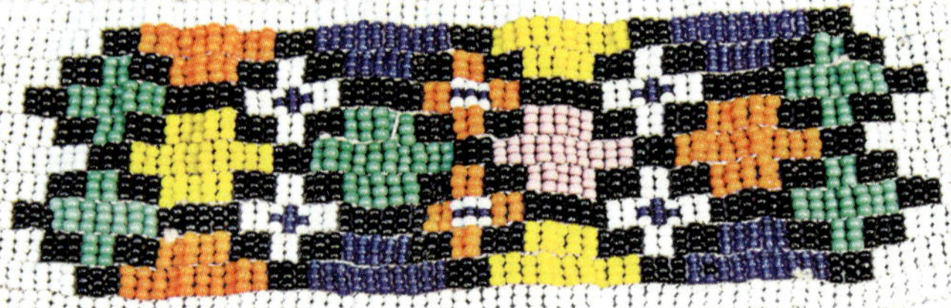

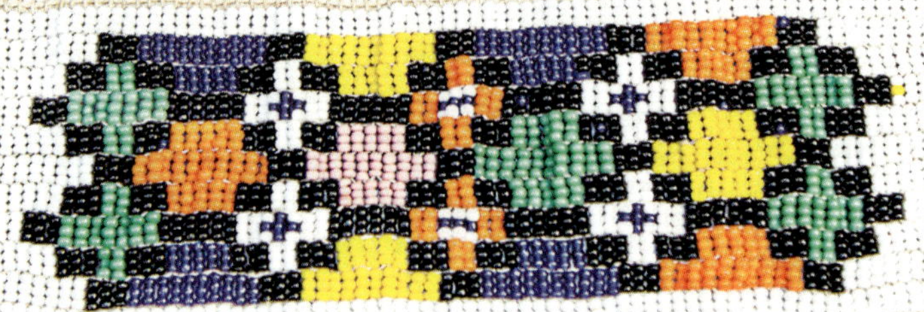

predominate. These are often enlivened, however, by complex patterns picked out in glittering coloured beads.

Girls who are not yet of marriageable age wear short red pleated skirts, but no headdresses. This is in contrast to the uniforms of the older girls who wear black skirts and multi-coloured beaded headbands. Like the married women, the young women wear white beaded anklets and their feet are bare. Both groups of girls wear heavily beaded and highly decorative frontal aprons below their circular beaded waistbands, as well as narrow strings of white beads below the knee and around their upper arms.

To complete their outfits both sets of girls carry small replicas of a Zulu shield, and in the case of the older girls, a black umbrella similar to, but usually smaller than, that carried by the married women. The symbolism of the small, but important, differences in the uniforms worn by younger and older girls is clear: the latter are moving towards marriage as their headbands indicate and, in particular, the colour of their skirts, which echo the characteristic black leather of the longer skirts worn by married women.

In contrast to the women and girls the dancing dress of men and teenage boys, although it may contain some beadwork, is characterised by a predominance of animal skins and feathers, which were once the defining characteristic of the dress of Zulu warriors. Many of the youths, however, may wear beaded anklets and either bands or single strings of beads around their necks. Some of these may be a reminder of the beaded love tokens worn by youths in the past. Older men and elders in the Church might wear a small framed photograph of Isaiah Shembe suspended on a string of beads around their necks. It is often referred to as *ifoto*.

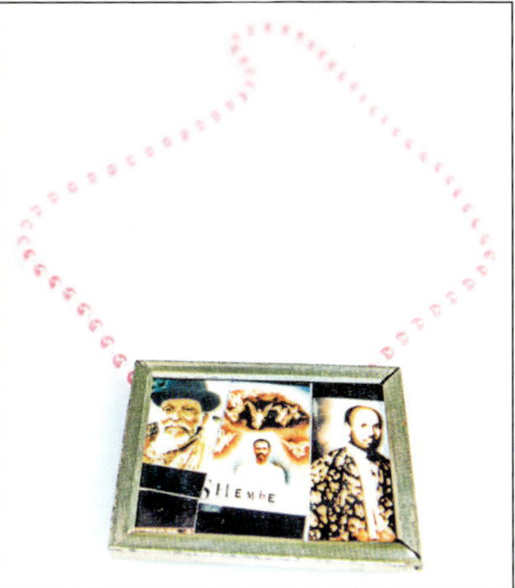

An *ifoto* with photographs of the prophet and church leaders. (AN) (Preston-Whyte Collection)

As each regiment dances it is watched intently not only by members of the public, but by the dancers who wait in the wings for their turn, and who comment both on the dancing itself and on the details of the costumes and beadwork worn by each of the dancers. Apart from those wearing western dress, the crowd is almost as colourful as the dancers themselves. This is a day not only of worship, but also a celebration of the past. Those who do not already own beadwork themselves may purchase a bead necklace or bracelet from one of the small informal stalls situated on the fringe of the crowd of attentive but often noisy spectators. Here and there adolescents and groups of excited children wearing a few strings of beads attempt to emulate the dancing. Babies, who often wear a single stranded bead necklace or bracelet, are tied to their mothers' backs in slings made of brightly coloured towels or brilliant pieces of coloured material.

Symbols, Design and Meaning

While white is symbolic of Christian purity, Ngubane, in *Body and Mind in Zulu Medicine* (1977), points out that white also has important positive connotations drawn from traditional Zulu cosmology. In this way Nazarite beadwork speaks with different voices, each of which may have not only a different, but a situational reference and meaning. The use and importance of white beads is echoed in the colour of the white cloth smocks worn by both men and women of the Church for regular daily and weekly prayer.

It is in the contrast between the background of white beads and the wide yet distinctive range of complex patterns made with brilliantly coloured and often sparkling beads that the variety and beauty of the beadwork characteristic of the Nazareth Church lies. Most of the items incorporate complex and often ornate geometric designs. Some of these are repeated again and again, while others appear less often and may be unique to particular beaders. As is the case with much Zulu beadwork, some of the designs and colour combinations point to the

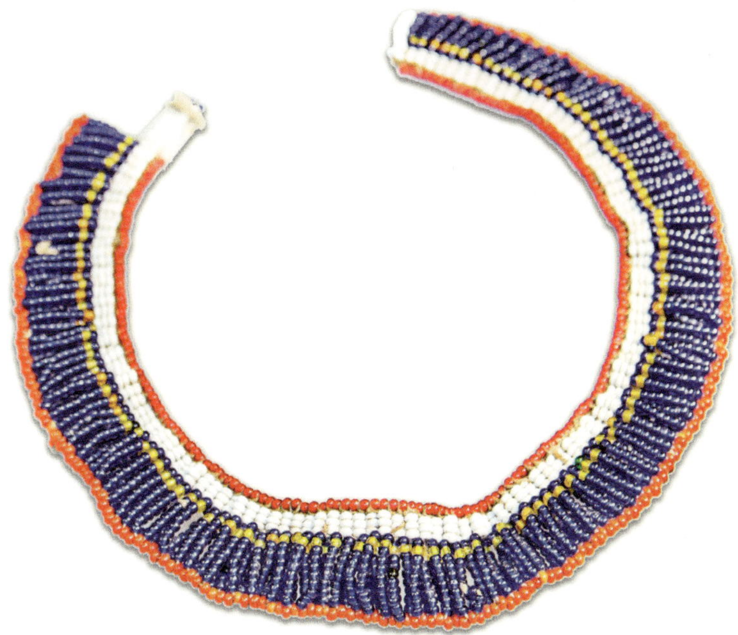

geographical area from which the maker comes, but this is
by no means necessarily the case and may be overridden in
importance by the colour symbolism in which the colour white
predominates.

Bead makers are free to experiment and innovate with both
design and colour, but probably most of the images worked
into beadwork bands have symbolic relevance either to Church
teachings or to the Zulu past. In some cases the message may
be complex and multi-vocal, in that it can have more than one
interpretation and the appropriate meaning is derived from
the context of its use. Thus the image of a Zulu shield may
celebrate the prowess of the Zulu warriors of the past, but it is
also reminiscent of the small shields carried by women and girls
on the dancing floor.

Many of the designs used in Nazarite beadwork are drawn
from the everyday life and experience of the makers. In some
it is possible to see what may be the outline of a fish or some
other common object. In others, however, it is impossible to do

more than hazard a guess at what might have been intended
by the bead maker. What looks to the outsider like a razor blade
may have a totally different meaning for the maker. It is even
more likely that the motif may have been an experiment with
form or a shape dictated by the possibilities or constraints of
a developing design. Sometimes letters of the alphabet and
numbers are introduced into beadwork patterns but, as many
of the members of the Church have had little or no education,
it is likely that it is the shapes and the possibilities many of these
devices offer in terms of pattern making that underlie their use,
rather than an attempt to convey a message of any description.
It is also possible that many of the motifs are the result of
experimentation and if the results are not pleasing to the maker
or her audience, they are not repeated.

It is for these reasons that beadwork designs tend to differ
from woman to woman and while some motifs are repeated
again and again, others which are less pleasing to the eye
of the maker seldom appear more than once or twice in
her beadwork. As new varieties of beads and bead colours
have become available, individual and often highly personal
variations have increased in number. The result is that new
designs are created almost annually and co-exist alongside the
older but still popular designs of the past.

Older Nazarite beadwork tended to incorporate bright primary
colours woven into a network of cross-like symbols. However,
translucent beads, some of which have a high and shiny lustre,
have now become widely available and beading patterns
have not only diversified but innovative new patterns have
tended to develop. Some have even come to resemble trendy
fabric designs and may give little evidence of overt religious
symbolism. What links most recent beadwork to that of the
past is the predominance of long narrow geometric designs,
which are dictated by the shape of the beadwork bands that
are tied around various parts of the wearer's body. Within the
constraints of this shape, however, there is ample opportunity

both for the development of complex designs and for the
subtle manipulation of different coloured beads and sometimes
of beads of different shapes and designs. Small brass studs
and even safety pins may be added to enhance the impact of
an item of beadwork and, on occasions, the finished article
is decorated with pompoms made of coloured wool or even
feathers.

Prayer uniforms

Everyday Church wear for men and women is a plain white
smock, known as *umNazaretha*. In addition to their white
smocks, married women often adopt simplified versions of
the traditional circular headdress of a Zulu matron. Squares of
beading may be attached to the headdress and most women
wear beaded anklets. The women may also wear white shawls
over their shoulders as a sign of respect towards God, the leader
of the Church, and senior members of the Church community,
symbolic of how in the past married women wore these shawls
as a sign of respect towards their husbands. These symbols of
membership may also be worn with everyday western dress as
the women go about their daily lives, and immediately identify
the wearers as members of the Nazarite community. For
worship men wear a white smock over their normal shirt and
trousers, but seldom wear bead ornaments other than a string
of plastic beads with a photograph or collage of photographs of
the prophet hanging from it.

Beadmaking and moneymaking

As in other parts of KwaZulu-Natal, it is the women of the
Church who are the bead makers. Proficiency in bead making
and the ability to weave the complex and original patterns that
conform to the traditions of the Nazarite Church are much
admired and honoured within its community. Furthermore,
because bead making is perceived as a religious obligation
of both women and girls, the latter learn the skill from their
mothers as they grow up and prepare for womanhood and
marriage. During the July festival groups of young girls often

spend time together practising bead making and learning from
each other how to weave the complex patterns and designs
characteristic of Church dancing regalia.

In addition to the making of beadwork for their own use, the
skill of beading is now put to good use in the more mundane,
yet for many critical, sphere of making money. Because many
of the women and girls belonging to the Nazarite Church
have had little or no education and, at one time, spoke only a
smattering of English, they did not find it easy to compete for
even the less skilled and lower paid jobs on the labour market.
In the early days it was also frowned upon for women to seek
employment not only outside the home, but to travel to work
beyond the confines of the land occupied by the Church.
The sale of beadwork, either to other members of the Church,
or more recently to holidaymakers and tourists has, however,
provided an increasing number of women with a welcome if
limited, and often seasonal, source of income.

It was when visiting small country towns and, in particular,
the city of Durban in order to buy the beads required for
decorating their Church uniforms and dancing regalia, that
women came to appreciate the potential that beadwork held
for providing them and their families with a source of income.
In Durban members of the Church saw other beaders offering
their work for sale to tourists on the beachfront. Some also
discovered beadwork for sale in the curio stores situated in
the foyers of large beachfront hotels as well as in other areas
of the city frequented by holidaymakers and tourists. In time
a few enterprising women offered their own beadwork for
sale to the managers of beachfront curio stores, while others
joined the ranks of the numerous itinerant hawkers who were
selling beadwork and other local crafts to the tourists on the
beachfront itself.

In order to compete in the already overcrowded tourist market,
many of the women adapted and simplified their beadwork to

conform to their growing understanding of what attracted both holidaymakers and tourists, and, as important, of what the latter were willing to pay for beadwork. Based on this experience they began to make relatively inexpensive, but what turned out to be extremely popular, curio beadwork. Much of this retained the distinctive preponderance of white beads and the geometric designs characteristic of Nazarite beadwork. This distinguished it from much of the other bright and often garish tourist beadwork on sale on the beachfront and in other places in the city.

Prospective buyers were often intrigued, not only by the unusual and distinctive style of Nazarite beadwork, but also by the simplified beaded headdresses worn by some of the bead sellers. A few prospective buyers noticed other items of beadwork peeping from beneath the western garb adopted by the women when visiting town. When tourists, in particular, expressed an interest in buying these items of what they referred as 'real bead work,' a number of the beaders responded by making simplified copies of their own beadwork, specifically for sale to holidaymakers and tourists. This move proved extremely successful, and their sales rose accordingly.

Growth in the tourist market

As the numbers of holidaymakers and tourists, not to mention local Durbanites, making use of the city's beachfront playgrounds grew, so did the numbers of craft sellers. By the 1980s the latter had come to constitute an increasing traffic hazard as they pressed their wares not only on passers-by, but on the drivers of passing cars. The municipal authorities stepped in and set aside specified beachfront areas for the use of traders. Stalls were erected and leased at a nominal rate to craft sellers including members of the Nazarite Church. In general, it was mainly women who had some knowledge of English who ran the craft stalls, and much of the beadwork made by members of the Nazarite community was made not by the stall holder herself, but by other members of the Church on whose behalf she negotiated the price with prospective purchasers.

Over time many of the beachfront stalls came to stock a wide range of craft items made by members of what tourists had come to recognise as the Shembe Church. These included woven grass mats similar to those used by members for prayer, and small replicas of Zulu shields and the ever-popular assegais and fighting sticks carried by members of the Church when dancing. In many stalls these images of the 'Zulu Past' now lie side by side with other genuine Zulu beadwork interspersed with cheap beaded costume jewellery, much of which often turns out to have been imported from the East. More expensive items of Church regalia such as the cowhide skirts worn by Zulu matrons and their characteristic round headdresses are sold in upmarket curio shops, along with more expensive beadwork made by a number of the income generating craft development projects which will be discussed in the next chapter.

Women members of the Nazarite Church are not generally encouraged to mingle with the members of other churches and, for this reason, many live fairly restricted lives. The selling of handicrafts, was, however, made an explicit exception by Amos Shembe when he took over the leadership of the Church. In this way he not only encouraged women to make handicrafts for the market, but opened the way for experimentation and the development of a distinct genre of tourist art based on the traditional beadwork colours and designs of the Church.

From tourist to fashion beadwork

It is not only in the field of cheap tourist beadwork that bead makers from the Nazareth Baptist Church forged a niche market. Always on the lookout for new ideas and markets, a number of the bead makers explored the shopping arcades of the inner city behind the beachfront. Here they found a number of up-market curio shops that offered imported beaded jewellery alongside local South African beadwork for sale. Occasionally the managers of these shops bought what they referred to as 'genuine Shembe' beadwork from the women, including the complex and beautiful beadwork made and worn for dancing. The prices paid for these items, though considerably higher than those paid by tourists for necklaces and bracelets on the beachfront, were hardly commensurate with their intricacy and the work that had gone into making them. One shop, however, was different.

The African Art Centre, which is described more fully in Chapter 5, was a project of the South African Institute for Race Relations. Particularly under the guidance of the director, Jo Thorpe, the bead makers were soon not only making beadwork specifically to sell to the Art Centre, but experimenting with new beaded jewellery that extended the boundaries set by the traditional expectations of their art. White beads still predominated and formed the background for increasingly complex designs for which there was soon a growing demand from the regular customers of the Centre and also from South African and international buyers.

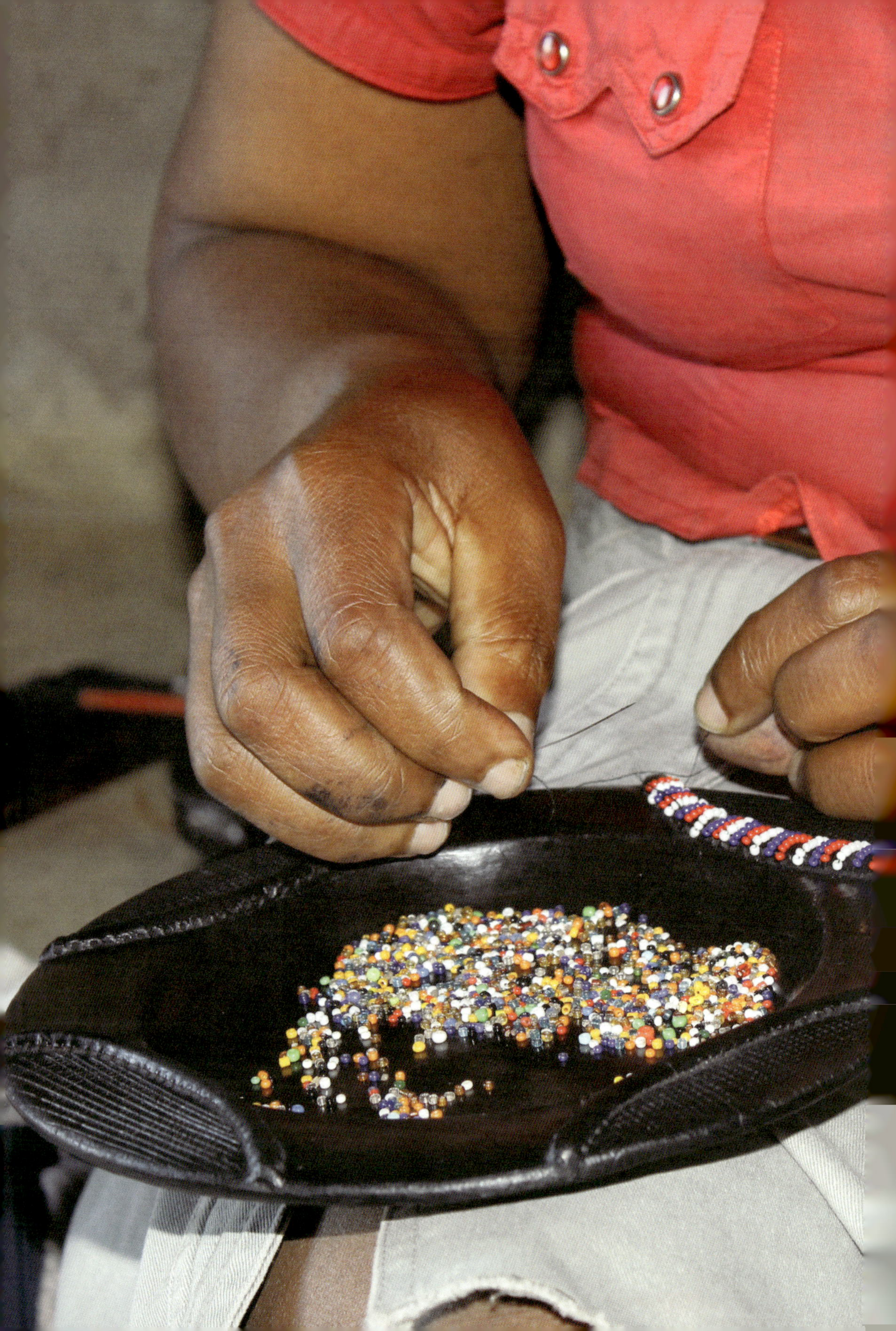

speaking with beads: Zulu bead making, bead colours, messages and meaning

UNTIL FAIRLY RECENTLY Zulu beadwork was the preserve of women, and despite the entry of a few men into the commercial craft arena over the last decade, women still make up the overwhelming majority of Zulu bead makers. Bead making is, indeed, regarded as women's work, just as wood carving and metal work are the domain of men. In the past, and today in traditional families, mothers and older women teach each new generation of girls to bead and young women and girls often develop proficiency in beading by practising together, particularly as they reach the age of courtship and marriage when these skills begin to be put into everyday use. Basic beading skills are soon acquired and proficiency usually comes with practice. Outstanding and unusual skill in beading is a gift that is not necessarily shared by all women, and those who excel in the use of colour and novel and intricate designs are honoured for their command of the art. Today bead making is one of the few traditional skills that provide women with the ability to make money.

The tools and materials used in Zulu beadwork have changed over time, but because the basic form of the constituent material, a bead with a hole in it and some form of thread, the techniques of threading have remained much the same. Older beadwork is usually easily identifiable by the use made of various kinds of string, cotton or some string-like material on which the beads are threaded, and by the fact that the string is looped to make a fastener

Main centres of Zulu beadwork production.

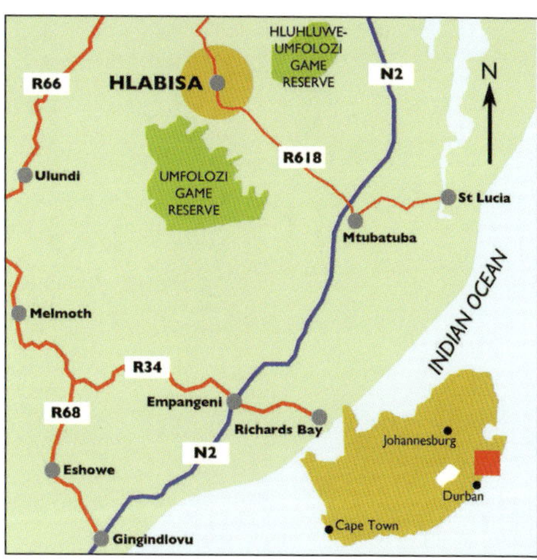

which is slipped over a single small bead. Modern beadwork and the majority of that made for the market, including that emanating from commercially oriented projects, makes use of more durable materials such as gut, and in most cases metal fasteners have replaced the loops of the past.

Special beading needles, some of which are curved, are used and the bead maker usually works from loose beads which are drawn up by the needle from a small container which is placed within easy reach. Depending on the pattern or design, the beads are sorted into appropriate colours and sizes.

Bead colours, messages and meaning

Zulu beadwork made and worn in traditional communities was, and still is, largely characterised by regional differences in both the patterns and the colour combinations that are used. In this sense, the beadwork 'speaks' not only of the wearer's social status and background, but also of the colour preferences that have developed in particular areas over time. The beauty and intricacy of the beadwork made in the Msinga area for local wear rather than for the market during the mid 1950s and early 1960s is such an example. It was described to the anthropologist, Frank Jolles (1991; 2010), in the following terms:

> *Isishunka* is generally made up of seven colours – white, light blue, dark green, pale yellow, pink, red and black.
> *Isithembu* consists of five colours – light blue, grass green, bright yellow, red and black.
> *Umzanzi* patterns contain only four colours – white, dark blue, grass green and red.
> *Isinyolovane*, is a combination of colours that do not dominate in any of the other styles.

Bands of coloured beads were sometimes decorated with studs and even small locks and it was in these elaborations that the creativity of the bead maker surfaced. Over time, and particularly as new bead colours became available, the number of personal innovations increased, with the result that, although the basic stylistic designs remained fairly constant, later beadwork was often enlivened by new colour combinations which allowed for ever more complex, innovative and idiosyncratic designs. The *umzanzi*, for instance, was often subtly changed by the use of black beads which provided a striking contrast to the other bead colours used. This was particularly the case when black replaced the more usual blue. Other bright new colours such as orange sometimes replaced red. Even more striking were the geometric designs that began to appear in Msinga beadwork in the late 1950s and early 1960s. Taken together, these changes led to the development of a new style of beading referred to locally as *isilomi* or *isimoderni*. Indeed, other new fashions, referred to as *imfesheni*, began to appear as beaders sought to outdo each other not only in innovative, but ever more complex designs.

Side by side with the exquisite and intricate beadwork intended for personal use was that made for sale, initially for the growing external tourist market and later for the fast growing fashion market. Much of the appeal of contemporary tourist and fashion beadwork and particularly that of the plethora of necklaces and so-called Zulu love letters, lies in the widespread belief that these items carry messages that can be read if one only knows the code. Caution is, however, required when attempting to ascribe a fixed or widespread meaning to the bead colours or colour combinations used in Zulu beadwork. It is likely, moreover, that where colours once did form the basis of a 'code' that could, in very general terms, be 'read' by the recipient, any such code was by no means universal throughout Zululand or over time. In addition, just as patterns and motifs differed from place to place, so the meaning of particular beads might be, and often was, affected by their place in the overall pattern of the beaded item.

For these reasons, interpreting the meaning of beadwork items and, in particular, the so-called 'genuine' Zulu love letters sold in tourist shops and wayside markets should be treated with extreme caution. In some cases a simple, generic

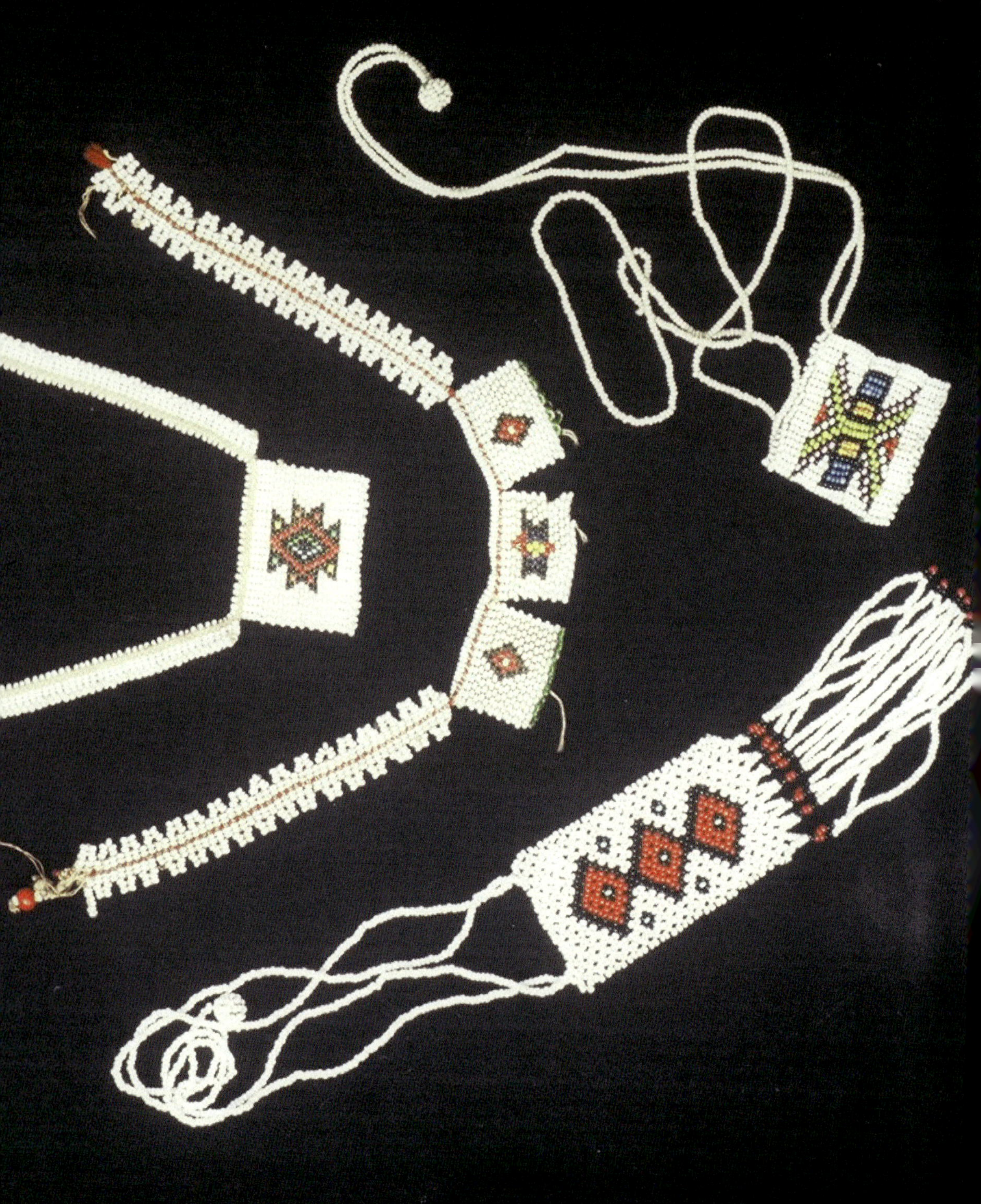

translation is attached to the 'love letters' produced by the increasing number of projects run and sponsored by local and international income-generating agencies. But even these are cryptic at best and designed to please the buyer rather than reflect the subtlety and possible meaning of the genuine article.

Do bead colours convey meaning?

With this caution in mind, it is fortunate that we have at least one early source upon which to draw in attempting to re-create the manner in which the colours of beads may originally have conveyed messages for those to whom bead ornaments were given. Based on fieldwork carried out in 1948 in the Bergville area, Twala (1958) lists the meanings attached by her research participants to the following bead colours.

> *White – I say this with an open white heart.*
> *Blue – I say `Oh' for the dove that picks food.*
> *White – In the yard at your kraal.*
> *Red – I envy also the one who enjoys your fireplace.*
> *White – Although my heart may be pure.*
> *Pink – You are poor.*

Grossert (1978) warns, however, of the difficulties inherent in reading Zulu love letters and stresses that their symbolic nature may make them open to different and even very personal interpretations. He points out that because each article was intensely personal, it could probably be reliably understood only by its recipient, or possibly by close friends of the maker. It is probable also that such letters were open to subtly different interpretations depending on the parties concerned, and the occasions on which they were made. He does, however, concur with Twala that white is – or was – usually used to indicate love, but warns that when used with black, the message may suggest that difficulties face the lovers. Ruby red means much love in spite of poverty, but pink imputes abject poverty to the lover, particularly with respect to his inability to pay *lobola* (bridewealth) for his bride.

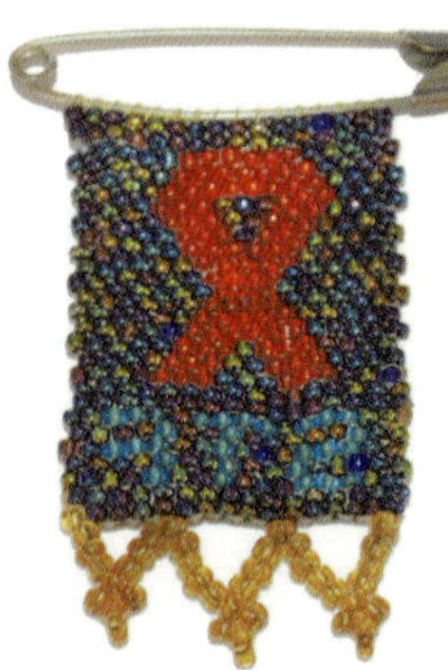

A particularly beautiful AIDS pin in vibrant, glittering colours. (MP-W)

Grossert also suggests that the numbers and proportions of a particular colour combination may once have had meaning. He stresses that beading was a form of symbolic language, but that – even as he wrote – it was changing and dying out. Certainly Zulu love letters made for sale and not for a lover lose their intrinsic communicative meaning and function; if they speak at all, the language is that of the marketplace and their objective is now purely commercial. It must be stressed, finally, that the 'colour coding' once used in genuine Zulu love letters cannot be automatically extended to other contexts, and should not be used to impute meaning to the beaded garments and regalia worn either in the past or today. When dealing with beads and Zulu beadwork, however, there are invariably exceptions to every rule.

During the 1980s, as the South African HIV/AIDS epidemic began to cast its shadow over the country, a number of local bead making projects designed and marketed HIV/AIDS dolls and small beaded lapel badges carrying the looped red ribbon symbol on a white background, drawing attention not only to the seriousness of the epidemic but also to the necessity of practising safe sex. Large and small HIV/AIDS dolls were on sale in many venues across the country, and delegates attending the 2007 International HIV/AIDS Conference held in KwaZulu-Natal received a beaded lapel badge in the standard conference package.

A number of other NGOs which took as their mandate the importance of raising awareness of the dangers of HIV/AIDS were also established at this time. Among these was *Siyazama*, discussed more fully in Chapter 4, and the Hillcrest HIV/AIDS Centre or *Woza Moya*, as it is now known. *Woza Moya* was situated outside Durban on the edge of the beautiful Valley of a Thousand Hills and was dedicated to fighting the epidemic among the local black inhabitants where the

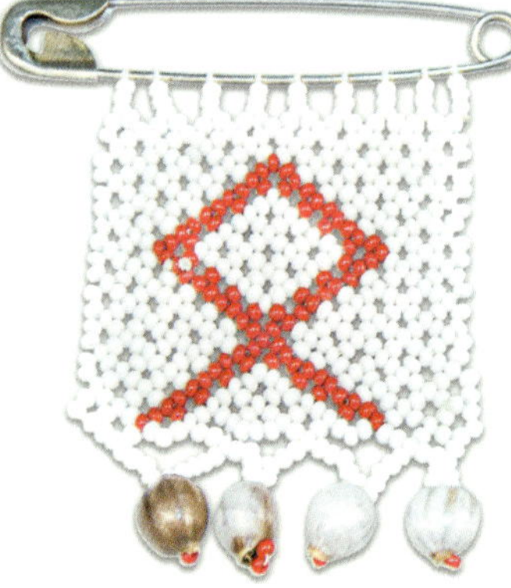

AIDS pin incorporating seeds – from Woza Moya. (AN) (Preston-Whyte Collection)

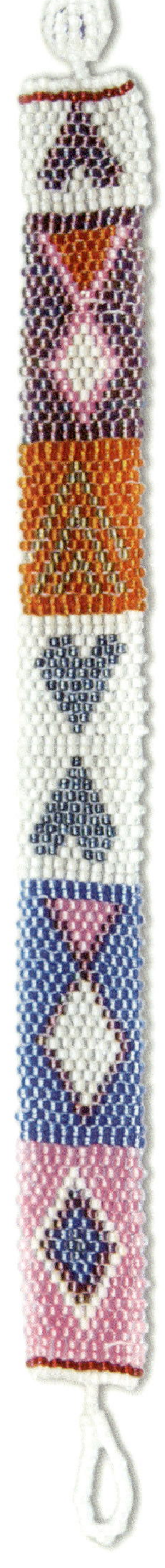

infection rates in some sections of the population was then in the vicinity of 40 - 60 %. The focus of the project was, and still is, on developing skills that will provide an income for impoverished local families. Beadwork was one of these and now, some 21 years later, the project is still active and its beautiful beaded jewellery is widely available in South Africa. The difference that the project has made in the lives of many families affected by HIV/AIDS was summed up by one of the beaders, Gogo Francesca, who is responsible for single-handedly feeding, clothing and educating her children:

> *I had nothing before I came to Woza Moya – even food.*
> *By making crafts I have been able to take care of my family…*
> *I am happy… my dignity has been restored.*

Idoli

Second only to Zulu love letters in popularity with tourists are the so-called Zulu dolls, referred to by their makers as *idoli*. These range from relatively small to, in a few cases, almost life-size dolls. Klopper (1982-89:32-38) argues that although traditional dolls appear to have been made in a number of neighbouring South African societies, they were not common in Zulu-speaking groups before the advent of a tourist market, which provided the impetus for their development and proliferation.

The very term *idoli* suggests that these beaded dolls, although they may have a distant ancestor in indigenous African 'dolls' made in many areas of South Africa, are first and foremost creatures of the modern world and, in KwaZulu-Natal in particular, of the contemporary tourist milieu. With the promotion and subsequent growth of tourism in many parts of the country, the number, popularity and variety of these dolls has burgeoned.

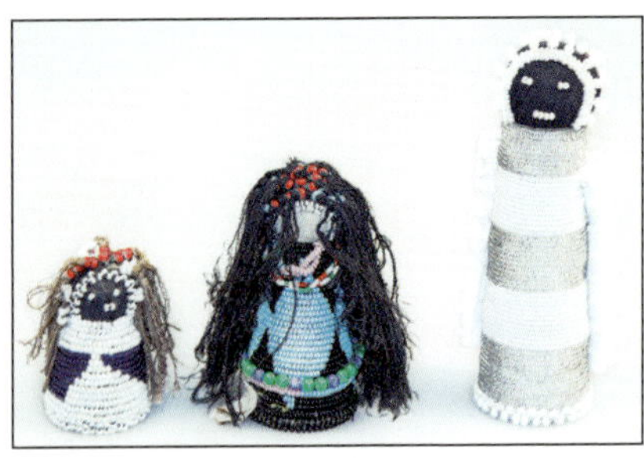

Three small 'Zulu Dolls' or *idoli*. The two dolls on the left date from the 1960s and early 70s. The doll on the right – a trend of making white dolls – are often referred to as 'Angel Dolls'. Keats Drift area. (AN)

In his exhaustive review of local African dolls in the Dulger-Collection in Munich, Jolles (2012) includes a fascinating and detailed discussion of this popular bead form in Msinga, one of the province's vast, primarily rural and impoverished districts. Beginning in the late 1970s and 1980s, these dolls were – and continue to be – made largely by a number of related women and a few men living in the KwaLatha district of Keat's Drift. After tracing the range and evolution of indigenous figurative dolls made by young women purely for personal use, first as playthings and later as courting gifts, Jolles moves to a discussion of the evolution of dolls aimed specifically at the growing tourist market.

He notes the surprise with which local doll makers in Keat's Drift greeted the interest aroused by their dolls amongst some of the white travellers passing through the district. They recounted to him how one motorist who stopped to examine the dolls advised the makers to add eyes to the faceless images in order to attract buyers. Following the motorist's suggestion, doll maker Hluphekile Zuma added two single beads for eyes, but left the rest of the face blank, thus largely defeating the objective of making the doll more lifelike.

Clearly the objective of courting dolls was not realism, but rather to alert the intended recipient to the doll maker's romantic interest in him. Young men often wore these romantic trophies proudly, some even sporting a number of them to indicate their popularity with women. Jolles comments, somewhat wryly, on the imbalance of the interaction. While the public display of a number of such dolls drew attention to the popularity of particular men, for young women there was no surety that the giving of the doll – although a subtle attempt to initiate a long-term relationship with the youth concerned – would be favourably received and acted upon.

Courting dolls were, and still are, made using a number of distinctive patterns. Early dolls consisted of a long string of beads wound round and round a stiff cloth core to form the body of the doll. The colours used were often those of the clan to which the maker belonged. Although the face was left blank, the head was covered by long, black twine to which white beads, sometimes mixed with blue and red beads, were attached to form a headdress resembling that of a diviner. A long, beaded loop was attached to many dolls for carrying them over the shoulder, or, alternatively to hang them on a wall in the homestead.

In some later dolls' headdresses, a number of regional styles and colours occur; these seem to have been particularly popular with tourists who eventually came to make up the bulk of the makers' market. In some parts of Msinga the dolls sported the large circular headdresses of married women typical of the area. Jolles comments that this innovation marks a radical change in design, as it moves the new style dolls out of the arena of courting into representations of the world of married women.

As the market for beaded African dolls increased, so did the number of beaders making them. Msinga dolls came into competition with dolls from other areas, not only in KwaZulu-Natal, but from elsewhere in South Africa. Beaders began not only to diversify but to dress their dolls in more and more elaborate costumes in order to maintain their hold on the market. A number of the Msinga doll makers increased not only the range of their costume design, but also the size of their dolls. Jolles shows one of the Msinga doll makers alongside dolls ranging from small to almost life size. A new market opened up at South African and other international airports where dolls from KwaZulu-Natal had to compete with dolls from other regions in the country, in particular with the ever-popular Ndebele dolls with their bright, stylised colours. This put a premium on continual change and innovation.

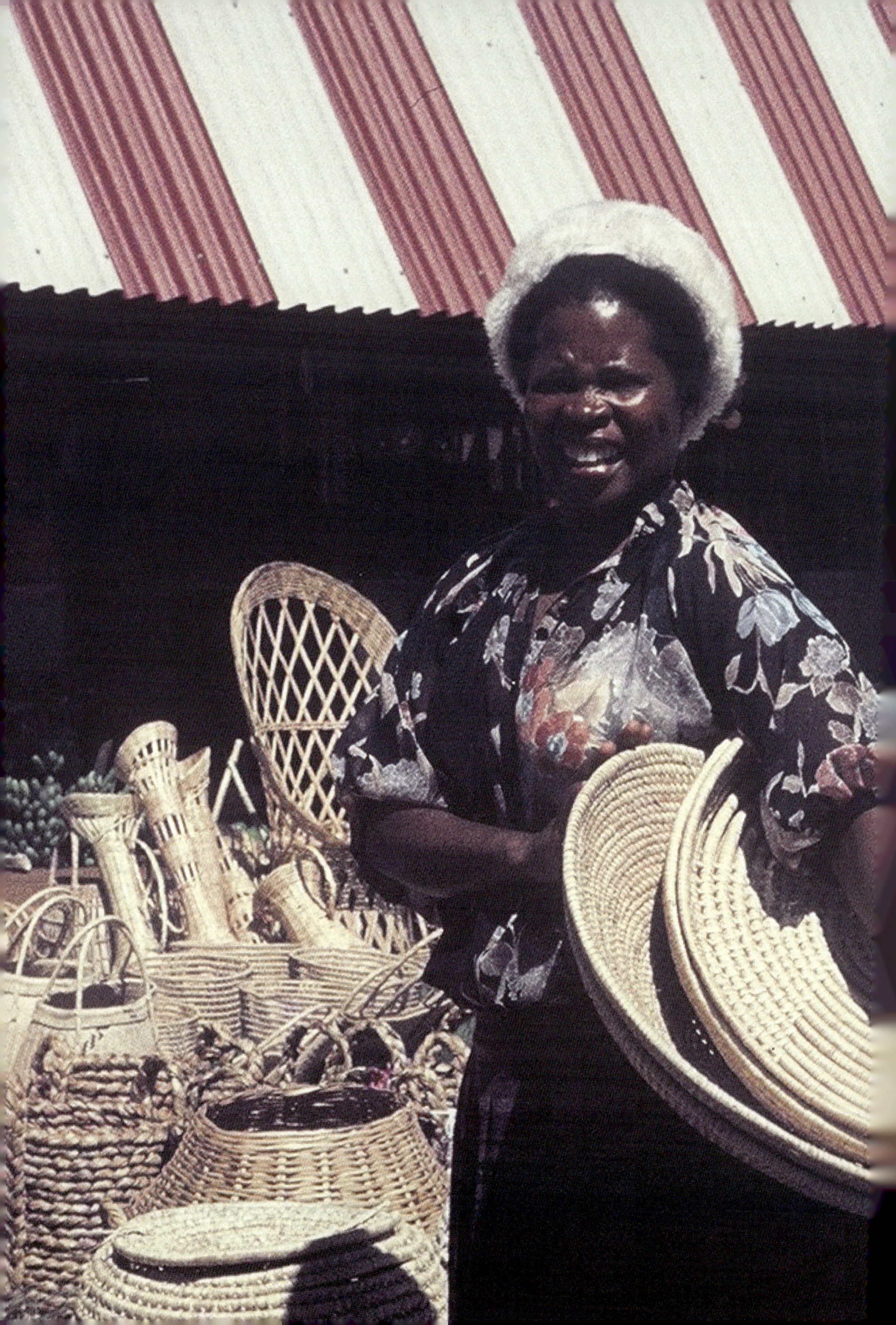

new beadwork frontiers

CONTEMPORARY ZULU BEADWORK is not a static arena nor is it a mere relic of the past. Signs of innovation and change are to be found on all sides as beaders respond not only to new markets, but also to changes in the social milieu in which they live and which their beadwork often comes to reflect. Once a local craft serving the needs of a limited and largely internal demand, Zulu beadwork was transformed during the late 1950s and early 1960s in response, first, to the development of a market for tourist beadwork, and secondly to the intervention of a number of development agencies committed to using beadwork as a vehicle for providing rural women with a source of regular income. Most of these agencies were intent also on raising the standard, design and durability of local beadwork in order to make it attractive to both a national and an international market. As a result an increasing number of rural women were drawn into bead making so as to take advantage of a growing and constantly diversifying external market. This market placed a premium on innovation and creativity in design and in the development of new forms of beadwork. These factors paved the way for the long-term sustainability of both an internal and fast growing external market for Zulu beadwork.

It was fortuitous that these changes coincided with an increase in both local and international tourist traffic along the coastal and inland highways of KwaZulu-Natal. In response to this, roadside stalls selling tropical fruit sprang up at the side of all major roads and highways and particularly at busy crossroads. At first most of these stalls were fairly small and stocked local fruit and vegetables, most of which was delivered to stall-holders by local middlemen. Soon, however, stallholders began to stock local craft such as clay pots, wood carvings and beadwork. Because of where they were situated, these stalls became a traffic hazard and traffic police regularly raided and closed them, while at the same time confiscating and often destroying the goods on display.

Realising that the destruction of the stalls threatened the
livelihood of many rural households, the provincial authorities,
working through the KwaZulu Development Corporation (KDC),
stepped in and provided funding for the building of a number
of large roadside curio markets. In these markets, the largest of
which was situated at Umgababa on the KwaZulu-Natal South
Coast, craftspeople rented stalls where they could display and sell
their wares. A number of stallholders found it more lucrative to
scour the interior for local craftwork rather than to rely on what
they or their family members could make. In time the popularity
of these markets increased the demand for all forms of craft
in the region, and particularly for beadwork. A visit to one or
more curio market soon became a mandatory part of the tourist
experience. Because of their portability, colourful beaded belts,
necklaces and bracelets were much in demand and the sale of
beadwork soon outstripped that of larger items such as clay pots
and woodwork. Tourists even tried to buy the beadwork on the

Local roadside
market, North Coast
late 1950s. (RP-W)

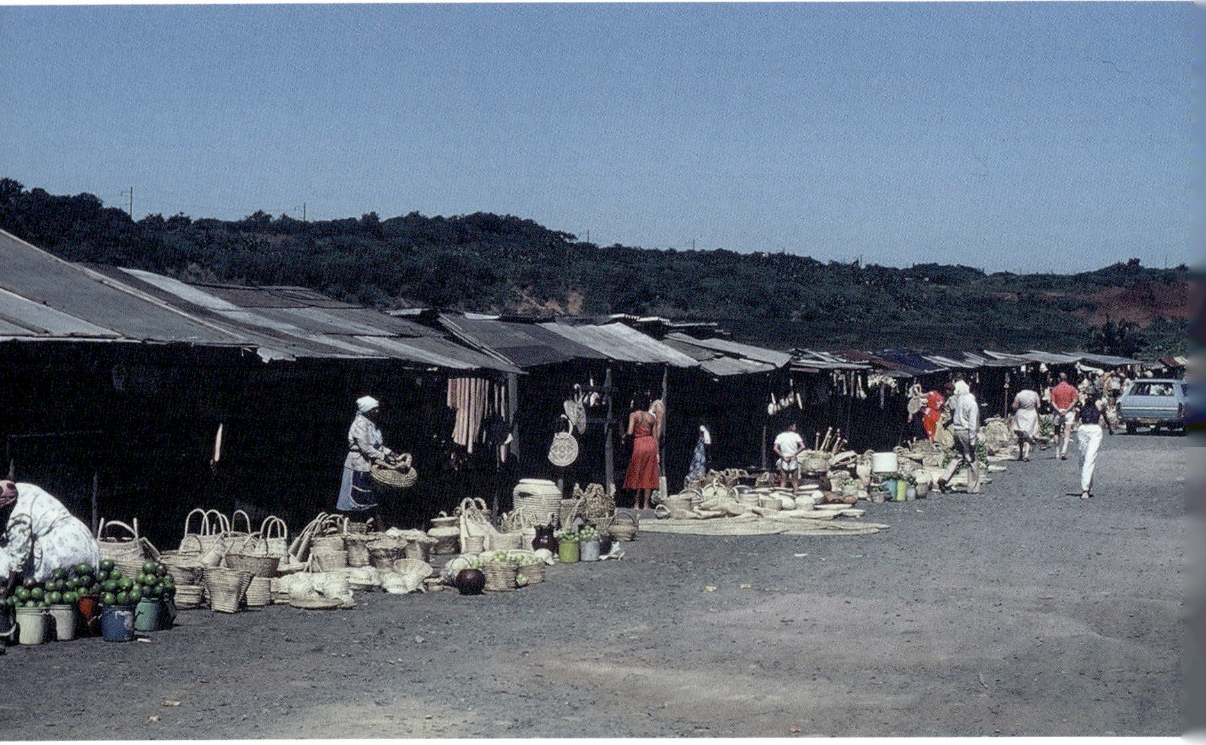

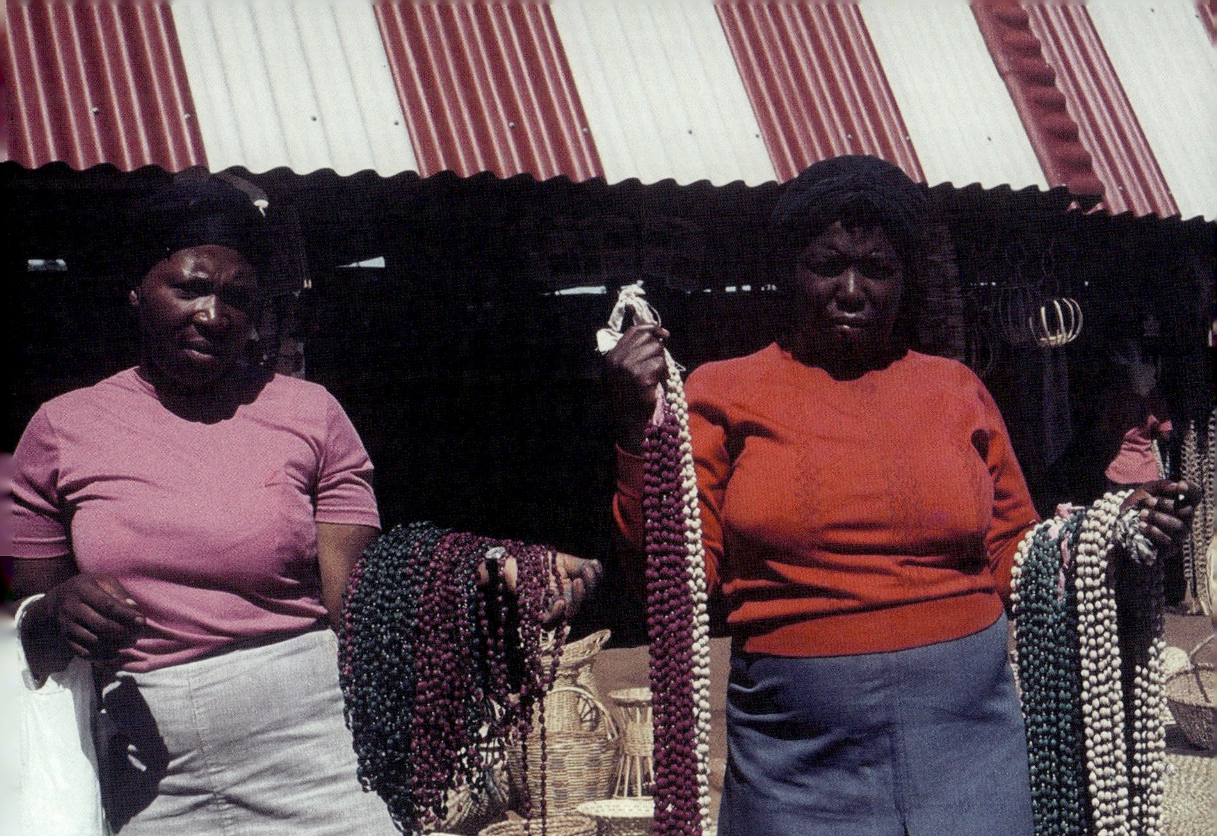

traditional dress worn by craft sellers. This encouraged traders to increase the range and amount of beadwork that they stocked.

A number of stallholders responded to the growing popularity of local beadwork by sourcing the most popular items from inland bead makers specifically for sale to tourists. Because they soon realised that the items most in demand were relatively simple and inexpensive, and that buyers seldom appeared to recognise quality beadwork, many began to stock goods that beadwork experts scathingly referred to as 'cheap tourist junk'. As holiday mementos, however, such trinkets served the purpose for which they were designed extremely well.

Observing that children emerged from many of the cars that stopped at the craft stalls and markets, stallholders began to stock small beaded animals, while others experimented with colourful hair bands and bracelets with tiny dolls attached to them. A few even offered Zulu 'fertility' dolls for sale to young women. Standard 'ethnic' craft ranging from Zulu stabbing

A range of popular 'ethnic' craft on sale at Umgababa in the 1960s and 1970s. (MP-W)

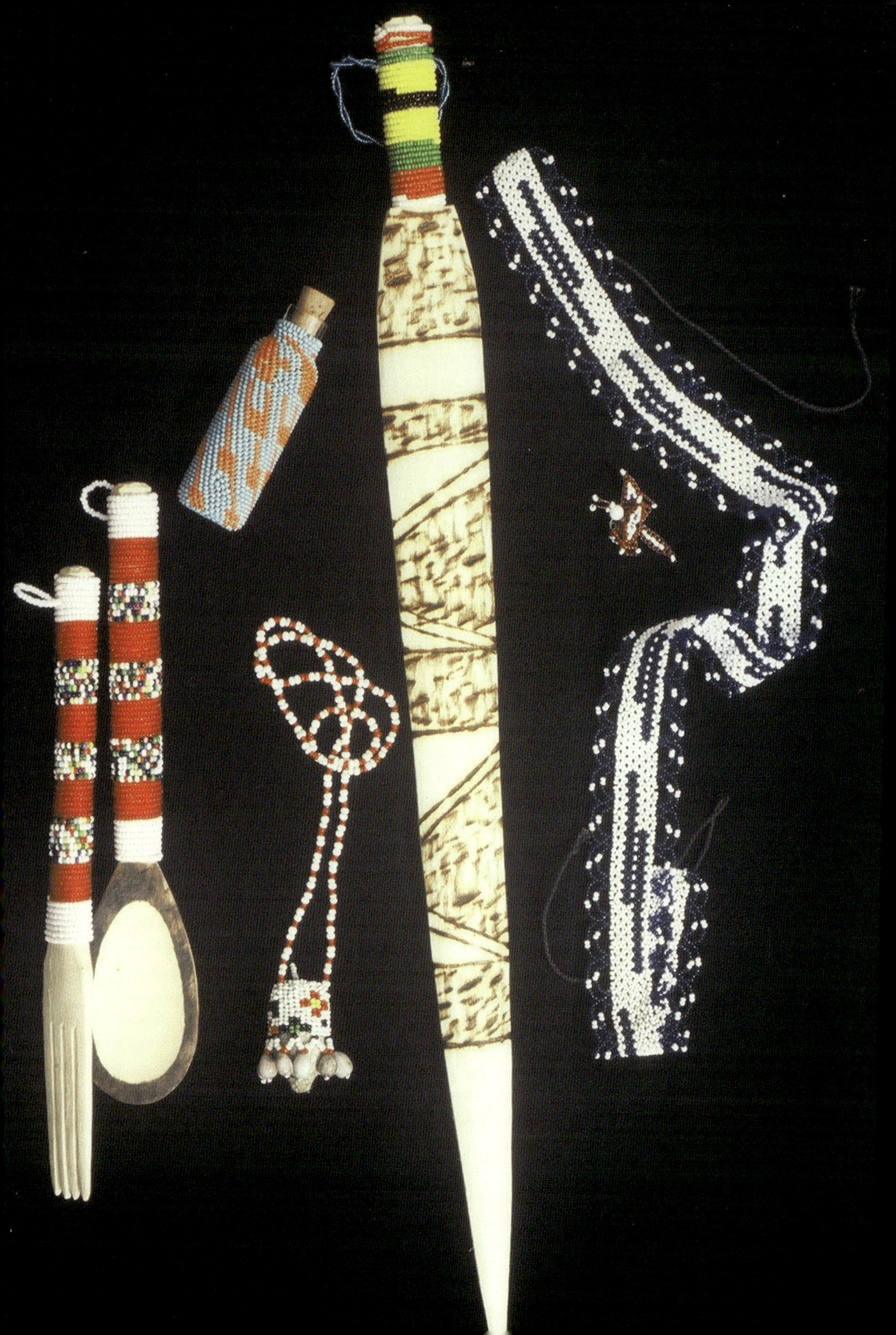

spears and assegais to beaded key rings, spoons and salad servers also appeared, and became extremely popular.

Success in the curio market is not necessarily dependent on novelty any more than it is dependent on quality or authenticity. Because, however, more discerning buyers do visit these stalls from time to time, the stallholders are continually on the lookout for particularly innovative items to combine with standard Zulu tourist fare.

The tourist boom along the coastal roads and highways of KwaZulu-Natal attracted the attention not only of local bead makers, but of a number of white South Africans who quickly responded to the money-making potential of 'traditional Zulu craft', including beadwork. Some enterprising individuals embarked on projects designed to produce craft on a large scale, with an eye to supplying the fast-growing curio market. Their motives were primarily financial, but some of the new craft entrepreneurs hoped also to provide the families of their farm workers and tenants with a source of much needed income, in order to supplement low-paid and often seasonal agricultural work. In some cases craft, and particularly beadwork projects, were aimed at assisting the families of severely handicapped men and women, most of whom were in no position to undertake heavy farm labour.

Two main operational models developed: in the first, small 'factories' were set up on white-owned farms and workers were paid a fixed daily or weekly wage, while in the second model, a simple cottage industry emerged in which craft items were made at home, often by more than one member of a family and craft workers were paid *pro rata* for each item. Beadwork aimed at the curio market was soon supplied to curio stores all over the province and was also stocked by a number of the stallholders at wayside markets who negotiated a somewhat lower price for their purchases than those paid by the white managers of urban curio stores.

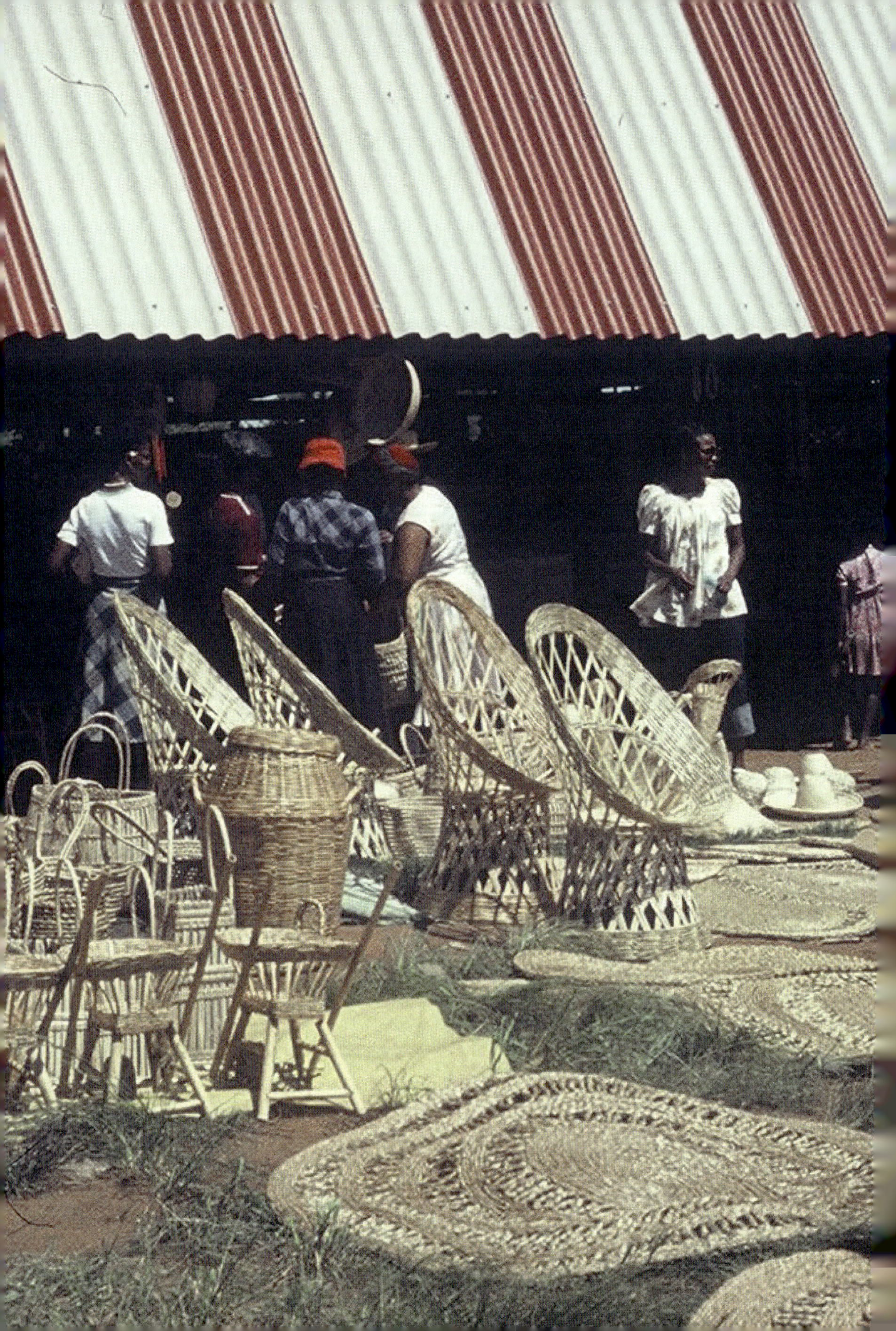

In time several enterprising white entrepreneurs moved into different and new tourist ventures. One was the staging of 'Zulu Dancing' and later the establishment of what were referred to as `Zulu Cultural Villages'. At these tourists were given a short talk on Zulu history and culture accompanied by demonstrations of beer brewing and the making of traditional crafts such as beadwork and pottery. The popularity of these shows, not only with overseas tourists but also with South Africans, lies largely in the skilful manner in which 'Zulu Culture' is packaged and presented as strange and exotic. An added bonus comes with the possibility of purchasing 'traditional' beadwork and artefacts such as the clay pots and beer strainers used in the 'cultural' presentation or replicas of them.

Roadside curio markets and Cultural Villages are by no means the only venues selling Zulu beadwork in KwaZulu-Natal. In Durban which is not only a major port, but also the centre of growing local and international tourist trade, curio stores and craft shops abound, clustering particularly in the vicinity of the major beaches and along the waterfront promenades. In addition to these formal businesses there are invariably large numbers of informal traders, some of whom have curio stalls on the beachfront from which they sell a variety of craft including Zulu beadwork. Most of the holidaymakers and tourists who stop to look at their wares assume that the stallholder has

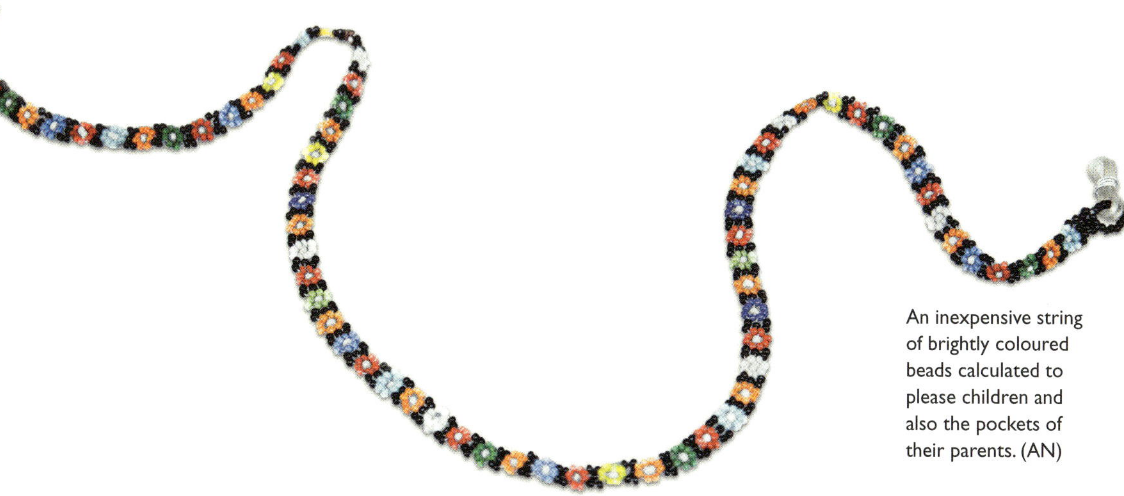

An inexpensive string of brightly coloured beads calculated to please children and also the pockets of their parents. (AN)

made the beadwork herself. She is, in fact, often an astute
businesswoman who collects her craft from rural makers
once a month, or more often in peak holiday season. Some
of the items for sale are often neither handmade nor, in fact,
hardly ethnic in character. Rather, they are cheap Taiwanese
or Chinese imports, such as bamboo sun hats, fans and highly
coloured tin trays, for all of which the traders have found that
there is a ready market. Many an unwary tourist has bought
what purports to be a 'Zulu' bracelet decorated with a small
beaded doll that was, in fact, imported from the East by local
middlemen and traders.

The reinvention of Zulu beadwork

A very different kind of Zulu beadwork to that made for either
personal use or for sale on the tourist market has developed
in recent years. This beadwork rivals traditional beadwork in
beauty and variety. As important, and unlike most of the makers
of early traditional beadwork whose names are now lost to us
or exist only in local legend, many of today's bead makers are
not only identified by name, but are publicly honoured for their
skill, originality and creativity. Their emergence is largely due to
a number of dedicated individuals who recognised the potential
that Zulu beadwork and Zulu beadwork skills had to provide
an income for both bead makers and bead sellers. The result
is a new beadwork genre that combines beauty with variety,
and has the potential to command prices far in excess of tourist
beadwork.

The agents, or facilitators, of these dramatic changes fall into
two broad categories. The first ranges from fellow South
Africans, some of whom were already active in promoting the
work of black artists and craftspeople, to farmers and rural
missionaries seeking a source of income for black families living
either on their farms or on local mission stations. The second
are the representatives of internationally based development
agencies who play a consciously interventionist role in
introducing changes in Zulu bead making and in other local

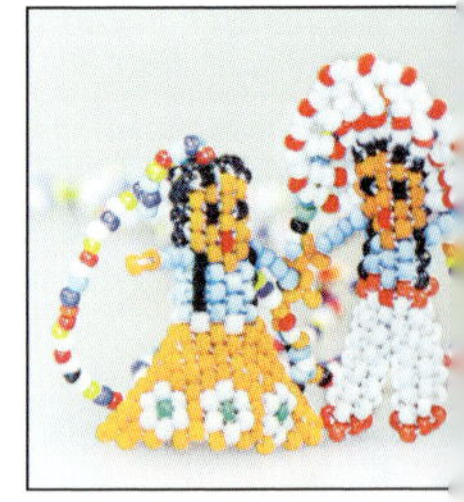

Two small popular
beaded 'dolls', on
the right is the local
version and on the
left an imported
doll originally made
to represent a 'Red
Indian'. (AN)

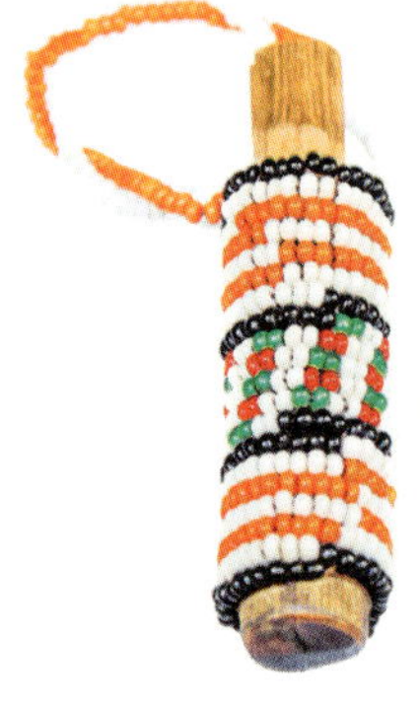

A Zulu 'medicine
bottle'. The original
of these bottles were
often filled with
protective herbs,
and this added to
their attraction for
tourists. (AN)

crafts, in order to increase their marketability and so provide a regular source of income for people with limited access to either formal or informal employment. While, in the latter context, beadwork skills have been used mainly to produce up-market jewellery, wall hangings and eye-catching beaded clothing, in time, a number of beaders diversified into making, among other items, a variety of beaded dolls and figurines. More recently, projects making fashion jewellery have been established and run by a new generation of black beadwork entrepreneurs. In this sense Zulu beadwork has not so much changed as been actively reinvented a number of times over the last two to three decades.

Early experiments in the production of beaded fashion jewellery

The objective of at least one of the early bead projects producing fashion jewellery was to design beadwork that would hold its own in the world of fashion, both inside South Africa and internationally. Projects like these were very different from the cottage industries started by local farmers in order to mass produce tourist beadwork. Novel designs and strict quality control were introduced by the project leaders, who insisted on the use of durable materials. These included gut instead of the far less long-lasting cotton on which to thread beads. Metal fastenings soon replaced the easily broken beaded loops of the past.

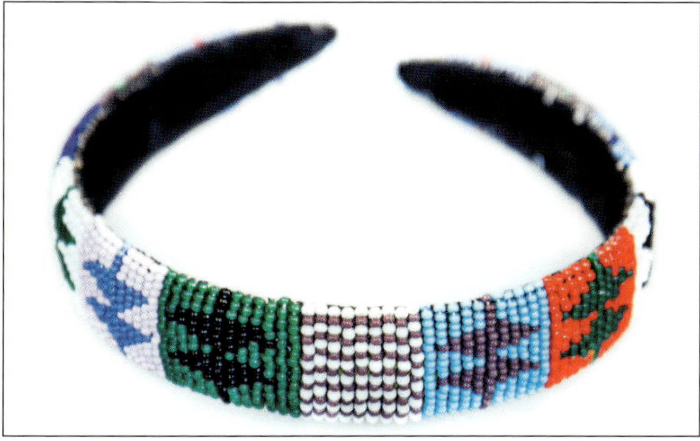

A brightly coloured and extremely popular headband for girls. (AN) (Preston-Whyte Collection)

An early but iconic example of the trend to internationalise Zulu beadwork was the initiative of Crena Bond, who developed the Mdukutshani Bead Centre on a farm near Tugela Ferry in northern Zululand. Here she introduced the use of a new variety of imported shiny beads in fashion colours quite different from those used in most curio beadwork. The glittering, long necklaces and bracelets, made in silver, gold, mauve and a funky brown by the women beading at Mdukutshani, caught the eye of a famous Paris designer, Christian Dior, and were used to complement and enhance his annual collection in 1982. The following year they appeared on the shelves of Harrods in London.

It was not only their designs and the impact of their beadwork that made Mdukutshani a pioneer project. The organisational model was that of a co-operative in which local women were provided with beads and paid piecemeal for the jewellery they made at home. Although the highest of standards were demanded, both in the choice and grading of colours and in general workmanship, the bead makers more than rose to the challenge and continued to produce ever more beautiful necklaces and bracelets.

Paradoxically, this turn of events eventually caused a number of problems for the project director; particularly when the output of project members threatened to exceed what the market, then largely seasonal, could bear. Beadwork piled up and had to be stored until new orders were received from existing distributors. Alternatively, new markets had to be found for the increased beadwork supply. In the interim the project experienced cash flow problems as the bead makers continued to produce high quality beadwork for which they had to be paid. These are common problems in many craft-based projects the world over, however small, and particularly to those that operate without wide-ranging marketing, planning and management structures. Some of them may be avoided, however, if the project is associated with and works

An example of the necklaces designed and pionered by Crena Bond and her team of beaders at Mdukutshani Bead Centre near Tugela Ferry. (MH)

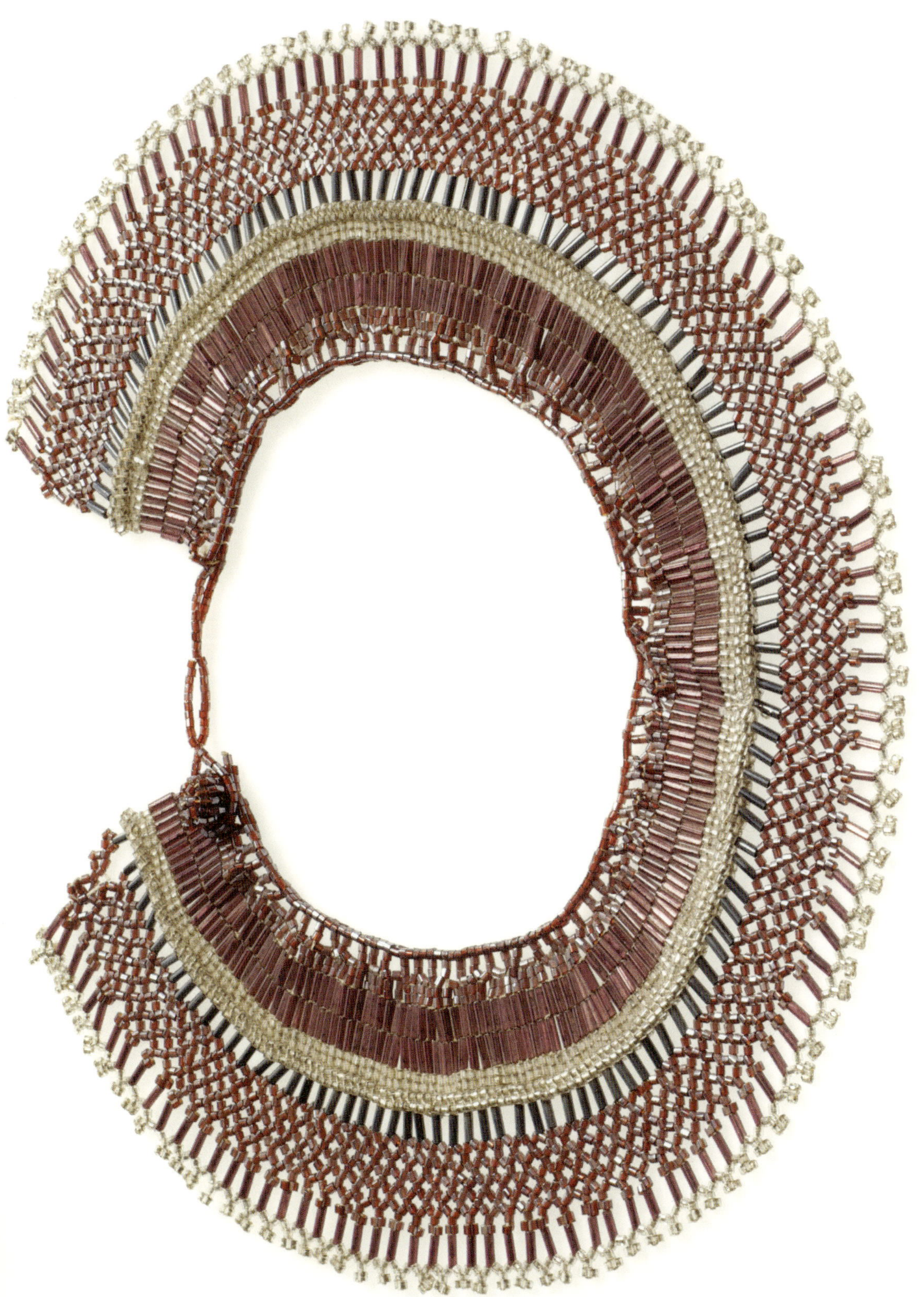

hand in hand with other similar, but not competing projects;
or is able to make use of the international links provided by
some supportive local and international funders to market their
beadwork. A number of Zulu bead projects have, in fact, been
initiated by international missionary associations in order to
provide money-making opportunities for local parishioners.

One such project was KwaZamokuhle, which, in contrast to
Mdukutshani with its array of shiny beadwork, concentrated on
producing beadwork that kept closely to traditional beading
styles and bead varieties. It was initiated
by missionary Ruth Johannsen, who relied
heavily on local and overseas missionary
networks in order to market the beadwork
produced by the project. The beadwork
was, however, also stocked by a few local
South African curio stores whose buyers
were dedicated to promoting examples of
well made traditional Zulu beadwork that
appealed to the more discerning buyers
rather than the average tourist. One of these
was the African Art Centre in Durban, which
is discussed in Chapter 5.

Questions of long term market viability

The question arises of the long-term
sustainability and, indeed, the viability of
relatively small beadwork projects. Many
are dependent on the entrepreneurial sense
and input of the founder or founders, and
particularly on how the project can maintain
its edge over competitors, many of whom
bring to the market increasingly novel
product designs and robust management,
together with well developed advertising
and distribution infrastructures.

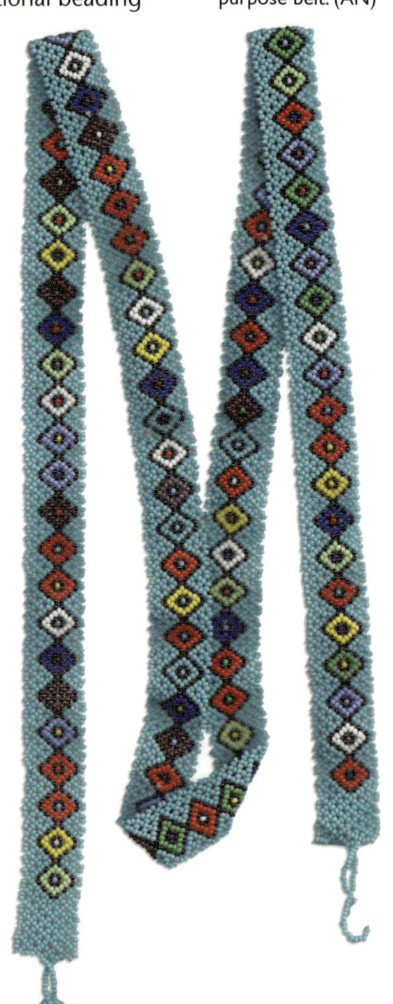

A narrow general-purpose belt. (AN)

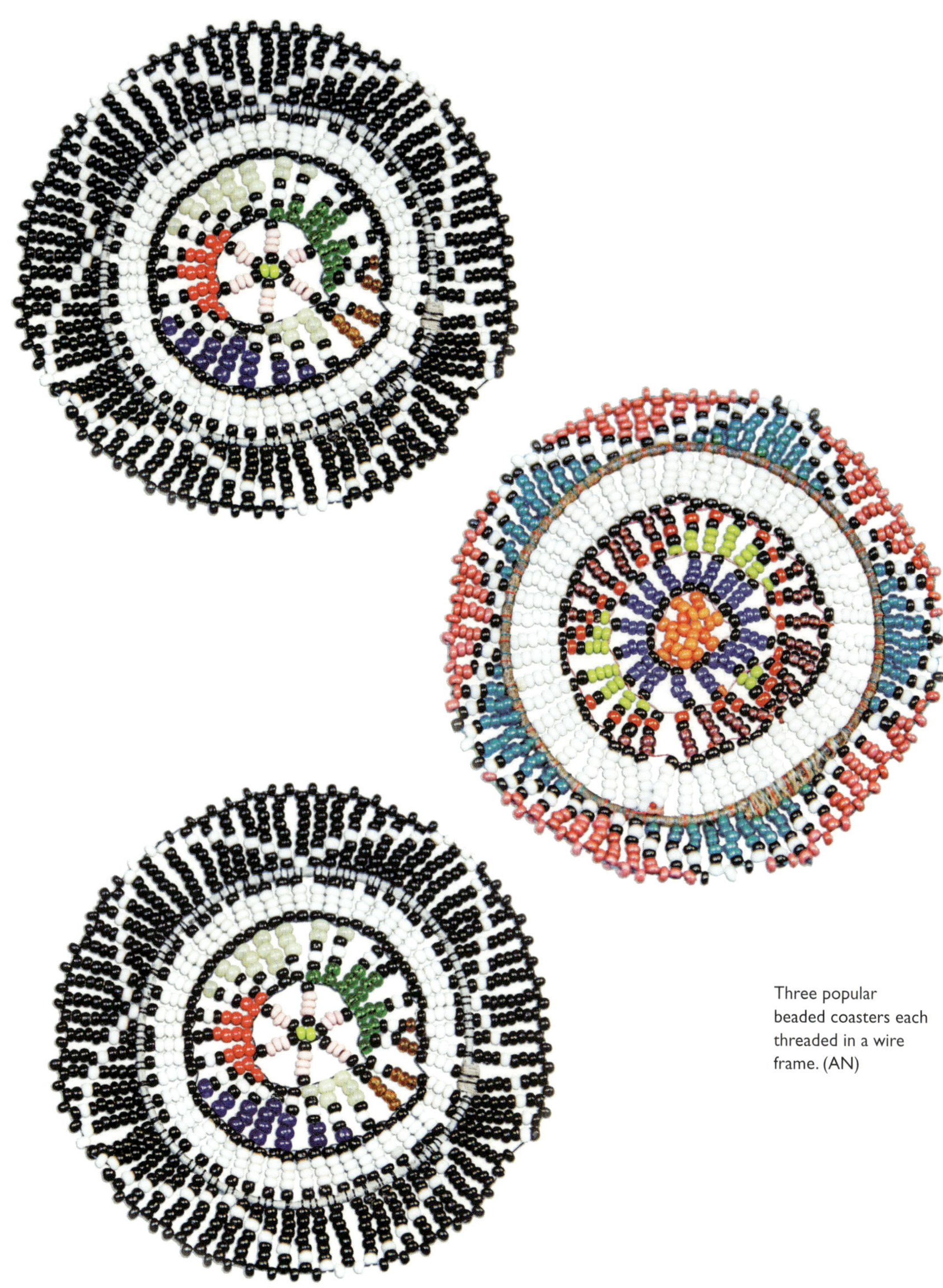

Three popular
beaded coasters each
threaded in a wire
frame. (AN)

South African beadwork as a whole is moving
beyond the point where relatively small,
philanthropically-oriented projects, which lack
the backing of sophisticated management and
distribution structures, can survive beyond the
short-to middle-term. There are a number of
ongoing beadwork projects whose viability is a
result of, in the one instance, being part of a larger
craft association, and in others, to operating under
the umbrella of a wider grouping of NGOs, which
includes a number of beadwork projects and affords
them mutually beneficial links. Examples of these
are discussed towards the end of this chapter and in
Chapter 6.

Yet another hurdle may lie in the future: currently
beadwork jewellery is in fashion, both in this
country and overseas. South African beadwork is,
furthermore, relatively inexpensive compared with
much other costume jewellery. How long beaded jewellery will
remain popular is, however, uncertain. The fashion market is
notoriously fickle and there is no assurance that Zulu beadwork
will not be replaced by some other fashion, or by an even
cheaper, mass-produced alternative.

The continuing versatility of Zulu beadwork is, however,
demonstrated by yet another beadwork project that has
recently sought to fill a specialised niche market. Sikanya Crafts
concentrates on producing specialty beadwork for both the
tourist and for what is referred to in the project's advertising
material as the 'gift' market. The project was started in early
2002 by Hazel Haines, and is run from her home outside the
small town of Eshowe in Zululand. Although relatively isolated,
the project is well known to local tour operators who bring
tourists to her home in order to buy 'genuine examples' of
Zulu bead work. Prospective buyers find the beadwork made
by Sikanya Crafts attractive; largely because of its innovative

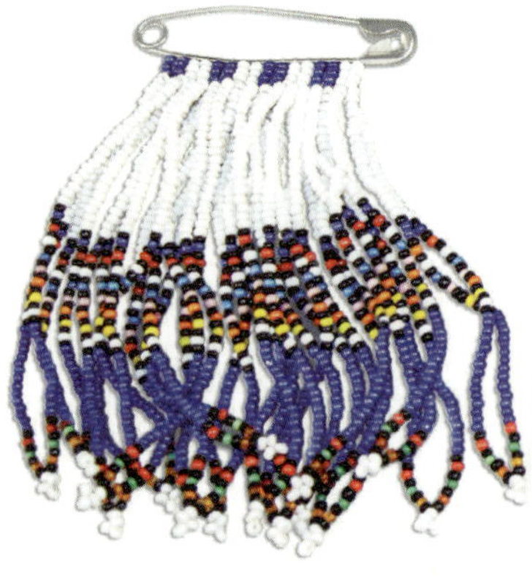

Beaded skirt or lapel pins.
(AN)

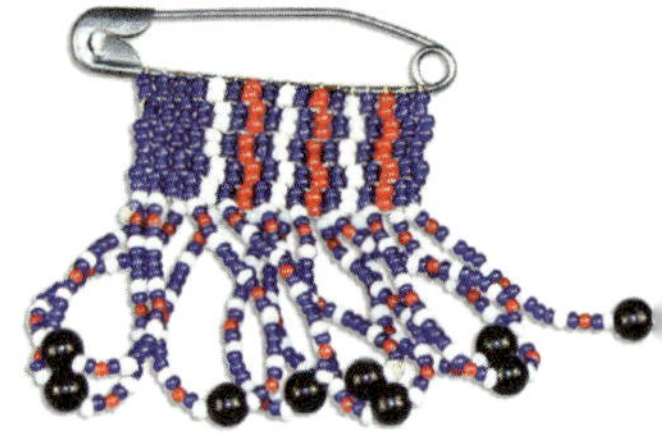

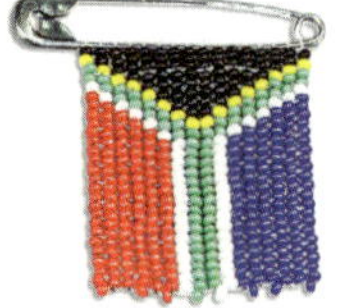

Beaded lapel pins
reminiscent of the
South African flag.
(AN)

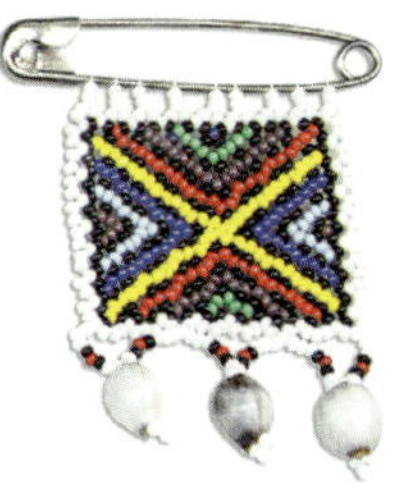

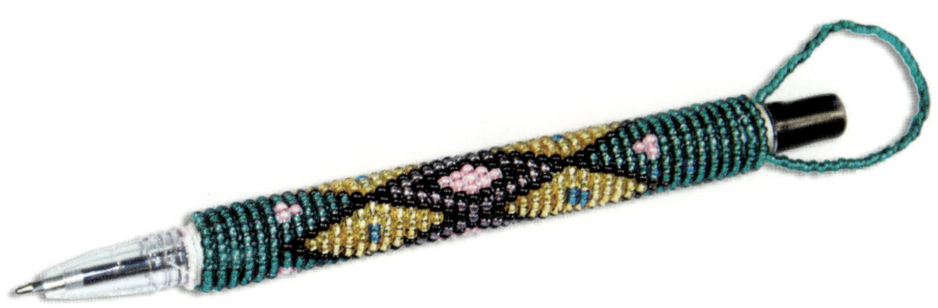

mixing of traditional and modern beading styles and colours. Glittering metallic beads are used to catch the eye, but are often interspersed with small buttons and beads made from local seeds. Variety and innovation are the keys to the success of the project.

Intermediaries and 'culture brokers'

As we have seen, the exercise of creativity in response to new market opportunities has led to the writing of a number of new chapters in the recent history of Zulu beadwork. Despite their skill and creativity, however, bead makers have seldom worked alone. In seeking to capture the nature of the often complex interactive process that exists between beaders and the commercial entrepreneurs who have helped in easing and streamlining the often demanding and uncertain route to the marketplace, it is helpful to borrow the term 'culture broker' used by Jules-Rosette (1984) to describe the role of such intermediaries. It is the latter who facilitate or broker the sale of items of one society's material culture to buyers from another. In the process, the original function of the item may be lost or replaced by what is often, but not necessarily always, a purely decorative function. Fashion jewellery has, of course, both decorative and commercial value.

In the case of tourist beadwork, 'culture brokers' are the middlemen who seek out rural bead makers from whom they buy beadwork in order to supply stallholders in wayside curio markets and other tourist venues in the province. The term may apply equally to the farmers who set up cottage industries in order to mass-produce curio beadwork and to the entrepreneurs behind the establishment of Cultural Villages. The development specialists in the KwaZulu Development Corporation, who funded the establishment and building of

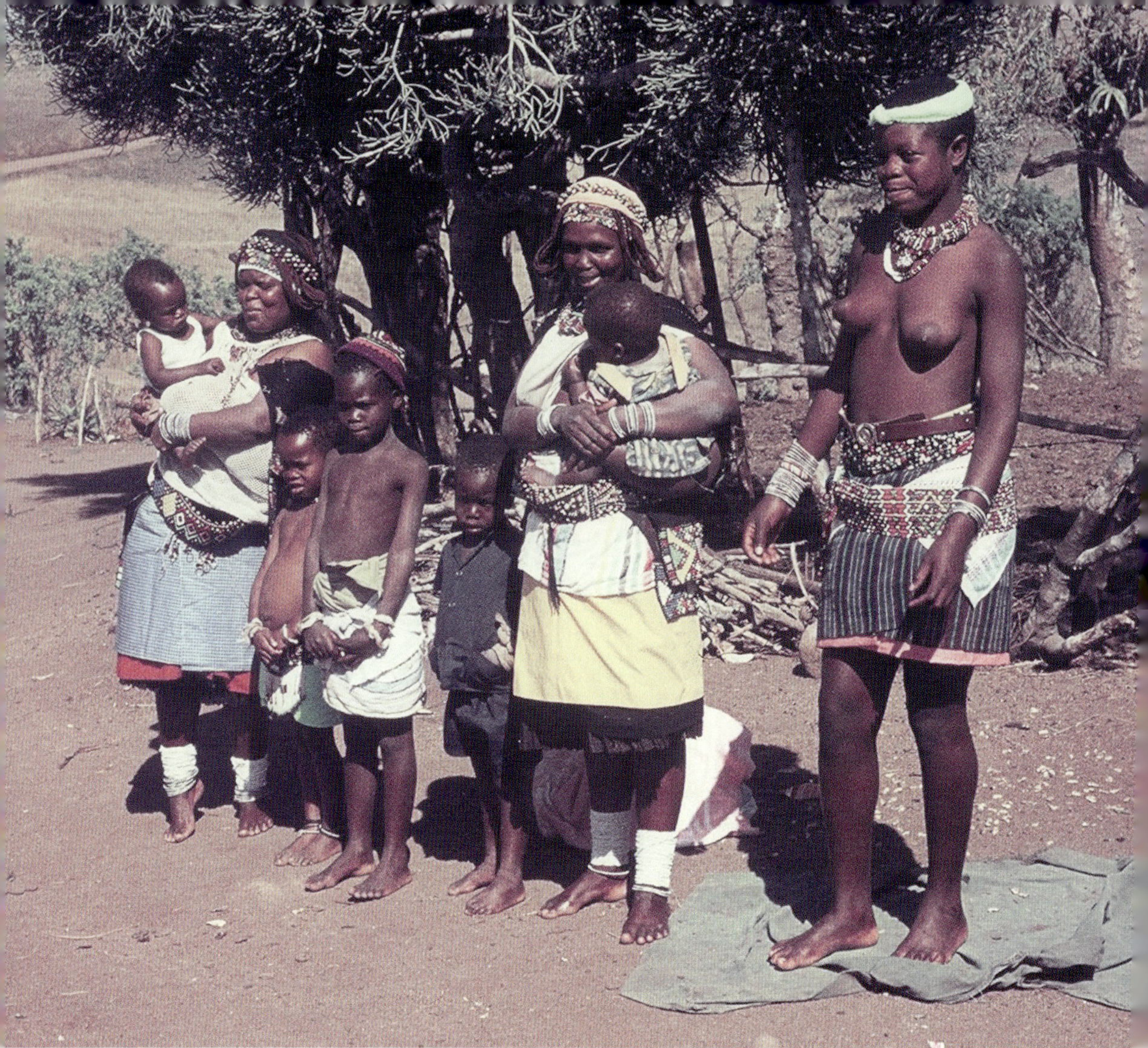

Dancers at the tourist 'cultural village'. (RP-W)

formal craft markets along coastal highways fall into much the same category, as do the directors and staff of income-generating projects designed to assist rural women to develop a secure and lasting income stream.

The *modus operandi* adopted by each 'culture broker' may vary, but all have a wide knowledge both of local craft and of what will attract potential buyers. Whether their motives are altruistic or merely to garner an income for themselves, successful 'culture brokers' have not only an understanding of external markets, but, in many cases, the financial resources necessary to develop and harness existing beading skills in order to produce

58

local beadwork that will attract a wide range of potential
buyers.

Although this book focuses on beadwork, a number of the
craft organisations discussed promote and sell a wide range
of Zulu craft. These include both the Zulu baskets and pottery
which have been the subject of earlier books in this series (van
Heerden 2009; Perrill 2011), as well as woodwork, tapestries,
wall hangings, leatherwork and embroidered clothing. In a few
cases, contemporary drawings and paintings are to be found
in up-market curio stores and in shops devoted as much to
black South African art as to local South African craft. In fact the
African Art Centre also sold art by white South African artists
and, indeed, took as its mandate the task of breaking down the
conventional distinction made between 'art' and 'craft'.

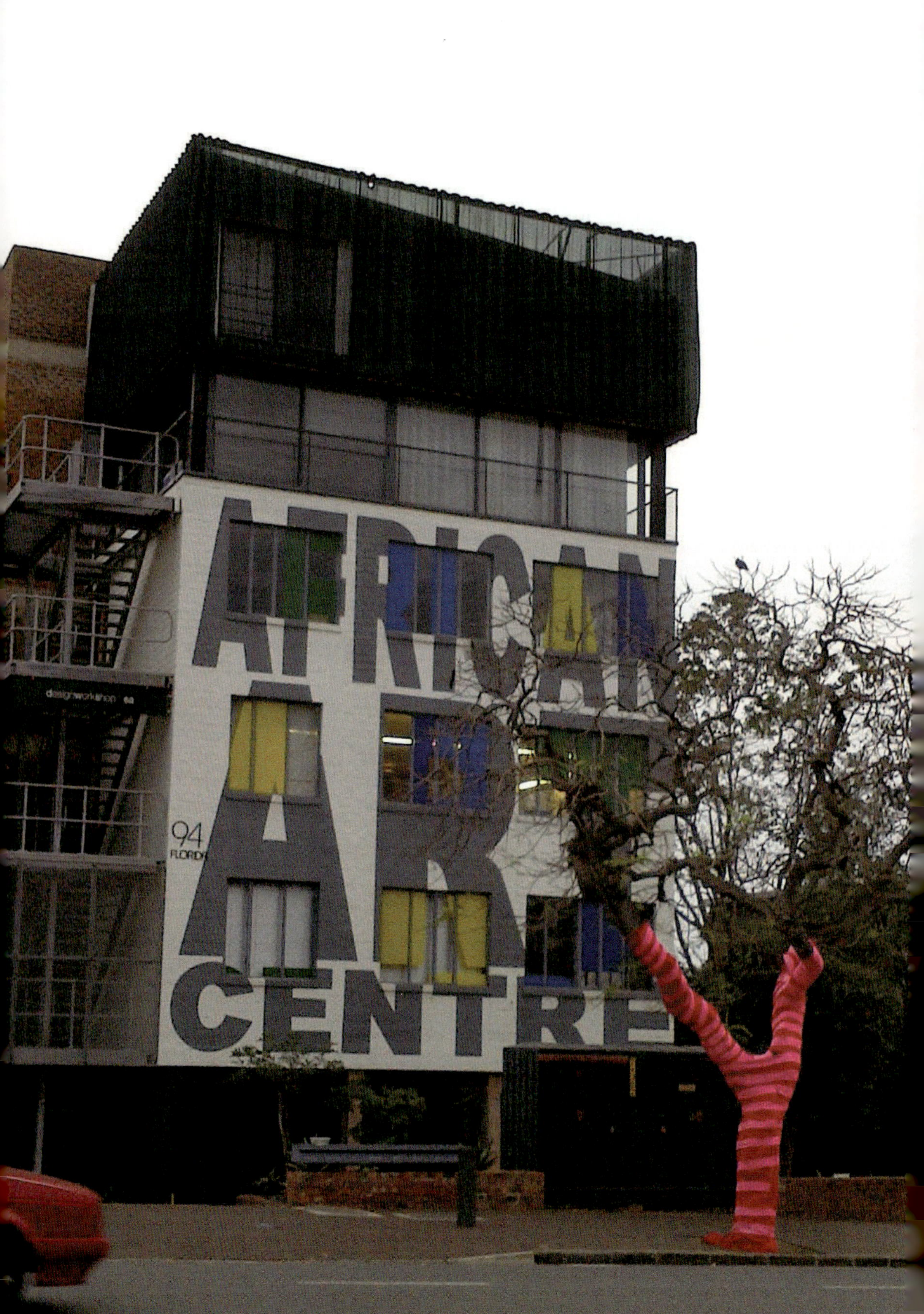

AFRICAN
ART
CENTRE
designworkshop 94
94
FLORIDA

5   Zulu bead sculptures:
the African Art Centre in the 1970s and 1980s

THE AFRICAN ART CENTRE (AAC) was established in 1959 as a project of the liberally-oriented South African Institute of Race Relations. It increasingly became the first port-of-call for many rural bead workers who visited Durban in the hope of selling their beadwork. The bead workers knew from experience that they were likely to receive a higher price at the AAC than they would by trying to sell their beadwork to passing motorists and tourists along the secondary road networks near their rural homes. They were also well aware that what they offered for sale to the AAC had to be of the highest quality, and that the Centre's manager Jo Thorpe, and her staff, would examine each item in minute detail before making a purchase. This demanding process constituted an important learning experience for the makers and helped to raise the standard of their work considerably. When an item was rejected, the staff at the Centre explained their decision with care and tact, so that the maker could, in future, satisfy their high standards.

Jo Thorpe's appreciation of originality equalled her exacting standards. Thus, while she admired and purchased items of traditional beadwork, and often bought these on behalf of collectors and museums, she encouraged innovation and her eye for novel colour combinations and balance was particularly acute. The prices paid to makers were related to the quality and originality of the item, but were, as the makers soon found, significantly higher than those they received either from curio store buyers or from beachfront curio sellers.

In cases where items were rejected by the staff of the Centre, their makers usually tried to sell them to the managers of nearby curio stores. Alternatively, they made their way down to the beachfront in hopes of a quick sale to tourists and holiday makers, despite the fact that the price paid for the item was often nearly half of what they had anticipated receiving from the AAC. While bargaining and even haggling over prices was the order of the day between bead makers and beachfront bead sellers, this was seldom the case at the AAC, where the atmosphere was one of appreciation and mutual respect between the bead makers and the staff of the Centre.

Beadwork was not the only local craft stocked by the AAC. Visiting the Centre was akin to entering Aladdin's cave. Huge woven grass baskets and clay pots stood on woven rugs and carpets, decorated with geometric designs that often echoed those on the baskets and on hand-woven grass bags. Woven hangings decorated the walls along with etchings and paintings by well-known black artists, while wood and bone sculptures lurked in the shadows. In one corner a mass of glittering beadwork jewellery, some of it made at bead projects such as Mdukutshani, provided a vibrant splash of colour to which many customers immediately gravitated. Bead workers, many wearing colourful traditional dress, were often found sitting

Crafter, Sizakele Mchunu at the African Art Centre, 1970s. (RP-W)

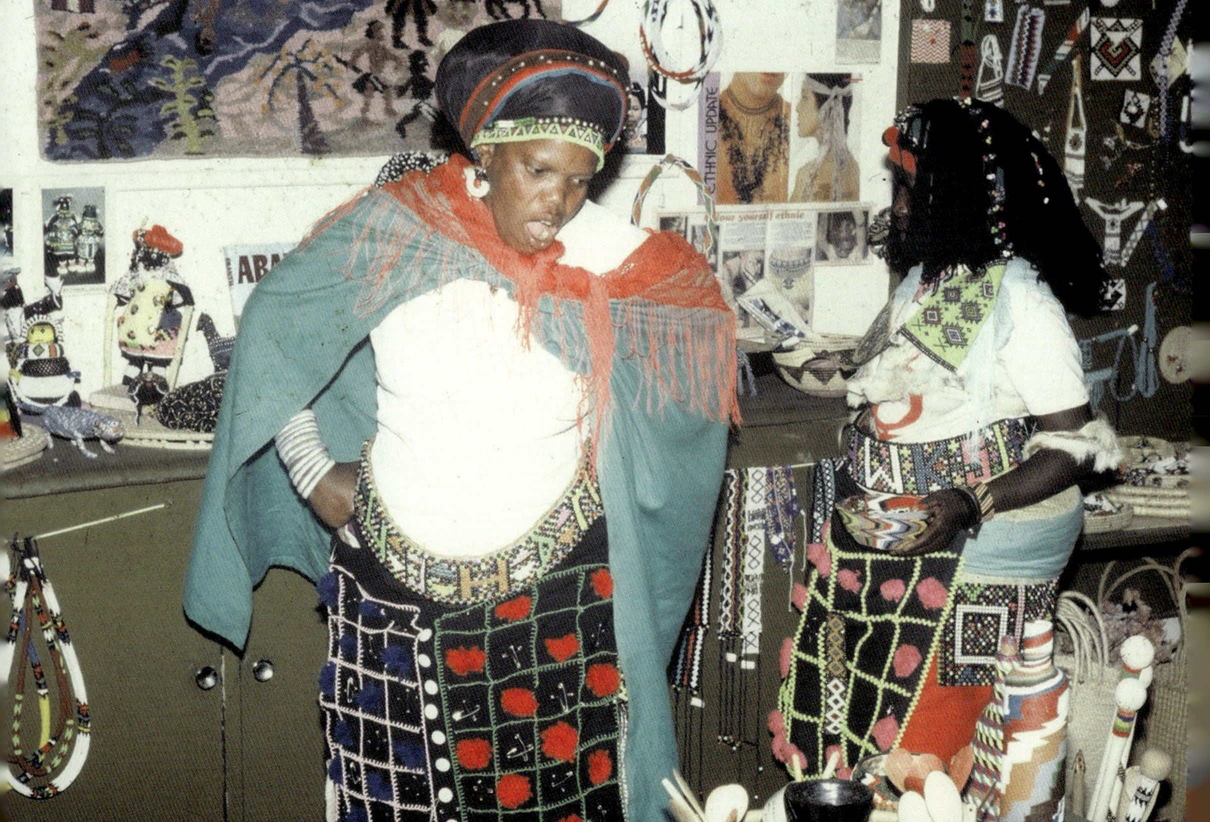

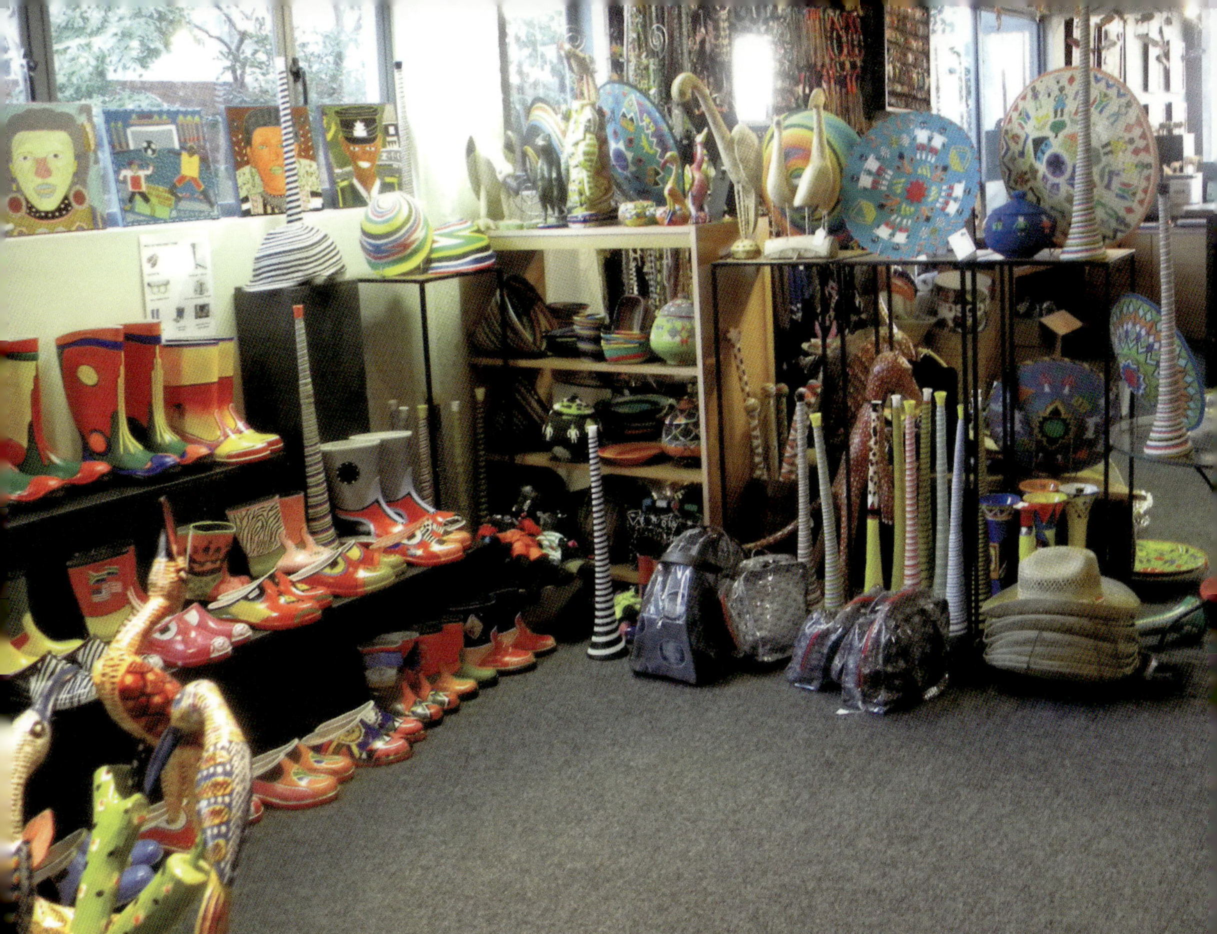

The shop floor and craft for sale in the African Art Centre in 2013. (RP-W)

on the floor mats relaxing and chatting or inspecting the beadwork and other crafts for sale. The atmosphere was noisy and convivial, in strong contrast to the usually more distant interaction between black and white people in South Africa at the time. In this open, stimulating atmosphere, novelty and innovation flourished among beaders as it did among the many other craftspeople who regularly gathered around Jo Thorpe at the Centre (Thorpe 1994).

Visitors were attracted not only by the vibrant and elegant necklaces and bracelets for sale, but by small beaded figurines often referred to as 'bead-cloth sculptures' or simply 'bead sculptures'. Made predominantly of cloth and supported by a light wooden or cardboard frame, bead sculptures were sometimes decorated not only with panels of beadwork but, as in the large doll mounted on a supporting wooden platform

Zulu Beadwork   63

made by **Kulumelaphi Hlambisa** in 1995, with a small piece of modern costume jewellery. Most of the earlier sculptures sold by the Centre were smaller and more delicate, but all showed the same eclectic use of beads and scraps of brightly-coloured cloth.

Some of the sculptures depicted household objects – for example the beautifully decorated radio by **Sizakele Mchunu**.

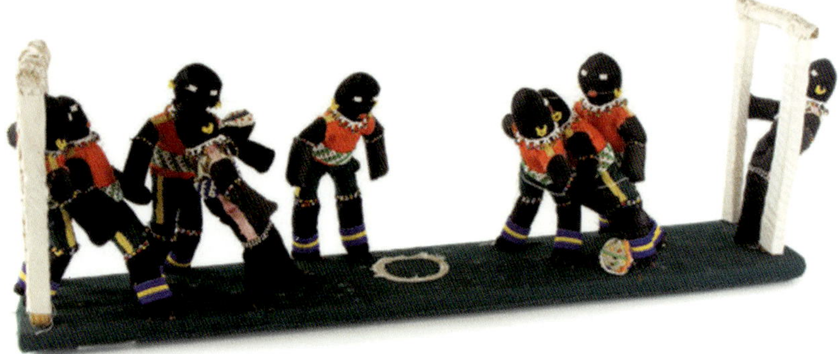

The Soccer Match by Sizakele Mchunu. (MP-W)

Others were, for many of the women, far more alien and intrusive objects such as the highly decorative helicopters made by **Gabi-Gabi Nzama** in 1987. Her home and those of a number of the other bead makers supplying the AAC was situated in the Nyuswa area of the Valley of a Thousand Hills. The area was then on the flight path of the police drug squad

Helicopter made by Gabi-Gabi Nzama. (MP-W)

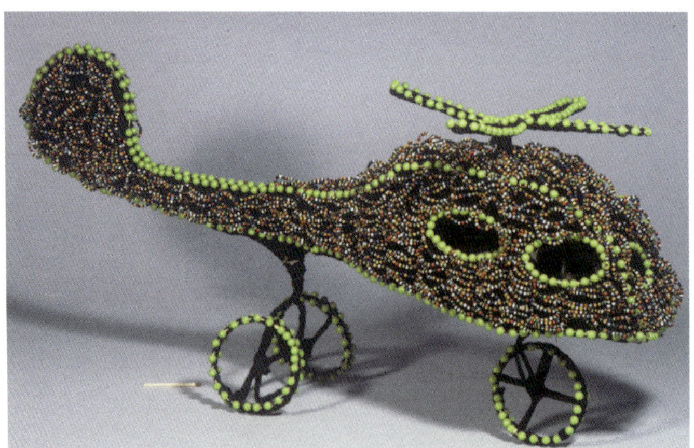

which regularly used helicopters to seek out illegal *dagga* (cannabis) fields hidden in the mountainous terrain where the bead makers lived. Gabi-Gabi explained that the windows of her helicopter were large and outlined in bright beads to emphasise, or perhaps to mimic or symbolise, the intrusive, prying eyes of the police.

In a book entitled *Resistance Art in South Africa* (1989), Sue Williamson suggests that some of the beaded helicopters brought to the AAC by Gabi-Gabi during the 1980s should be interpreted as examples of this genre of silent protest. Williamson reminds us that the AAC helicopters were made during a time of increasing political unrest and protest in South Africa and suggests that the 'all seeing eyes' of some of Gabi-Gabi's helicopters may have been a coded reference to the surveillance activities of the police helicopters,which the people living in the Valley of a Thousand Hills sometimes referred to as the 'eyes of the government'. In support of her argument she includes examples of two other bead sculptures made by the AAC beaders at much the same time. The first is that of a young man in what looks like a gray military uniform, and the other is of a youth holding a gun.

These are interesting suggestions and make a good deal of sense, particularly as the AAC was a project of the highly

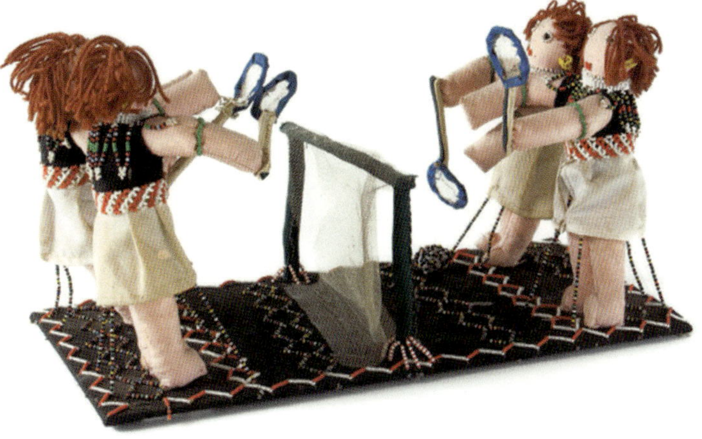

The Tennis Players by Mavis Mchunu. (MP-W)

vocal, anti-government Institute of Race Relations, and much of the art sold by the Centre fell into the category of protest art. It may, however, have been that Jo Thorpe, mindful of the safety of the bead makers, did not encourage them to join the ranks of the other artists whose politically-oriented work she accepted, and for which there was a good market, particularly from international buyers. Alternatively she may have sold the more overtly political bead sculptures privately to overseas collectors.

As time passed and the bead makers saw that there was a growing market for bead sculptures, some women began to make intricate and expressive beaded tableaux portraying their daily lives. In a work by **Mavis Mchunu** a game of tennis is portrayed and in another of her works we see a soccer game in progress, replete with lively players, goal posts and ball.

Sizakele Mchunu was among the most prolific and expert beaders. As her work gained increasing appreciation at the AAC, Sizakele experimented with making tableaux consisting of a number of figures, which rank among the most expressive

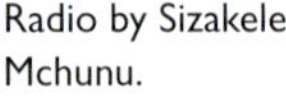

Radio by Sizakele Mchunu.

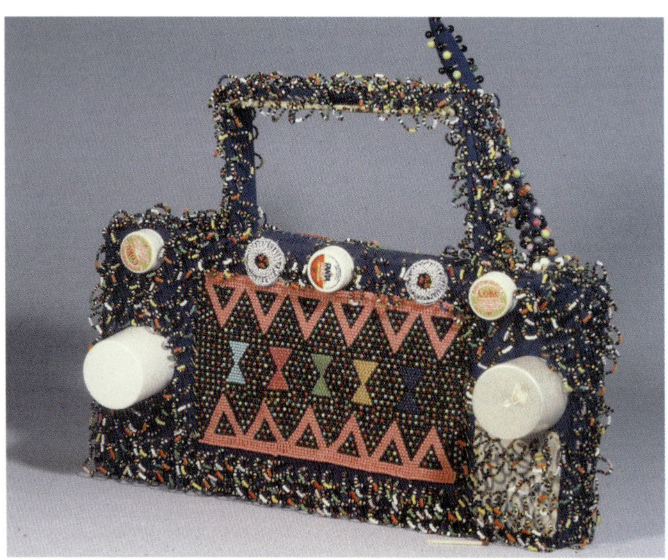

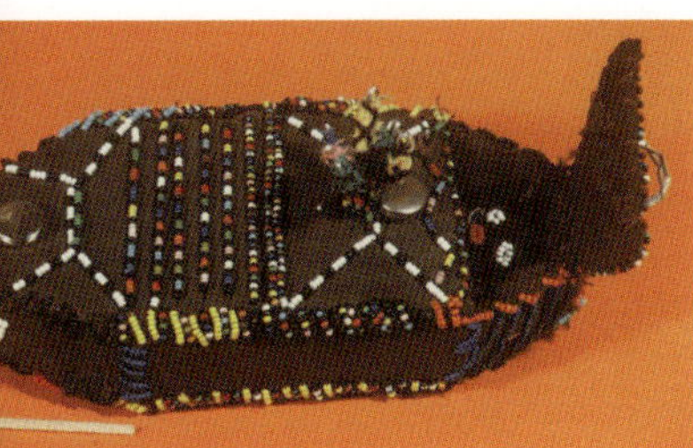

A diminutive coffin, the lid of which opens to reveal its small incumbent, by Sizakele Mchunu, *circa* late 1950s to early 1960s. (RO)

bead sculptures brought to the Centre. Many portrayed mothers and babies. In one she reflected the excitement of the birth of a baby to a traditional woman who is identified by her hair, which is dressed with ochre, and by her beaded clothing. The new mother lies on a high hospital bed attended by a nurse clad in an immaculate white uniform and veil.

Tragically, Sizakele herself lost her newborn baby and her sorrow was reflected in a series of sculptures portraying the event. One is of a tiny coffin, the lid of which opens to reveal the small head of the dead child. In another a grieving mother rolls in sorrow on a woven grass sleeping mat. Both sculptures are now in museum collections.

Completely different to the portrayals of daily life, but nonetheless extremely popular with many of the Centre's patrons, were and continue to be, the many small bird and animal sculptures, capturing the essence of the original with humour and appreciation.

The impetus to experiment, first with making beaded figures and later with tableaux, seems to have been largely a response to an overproduction of bead jewellery. One of the first women to bring a beaded 'doll' to the AAC for sale was **Thembi Mchunu,** whose tall, elongated figures were later to become extremely popular. Thembi explained how she came to begin making dolls and human figures. She decided to experiment with making a doll similar to ones she had seen made of felt by the members of a local sewing project aimed at providing an income for people who suffered from various physical disabilities. Thembi's doll was immediately bought by Jo Thorpe. Encouraged by this success Thembe soon began to experiment with making other kinds of 'dollies', and when these proved to be popular with the Centre customers, her example was followed by many of the other beaders.

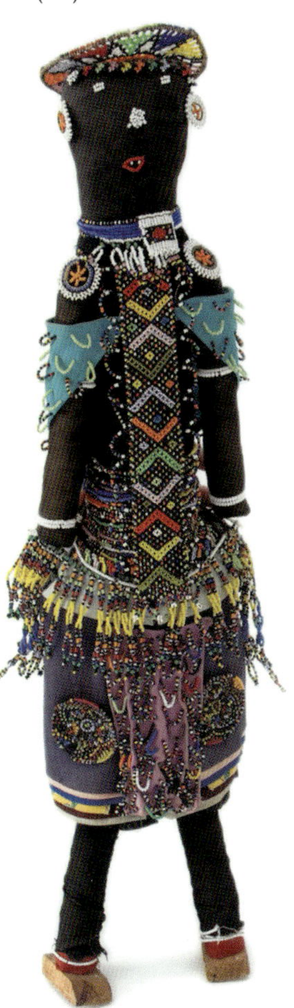

Beaded doll in traditional dress by Thembi Mchunu, late 1950s to early 1960s. (RO)

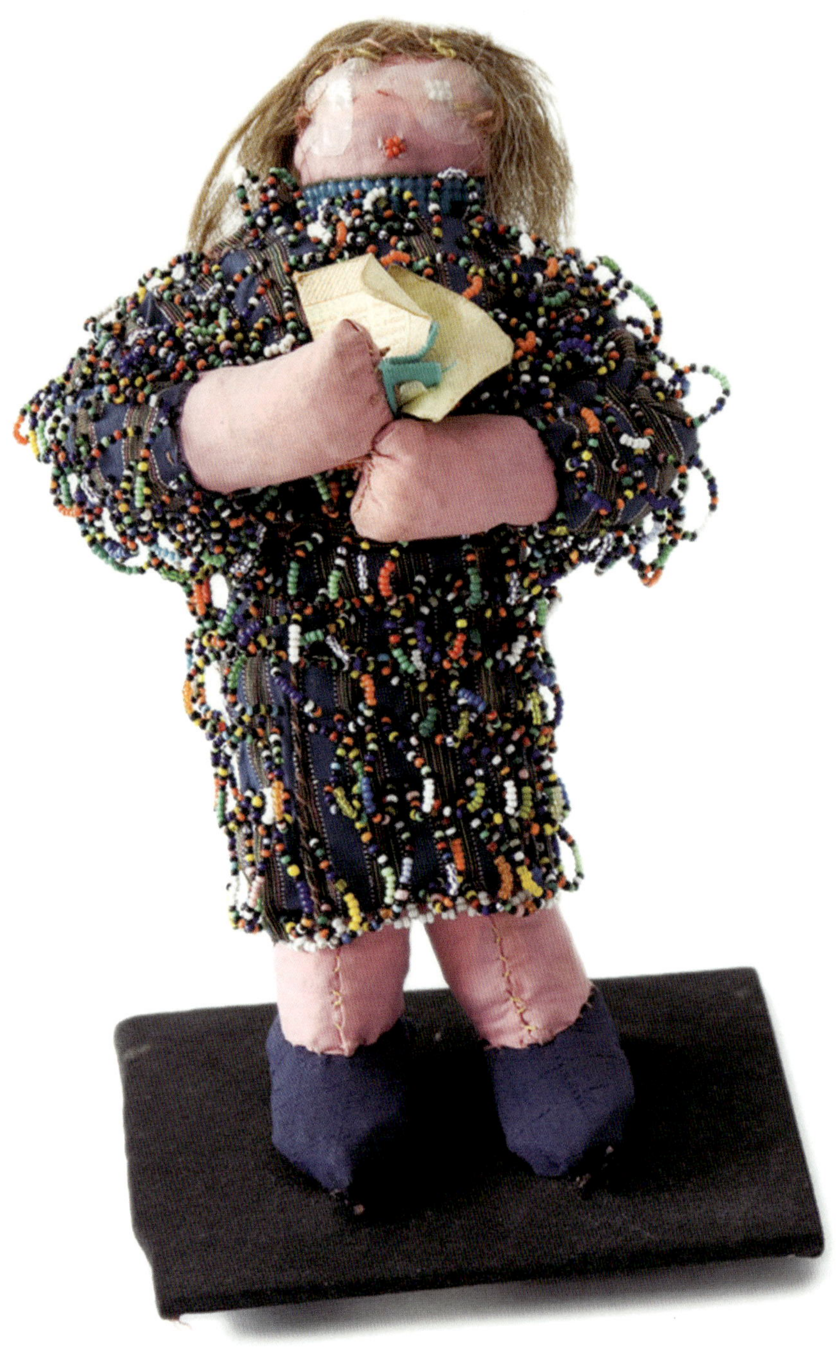

In many respects, it was the taste of the buying staff of the Centre and, particularly, that of Jo Thorpe herself that moulded not only the organisation, but the genre of bead sculptures. Indeed, Jo Thorpe fitted Jules-Rosette's characterisation of a 'culture broker' admirably. When Sizakele Mchunu brought a small beaded portrait of Jo Thorpe to the Centre, it was immediately christened 'The Culture Broker'. The figure wears a dress covered with beaded loops and stands with her glasses on her nose and pencil and pad in hand, as if ready to record the purchases made by the Centre staff. Jo invariably wore a profusion of beadwork, but Sizakele explained that her beaded dress was, first and foremost, an indication of the esteem in which she was held by the bead makers.

Most of the bead makers who visited the AAC had to make long and often complicated and arduous journeys by foot, in buses or occasionally, if they could afford it, in local taxis. However, because they anticipated receiving a good return from selling their beadwork, the journeys were treated as festive occasions for which they dressed with care in their best traditional finery.

During the 1980s and early 1990s many of the later and more complex bead sculptures were the work of a relatively small number of bead makers who regularly brought work to the AAC for sale. The group consisted of some twelve women made up of three smaller clusters of relatives who lived close to each other in the Inanda valley, which was then at least a two-hour journey from Durban. Although often influenced by the work of bead makers from other areas, each woman tended to specialise in particular subjects and bead decorations. Consequently, even though only one or two women from a particular cluster might make the journey to town bringing the work of the others for sale, members of the Centre staff were usually able to make an informed guess at identifying the maker of each piece and the women who had brought the beadwork into the Centre would often identify the maker by reference to other pieces of her work already on display.

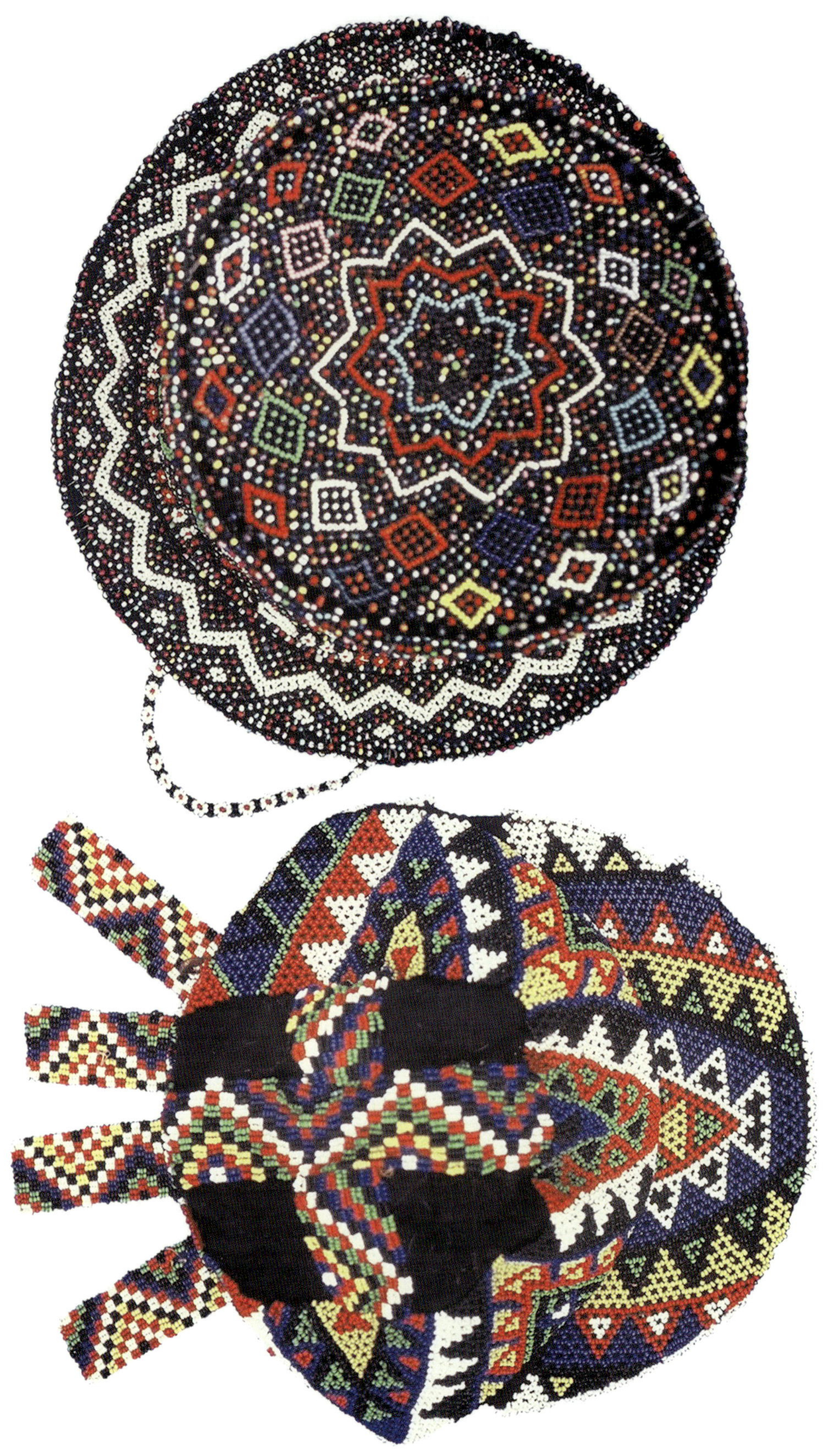

Bead makers' stories

Who were the women who, in venturing into Durban in search of markets for their craft, broke the mould both of traditional isolation and of the prevailing market genre of beaded tourist necklaces and bracelets? What, furthermore, were the events that precipitated their move in new directions and, in particular, what was the part played by members of the AAC staff in their role as 'Culture Brokers' in the development of bead sculptures?

The best way to answer these questions is to introduce each cluster, the women who participated in it and the type of sculpture each woman made. The following material is the result of interviews and visits to the homes of the three main clusters of bead makers during the 1980s. In this sense it is the story of an era that has passed. It was an era, however, that formed an important link in the story of the creation of modern Zulu beadwork. It was, moreover, an era that laid the foundation for many of the creative departures that characterise the diversity of contemporary Zulu beadwork. Here it is possible to provide only a short overview of some of the more prolific and skilled beaders who made up two of the main groups responsible for this transformation.

For some readers, following the description below may be complicated by the fact that some of the groups of beaders share the same clan or clan name and might be assumed to be closely related. This is not, however, necessarily the case, as clanship in contemporary Zulu society confers little more than the possibility of a distant kinship link. This may, however, be used as a basis for extending hospitality to and working with people who have the same clan name as oneself.

The Mchunu's and the Mlaba's

It was Thembu Mchunu who brought the first bead sculpture to the AAC for sale. At that time she was in her late thirties and had never married, devoting herself instead to her profession as a diviner and traditional healer. She and her young daughter lived with her parents in a large extended family in the Nyuswa region of the Valley of Thousand Hills, inland from Durban. In rainy weather the gravel roads often became impassable to most vehicles. As a result of her practice as a healer, the time Thembi could devote to beadwork was limited. Since many of the other women in the homestead were, however, also skilled beaders, the output of this cluster was both prolific and regular.

Representatives from the homestead usually visited the AAC every three weeks or so, bringing with them the accumulated beadwork made by the women of the family to sell. As with all purchases made by Centre staff, prices were individually negotiated with the family representatives. Staff took the opportunity to point out product faults to the women, and usually suggested how these could be remedied or avoided in future. It was not unusual for women from this group to take home as much as R200-R400 in one day for the beadwork they brought for sale. At the time this was a significant contribution to family income since it was considerably more than the wages paid to unskilled black women working in Durban.

Like the other young girls in the community, Thembi and her sisters learned to make beadwork when they began courting. Thembi, however, was called by the spirits of her ancestors to become a diviner and spent over a year away from home training for her profession. The training and practice of a respected profession provided her not only with personal independence, but also set her apart from other young women, many of whom were by then preparing to get married. Her position therefore gave her the confidence to follow a very different lifestyle to that of most of her peers. This did not exclude her from assisting her mother and sisters in making curio beadwork that was sold in small local villages and on the side of the road to Durban.

Venturing into Durban, probably to buy beads from local wholesalers, Thembi visited the curio shops near the beachfront

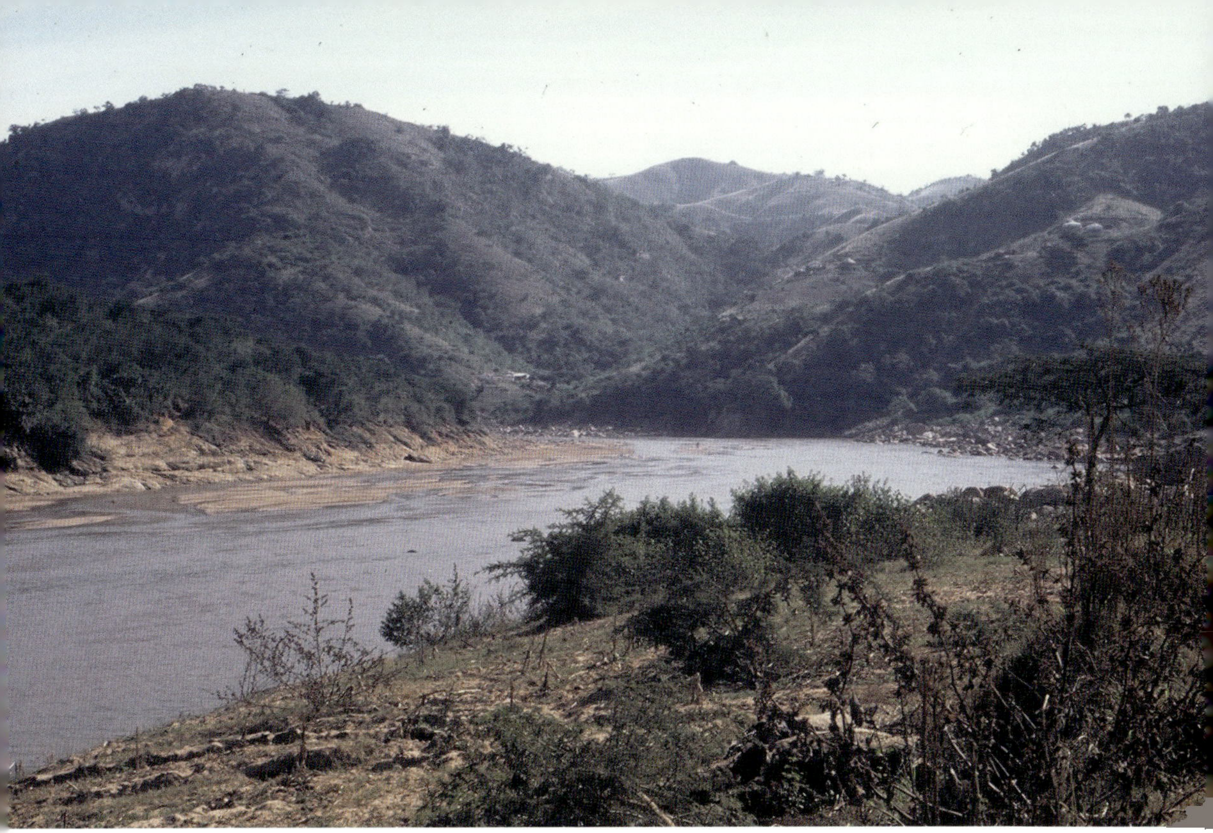

The journey along the side of the winding river to visit the homes of the Mchunu and Mlaba families. (RP-W)

A typical circular homestead perched on the side of the steep hills above the river. (RP-W)

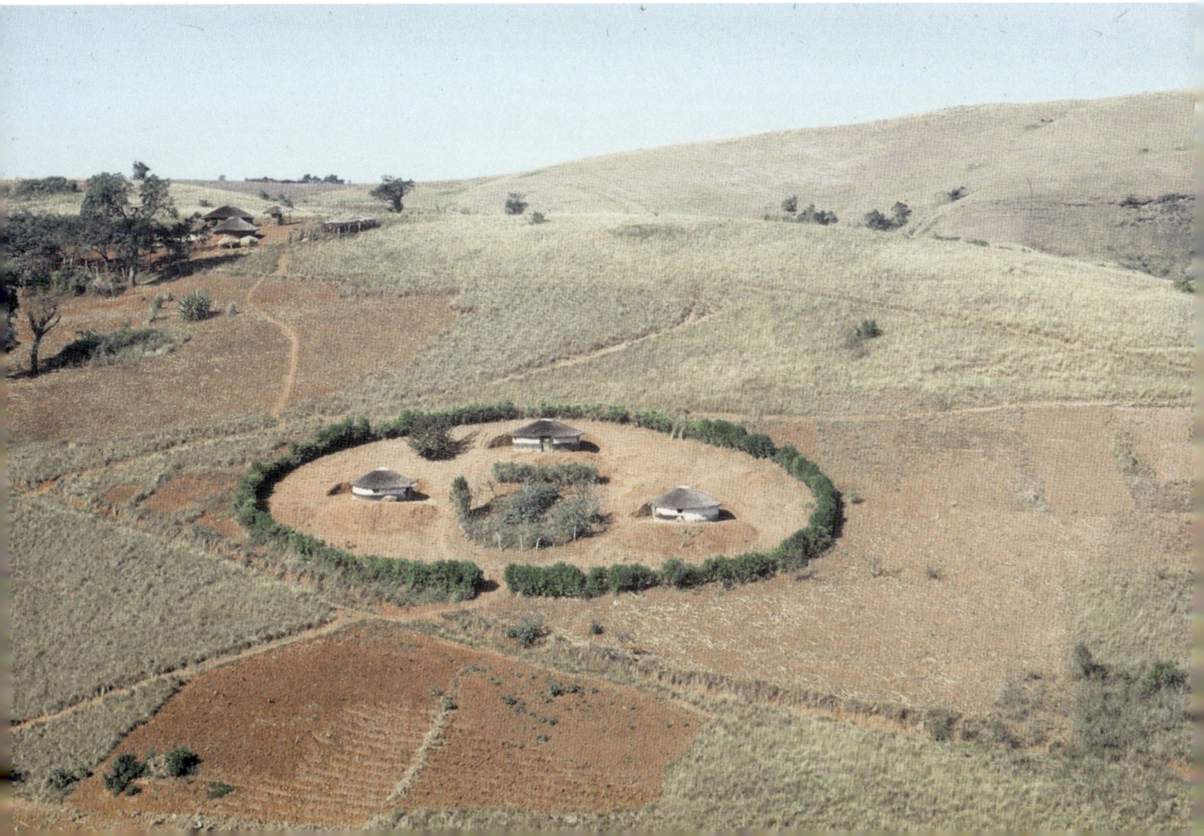

to see not only what they stocked, but also to test the waters
for future sales. She also attempted to sell beadwork necklaces
and bracelets on the beachfront itself, but was disappointed
by low prices and the often abusive haggling she encountered.
Eventually, she visited the AAC and she began to take her
beadwork, together with that made by her mother and sisters,
to the Centre for sale.

Although the Mchunu's beadwork was of a consistently high
quality, in time only some of what was offered for sale was
bought. When Thembi inquired why, Centre staff explained
that they had an oversupply of high-quality beadwork and
were limiting the amount bought from each seller. Thembi
then asked what other kind of beaded craft she might make in
order to retain her previously lucrative market. She had seen
small dolls made of felt for sale in the sister shop of the AAC
in Pietermaritzburg, which were reminiscent of those she and
her sisters had made from scraps of material when they were
children.

When she returned to the AAC some weeks later, Thembi took
a small, experimental bead doll along with the usual necklaces
and bracelets. It was bought immediately and Jo Thorpe
suggested that Thembi make more beaded dolls. In response,
Thembi made a whole array of dolls dressed in a range of
traditional beaded outfits, and with these a new and highly
saleable bead genre was born.

Thembi Mchunu's dolls were invariably tall and thin and
covered with intricate panels of traditional beadwork in bright,
primary colours that echoed those of her own ceremonial dress.
Many wore the typical beaded skirt and circular headdress of
a Zulu married woman, together with beaded necklaces and
earrings. Beaded chains were looped around their waists and
hips and most wore decorated shoulder scarves and other
typical bead ornaments. The dolls stood ramrod straight, arms
to the side balancing firmly on wooden feet and sometimes

on flat planks of wood that ensured that the doll would stand upright. The faces were usually indicated by beaded eyes, nose and mouth and, in this respect, they departed quite radically from the typical *idoli* made at Keat's Drift and discussed in Chapter 3.

Responding to the praise she received for this novel beadwork departure, Thembi commented to Eleanor Preston-Whyte:

I do not think I am clever...it is the other people who think I am clever. I just make dolls for money and people like them ... This makes me pleased, and I also enjoy thinking of new things to make.

Continuing this train of thought, but also in response to a direct question, she explained further:

I copy the people where I live when they dress up ....
I think about what I am going to make before I begin ...
I like to be alone while I do this. When I think, I get ideas both for my medicines and for my dolls ... (personal communication,1990).

Thembi's dolls proved to be, and remained, immensely popular with prospective buyers. Soon the other bead makers in her extended family began to experiment with making their own beaded dolls, but they seldom surpassed her arresting representations of the colourful traditional dress of the women living around them.

The 1980s was an exciting time for the AAC. Once it became clear that Jo Thorpe and her staff were willing and even eager to buy beaded figures, as well as the more usual bead jewellery, a number of the Centre's regular bead makers followed Thembi's lead and began to experiment with making not only a variety of human figures, but also a wide range of animals and birds. Horned buck, lions with beaded manes and sinuous snakes made their appearance on the shelves of the Centre and were greeted with enthusiasm by old and new buyers alike.

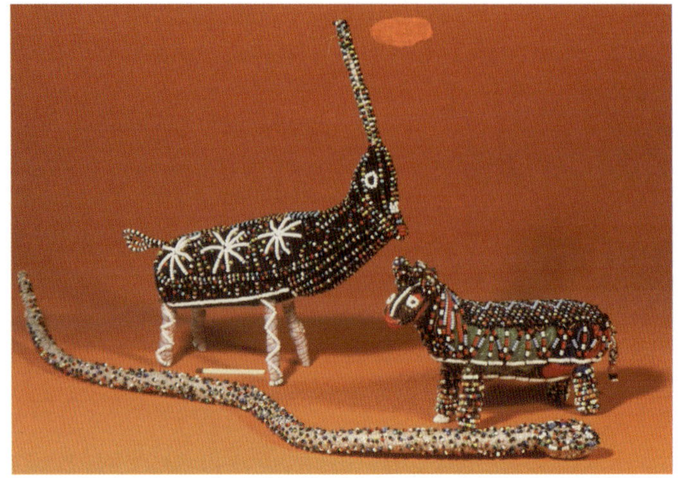

By 1987 Thembi Mchunu had an established reputation for making a variety of exquisite small beaded animals, while her close relatives, the Mlaba's, were experimenting with making not only small animals but birds as well.

As in the case of beaded dolls, the new generation of beaded animals and birds reflected the world and everyday events of interest to the makers. In some, human and animal figures were

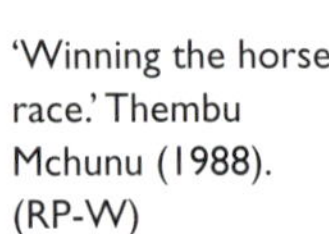

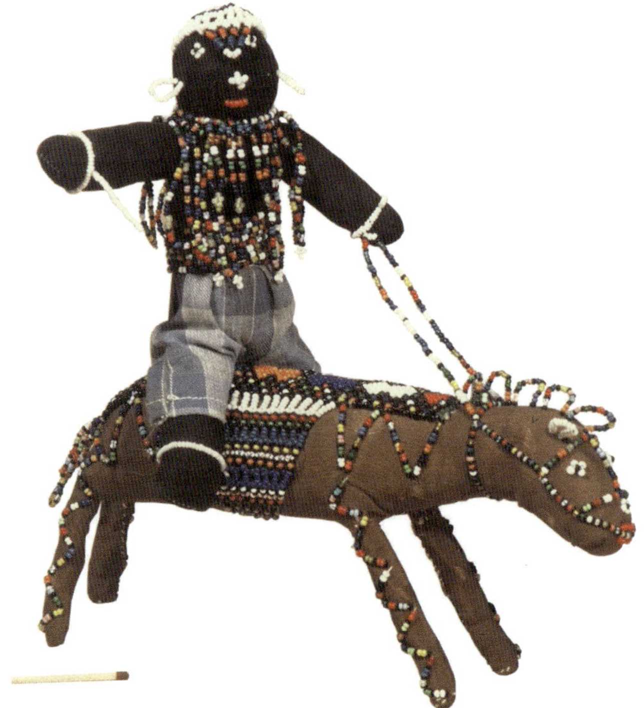

76

skilfully combined, as in the case of the galloping racehorse which is being urged onto the winning post by its excited jockey. This sculpture by Thembe Mchunu was made in 1986 and was clearly based on her observation of the activities at a racing stable situated near her home, where a number of the members of her family had recently found employment. Other bead sculptures made by women from this area portray canoeists battling the high waters of the Umgeni River which flows through the valley below their homes. An internationally known and famous annual canoe race known as the Mzinduzi Marathon takes place in these waters and it is the exertions of the canoeists that these sculptures depict.

Always at the forefront of the market, Thembi Mchunu moved on to experiment with making a wide variety of small birds and later animals, while both she and her sisters kept the AAC well supplied with numerous 'bugs' and other small imaginary creatures, all of which became extremely popular with prospective buyers. In many cases these innovative women experimented not only with new products but also with new ways to construct and stabilise bead sculptures. The **Mlaba's**, for instance, became well known for their representations not only of birds, but also of birdlike airplanes with extended wings built around and supported by a wire frame. It is possible that the first bird was made as early as 1982 by Thembi Mchunu's sister, Khulumelaphi, who had married into the Mlaba family. Khulumelaphi subsequently encouraged members of her new extended family to follow Thembi's example in moving from making beaded necklaces and bracelets to experimenting with new forms of bead sculpture.

A wide array of new and original beadwork subjects was soon developed by Khulumelaphi and other members of her new family. When asked where the ideas for her birds came from, Khulumelaphi explained that she had tried to copy the brightly coloured birds she often saw hopping around on the ground next to an old mulberry tree near her home. Another woman,

Hlalaleni Mlaba, began making beaded peacocks with delicate fan-shaped tails after seeing one display its colourful tail feathers in the garden of a white doctor she had consulted in a nearby small village. In explaining why she was so intrigued, Hlalaleni mimicked the peacock's dance with humour and accuracy as she herself danced backwards and forwards. Today, nearly thirty years later, her bead sculptures still enchant us not only with their vibrancy, but also with the close attention to detail that can only be the result of prolonged personal observation.

The Mchunus of Ndwedwe and Gabi-Gabi Nzama

We turn now to consider the beadwork made by the small but extremely creative group of women living in the Ndwedwe area on the other side of the Valley of A Thousand Hills from Nyuswa, the home of Thembi Mchunu and her family. One of them was **Sizakele Mchunu** whose bead sculptures were, as we have already seen, amongst the most beautiful and provocative brought to the AAC during the 1990s. Before her death, Sizakele Mchunu and her sisters, Mavis and Thandi together with her co-wife Celani Nojiyeza and Gabi-Gabi Nzama (the sister of Celani and Sizakele's husband) made up one of the most active and creative production groups associated with the AAC. From as early as the mid 1980s, they supplied the Centre with both traditionally based beaded jewellery of an extremely high quality, and then, following the lead of Sizakele, a constant array of exquisite and novel bead sculptures. Although each developed her own particular style or brand of bead sculpture for which she became well known,

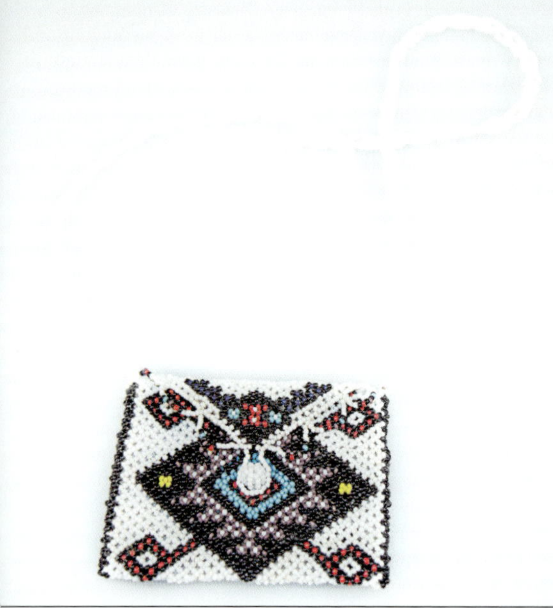

Small beaded purse with a geometric design. (AN)

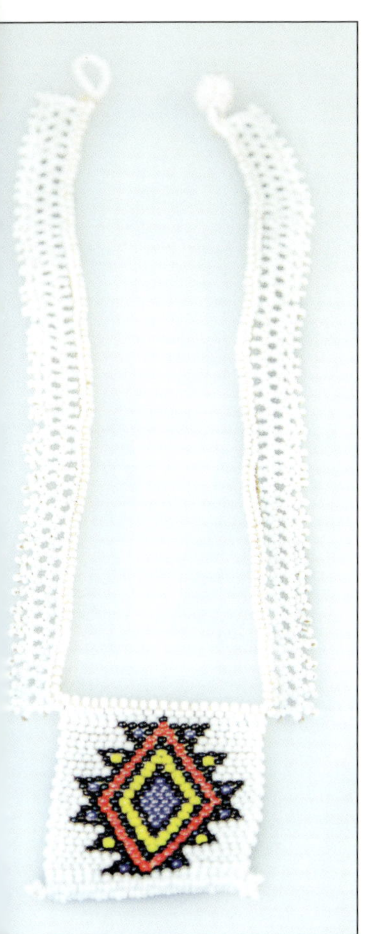

A matching beaded 'love letter'. (AN)

the women seemed to continuously stimulate each other to strive towards new creative heights; not only to attract customers, but to satisfy their own developing aesthetic sense. While the development of their art was to some extent guided by Jo Thorpe and the Centre staff, the final products were unique to their makers. The market responded positively and sales increased; indeed innovation and market success reinforced each other.

The journey from Ndwedwe to Durban is long and can be arduous and, especially in the rainy season, even hazardous. The bead makers from Ndwedwe often had to wade across the swollen Umgeni River to reach public transport, and could be cut off from the outside world for days on end.

Both Mavis and Thandi had limited primary schooling, but Sizakele had remained at home helping with the seasonal round of rural agriculture. It was from their mother that Sizakele learned bead making; Sizakele in turn taught the skill to her sisters. When Sizakele became the second wife of a local traditionalist, she taught her co-wife, Celani, to make beadwork.

At least one, and often all three, women travelled regularly to Durban to sell their beadwork with the AAC soon becoming their first sales stop. Because of the proximity of Gabi-Gabi's home to those of the other beaders, she sometimes accompanied them on these selling expeditions, but might also go alone or with other nearby beaders. After her marriage, Sizakele visited her paternal home regularly and the sisters continued to work together and, to some extent, each influenced the work of the others. Particularly in the case

of Mavis and Thandi it is often difficult to judge which of
the sisters made many of the early sculptures. This difficulty
is exacerbated by the fact that makers often took their
kinswomen's sculptures to sell in Durban, and the Centre staff
sometimes presumed that, with the exception of the distinctive
dolls made by Sizakele, the woman who had brought the piece,
was its maker.

In focusing on the bead sculptures that came to characterise
one of the unique developments for which the African Art
Centre became well known in the 1960s and 1970s, it is
important not to lose sight of the exquisite beaded jewellery
that the beaders who supplied the Centre continued to bring to
Jo Thorpe and her staff for sale. Typical examples are shown on
Page 81, and although their cheaper counterparts might have
been bought in local curio stores and roadside markets such as
those at Umgababa, the quality and colour co-ordination was

Two beaded bags
and a beaded purse
in contrasting colour
combinations.
(RP-W)

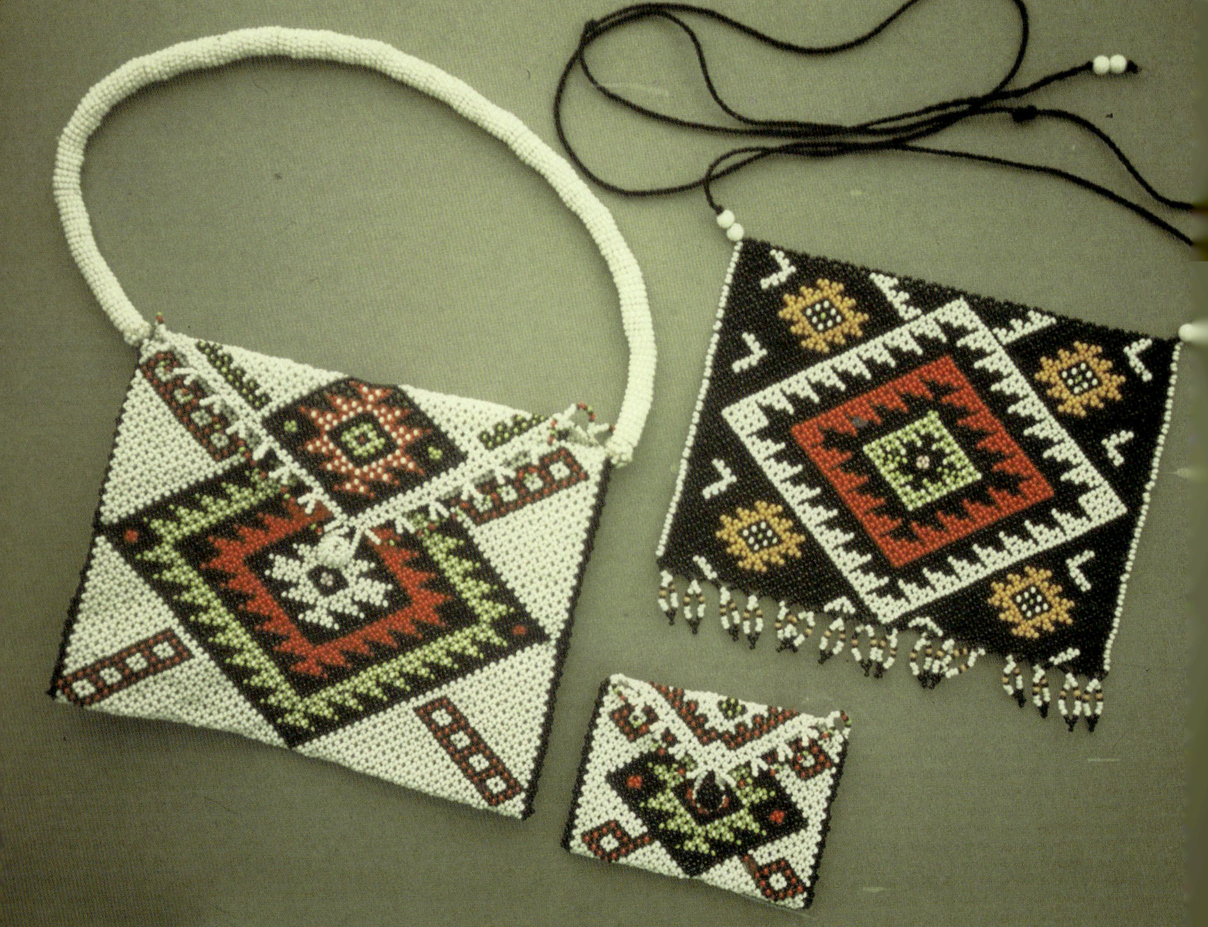

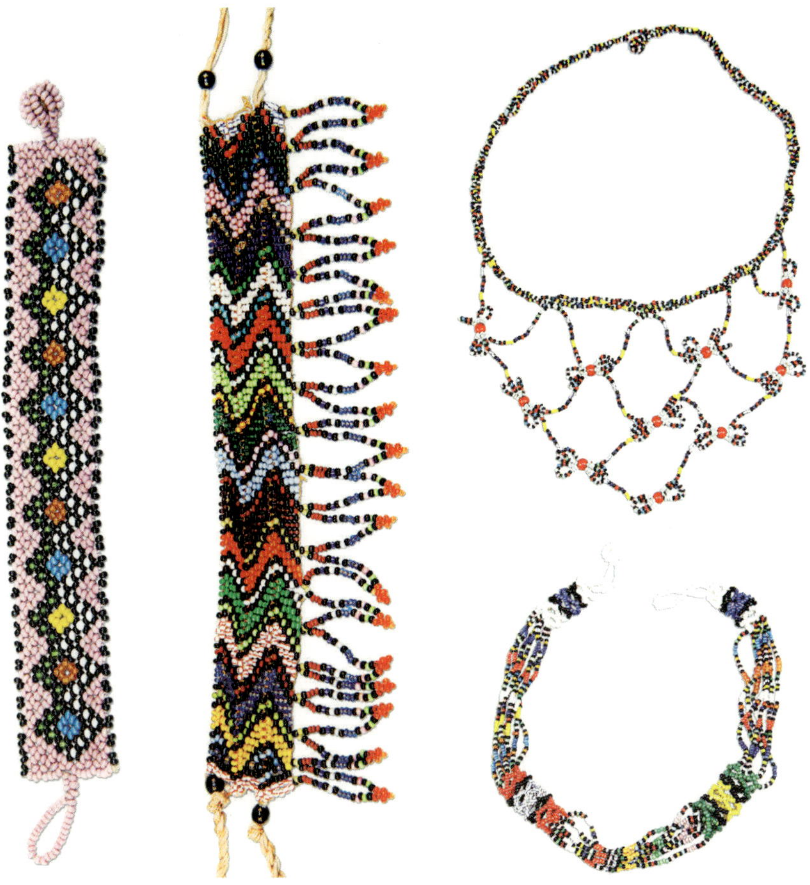

seldom as fine as that of the jewellery on sale at the African
Art Centre itself. At much the same time the African Art Centre
began to stock beadwork made by a number of specialist
bead projects that entered the field at this time and over the
following decades, including those discussed in the previous
chapter.

The collage of photographs provides a representative view of
the bead sculptures made by the five women from Ndwedwe.
While doing justice to the variety and ingenuity of each beader,
the photographs also demonstrate an overall coherence that
allows the individual items to be classified as part of a single
beadwork tradition. The bead sculptures that make up this

A variety of
necklaces, a beaded
belt and beaded
bracelet. (AN)

collage date from the 1980s, and are arranged roughly in the order they were acquired by the AAC.

The beaded figure tradition continues to flourish. The makers now include men as well as women, both of whom continue to experiment with a wide range of subjects, as works by **Caesar Mkize** demonstrate. The sale of beaded figures soon spread to other venues. They are now available not only in craft centres and curio stores, but also in department stores and on busy street corners in many South African towns and cities, as well as at tourist venues throughout the country. In many of these venues they rub shoulders with beadwork made in other parts of the country, particularly with the well-known Ndebele dolls, whose broad bands of vibrant colour have become a firm favourite with foreign tourists.

In KwaZulu-Natal beadwork made for the market has taken a number of different turns, many stimulated by projects aimed at providing an income for women and men. Unlike the original Zulu bead sculptures, some of the figures made recently are fairly large and constructed of wire with only a few beads to add colour and sparkle. It is unlikely that hawkers are the makers of these craft items, although sometimes one sees beaded animals being made on the side of the road while the maker waits for customers. In some cases wayside hawkers are supplied with goods by middlemen and often unsuspecting buyers purchase mass-produced replicas imported from the East as opposed to genuine local craft.

In contrast, the AAC has continued to sell both art and craft made by local artists who are known to their buyers; many of whom have earned the respect and admiration of the wider community of art lovers. In 1984 the AAC became an autonomous, non-profit organisation and moved its premises from downtown Durban to a more roomy and accessible shop in Durban's Florida Road where it is patronised by local artists and art lovers alike, as well as tourists seeking works of art rather than souvenirs. Here both fine traditional and contemporary Zulu beadwork are among the Gallery's specialties. Jo Thorpe's place as a major 'culture broker' has been taken by Hlengiwe Dube who continues Jo's tradition of supporting and mentoring local bead makers, as well as assisting them in finding markets for their work.

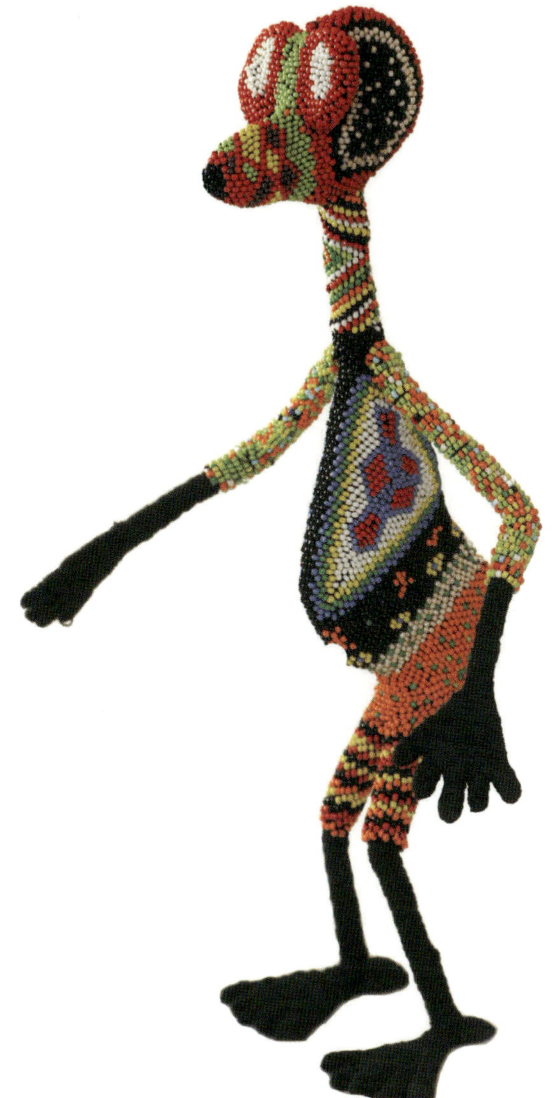

Figure by Caesar Mkize, *circa* 2010. (MP-W)

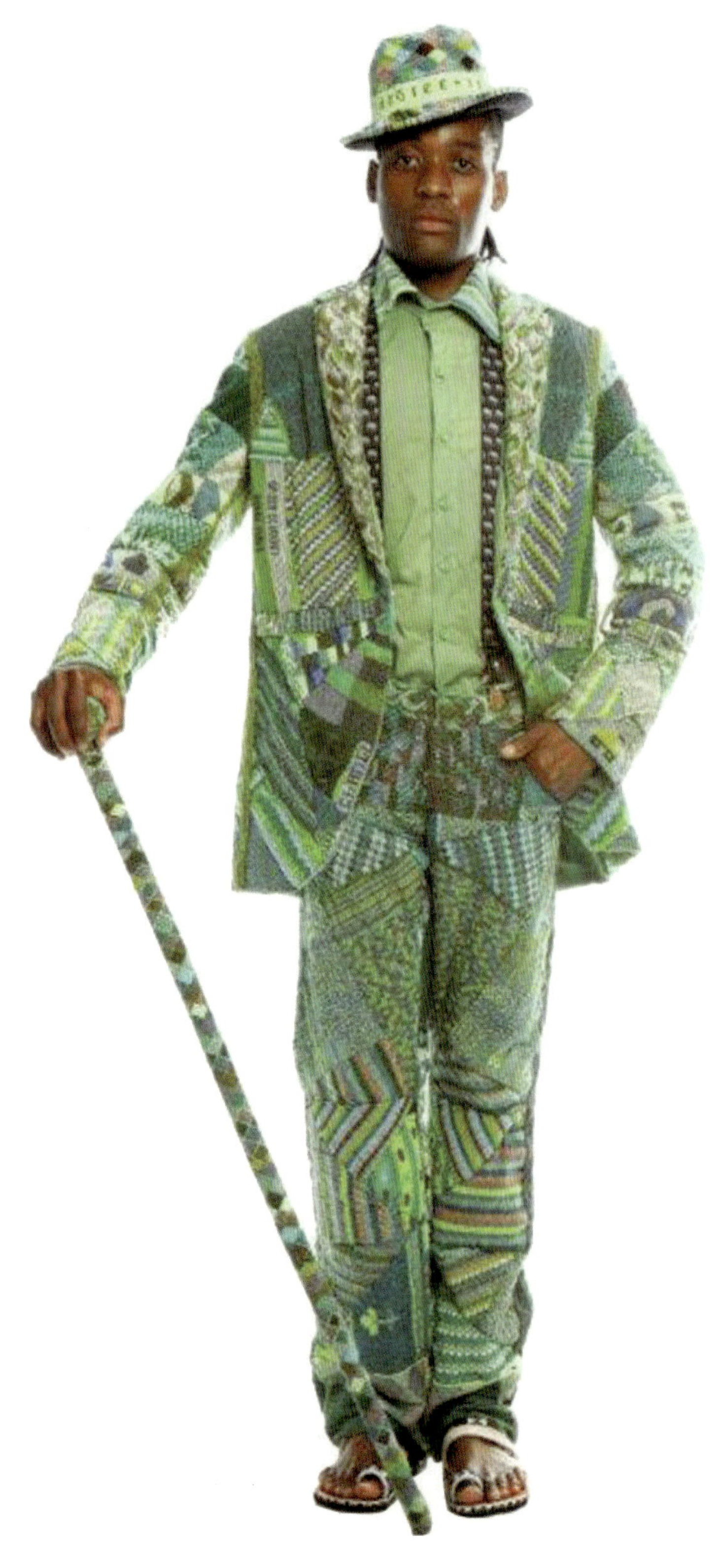

6   Zulu beadwork for the new millennium

THE START of the new millennium ushered in a minor revolution not only in the development of new beadwork styles, but in the increasing number of uses to which Zulu beadwork was put, and in the contexts in which it began to appear. It was also a time when the promotion of local beadwork began to characterise the development strategies of international funding bodies and local non-governmental organisations (NGOs) seeking to promote income generation among the rural and peri-urban poor in many parts of South Africa, including KwaZulu-Natal. Bead workers from different bead making projects in the province began to meet and network with each other, with the result that they not only shared ideas, but in some cases, collaborated in marketing and in seeking funding for related work.

On the negative side, inexpensive but unusual and attractive imported beadwork began to compete with local beadwork for a share of the local market. A number of the directors of beadwork projects that were currently producing fashion jewellery in KwaZulu-Natal realised that competition from imported fashion beadwork could only continue, and might even intensify. As a result these projects diversified the range of beadwork that they currently produced, and explored other uses to which beadwork might be put.

By the late 1990s Zulu beadwork had made its appearance in arenas as diverse as commercial art, interior design and decor. In one instance local beadwork was harnessed to give weight to a high profile public campaign to raise awareness of the increase in rhinoceros poaching in KwaZulu-Natal game parks. This use of Zulu beadwork to raise public awareness of social issues and to champion a public campaign is reminiscent of the early 1970s, when an inverted beaded red cross was used in the fight against HIV/AIDS.

On an entirely different front, local beadwork now features in
examples of contemporary public art, and is on display in a
number of local and national museums and also in the more
avant-garde art galleries across the country. In what follows we
feature some of the more prominent campaigns and occasions
in and on which Zulu beadwork continues to add verve and
colour to both important and everyday events and causes, both
in KwaZulu-Natal and elsewhere in the country. This is not,
however, to suggest that more traditional forms and uses of
Zulu beadwork are necessarily on the wane, as we will see in
the next, and concluding, chapter of this book.

In order to illustrate both the variety and the beauty of much
contemporary Zulu beadwork, we turn now to feature the work
of a number of very different Zulu bead making initiatives. Two
of these are based in small towns in rural KwaZulu-Natal and
the third, which consists of a loose, but mutually beneficial
association of a number of relatively small projects, is located in
the city of Durban. The first project to be discussed is a long-
established rural project that, although probably best known
for its fine basketwork, also produces a range of varied and
exquisite bead jewellery. This project is of particular interest
because it has avoided many of the problems that bedevilled
the management structures and distribution networks of a
number of the earlier projects that made beaded jewellery in
the province.

1. The Vukani Collection Trust and the Vukani Zulu Cultural Museum

The beadwork genre popularly known to its many local and
international admirers as 'Vukani Beadwork' has its roots in
the early work of Evangelical Lutheran missionaries, Pastor
Kjell Lofroth and his wife Bertha Lofroth who from 1972 were
stationed on a mission station situated at Rorke's Drift in central
Zululand. Although many local crafts, particularly basket
weaving, appeared to have virtually died out in the area, Pastor
Lofroth believed that it would be possible to revive these skills

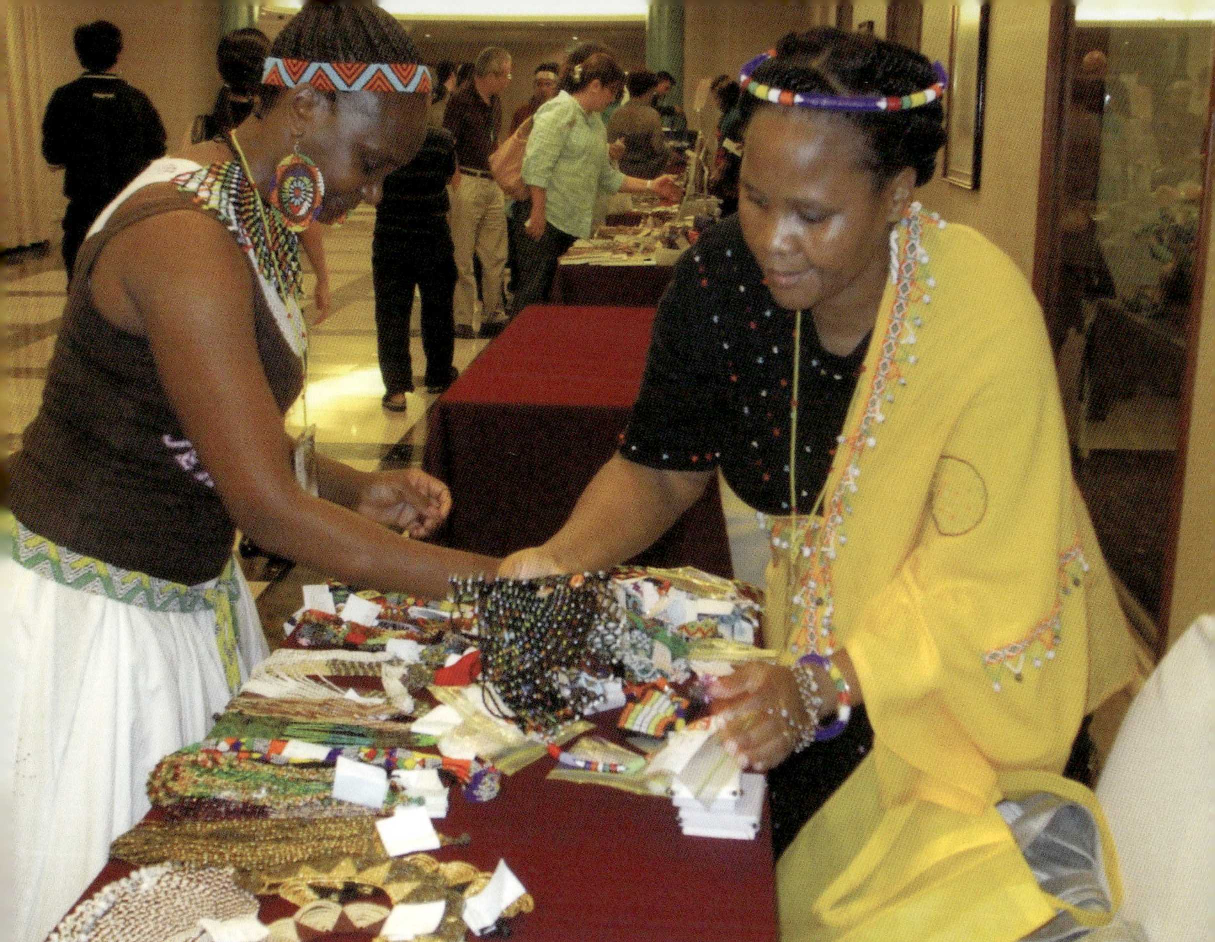

in order to develop an income stream for local people. This was sorely needed, as poverty was endemic, with many local men either unemployed or working as poorly paid migrant labourers in Durban and in other South African towns and cities. Although local women sometimes found employment as domestic workers either in nearby Eshowe, or as seasonal labourers on local farms, the opportunities for both were severely limited. A few of the younger women were, however, temporary labour migrants earning low wages in nearby towns and villages and, in some cases, as far afield as Durban.

In the face of considerable local scepticism on the part of church leaders and the community at large, Pastor Lefroth persisted in his campaign to revive and harness traditional weaving skills in order to provide a local source of income for both men and later, for women, living in the vicinity of the

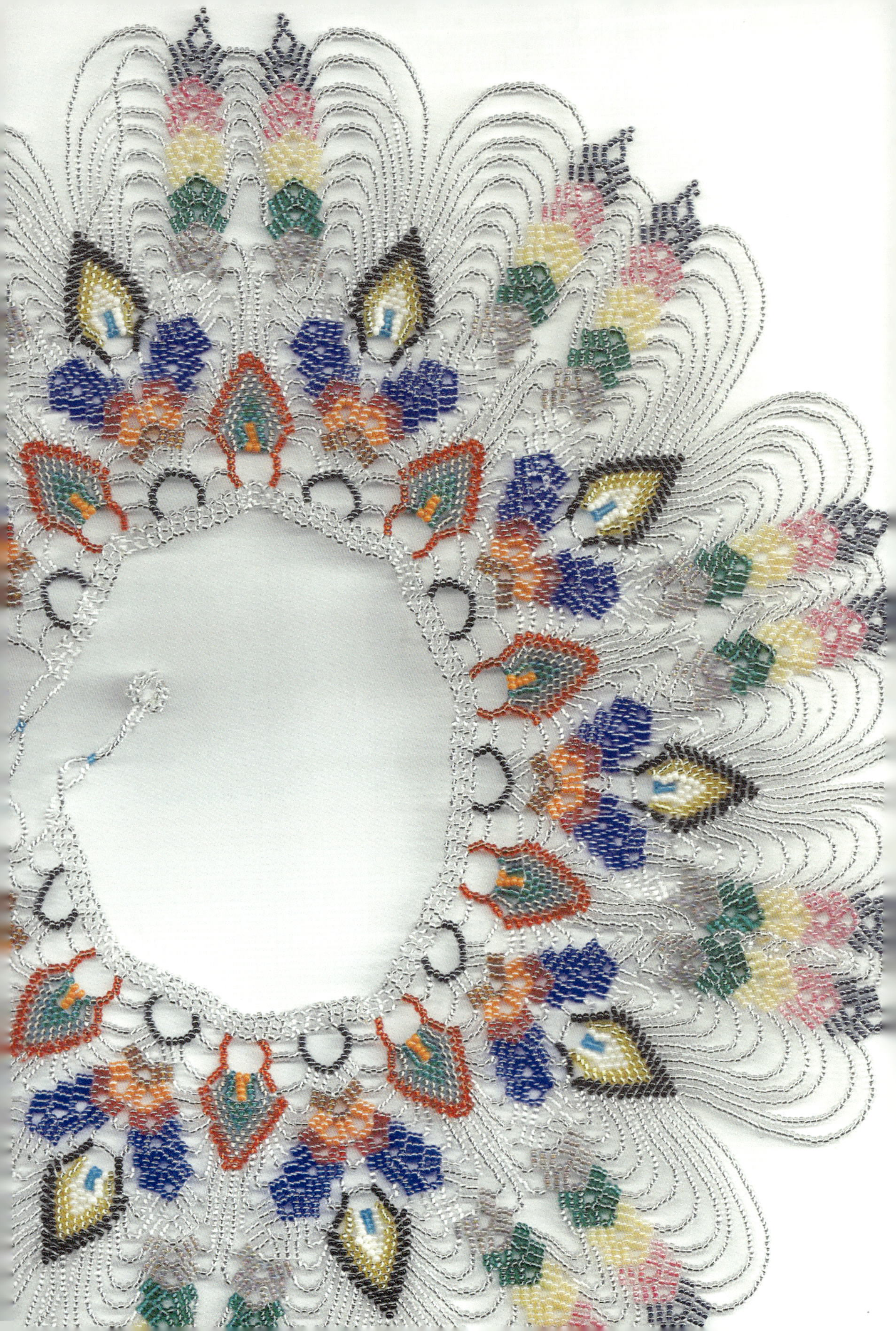

Mission. Under his guidance the Vukani Association was formed in 1972 with the aim of reviving craft skills in the area. Both men and women were invited to join the Association, which was run as a co-operative by a committee drawn from all participating members. The first chairperson of the committee was Mrs Cecilia Matiwane and more recently the position has been filled by Mr (Rev) Gabriel Shandu.

The organisation of the Vukani Association and its various successors continues to be based on a decentralised model. Members worked at home in their own time and the completed items were collected at specified times from agreed-upon collection points by Vukani field staff. Each item offered for sale was carefully scrutinised for defects before being accepted by the organisation's buyers and taken to Eshowe for pricing and sale to the public. As in the case of the Durban based AAC, the Vukani field staff under the leadership of Baba Elliott Dludla tutored new crafters in order to develop and maintain a high standard of weaving. Once in Eshowe each item was and continues to be graded according to quality, and priced before being allowed onto the open market.

Vukani craft was initially sold largely through Swedish and other church networks. In time a wide variety of local South African markets such as the AAC and a number of other up-market Durban curio stores increased the demand for Vukani products, particularly for their exquisite basketware. Beadwork was also accepted for sale by the Vukani Association, but does not appear to have featured strongly in the early days of the organisation. It was, however, to become, and has remained an important and distinctive feature of the organisation's later craft repertoire.

In contrast to basketry, beadwork, although also made in the homes of the local beaders, is brought for sale by the makers to the headquarters of the appropriate collection point. Most of the beaders now supplying Vukani with beadwork were initially contacted through church networks or through welfare organisations active in the area and were invited to bring their beadwork to the Association for possible sale. Although at first the beadwork was largely traditional in style, the impetus given by the opportunity to make a regular income from bead making provided the stimulus for the creation, not only of a number of new designs, but, as new varieties of beads were sourced with the assistance of the Association, for experimentation with increasingly novel and complex designs and colour combinations.

Beadwork is displayed alongside the other craft for sale in the local shop on the same premises in Eshowe. Today Vukani offers some of the most beautiful beadwork made in KwaZulu-Natal and its beaders command commensurately high prices for their work. There is a growing market of discerning buyers, both from within South Africa, and from abroad, who seek out and are willing to pay highly for the quality of their beadwork. It is not only the beauty of the finished product that potential buyers value. The strength of the twine used by the beaders,

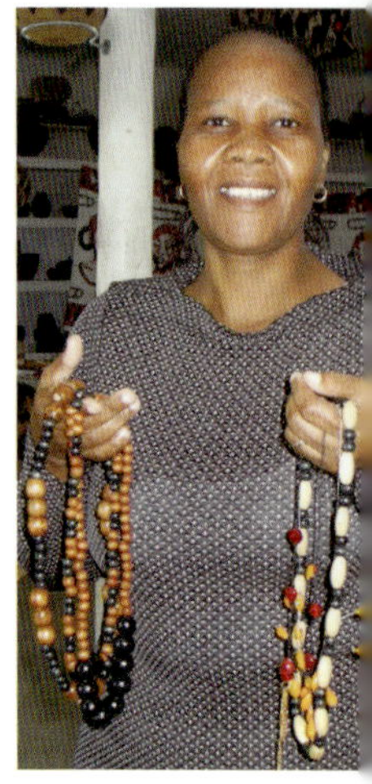

Simosini Doris Mwelase holding a number of pieces of Vukani Beadwork, circa 2013. (VG)

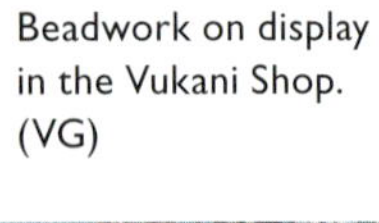

Beadwork on display in the Vukani Shop. (VG)

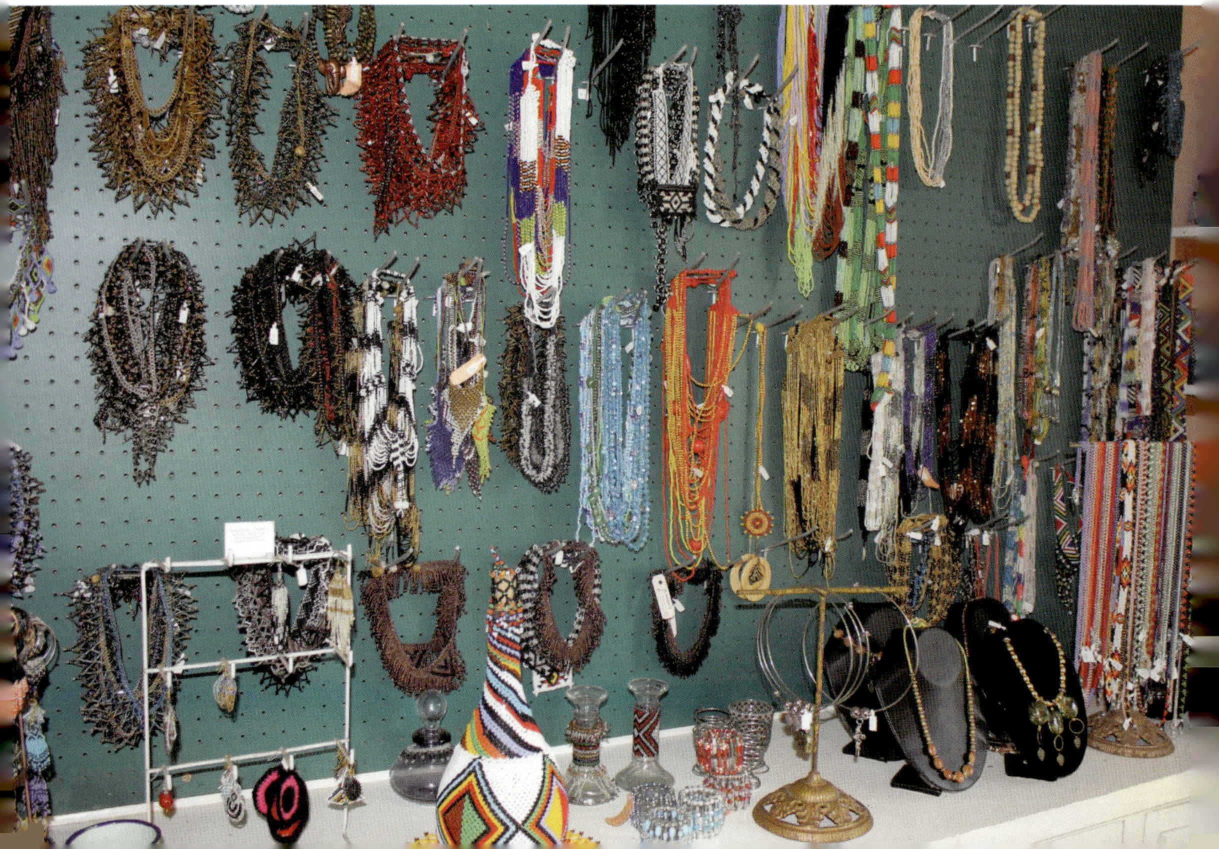

the uniformity and tension of the weaving itself, and the attention paid to finishing each item of beadwork with care, are valued almost as much as the intricacy and beauty of the designs themselves.

Income earned by the beaders selling to Vukani has made a significant difference to the welfare of their families. It has provided not only a noticeably better diet for household members, but has put ongoing health care within the grasp of many families who could not previously afford it. An increasing number of local children have been able to attend school and can now look forward to a future in which they, in their turn, will find gainful employment.

On a more personal level, the selling of their beadwork and the enthusiastic response with which it has been greeted, has brought Vukani beadmakers the personal satisfaction of creating objects that are admired not only for their intrinsic beauty, but for the skill that has gone into their design. Visiting the Vukani shop and Zulu Cultural Museum and mixing with an admiring public has widened the personal horizons of the beaders, and in one case, led to the opportunity to travel overseas to attend an international conference on beadwork. This is captured in the story told to us by **Simosini Doris Mwelase**, one of the Vukani Arts Association's most experienced and innovative beaders. A summary of her life history underscores the rewards and opportunities that belonging to a vibrant and supportive craft organisation can bring to otherwise isolated rural women.

One of nine children, Simosini Doris Mwelase was born in the Mahlabatini district of Zululand in 1961. Her parents could not afford to send her to school and she was married relatively early to a local man, but was widowed in 1998. By then she had five children and eventually five grandchildren. Simosini was largely responsible for much of their care and support and she badly needed additional income to help feed and clothe herself and the children.

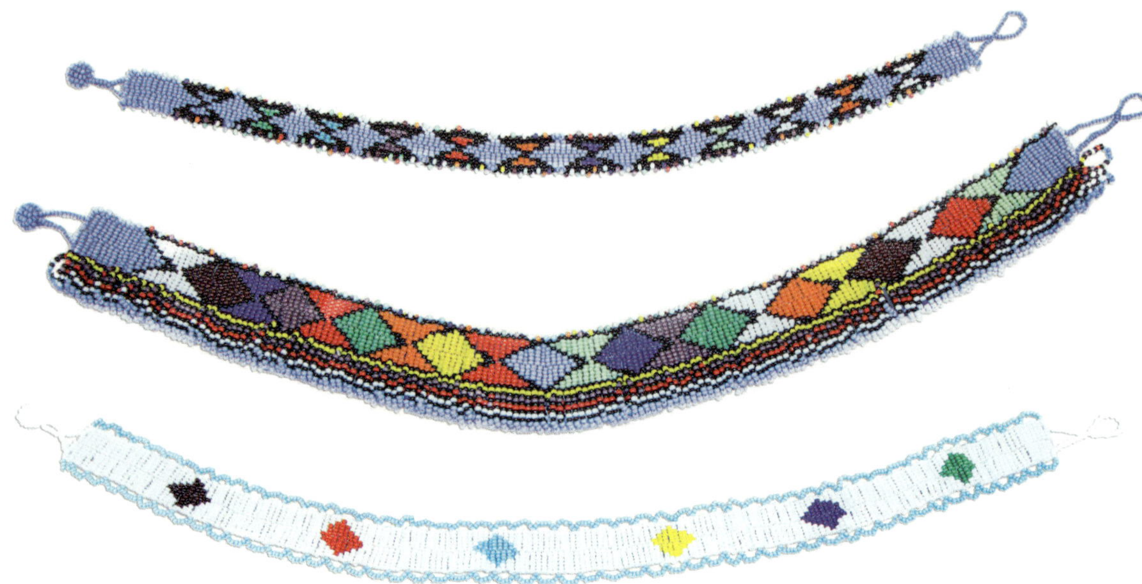

In 2002 a friend mentioned to her that in Durban the YMCA was teaching people to do beadwork in order to help them make a living. Apparently for an initial outlay of R10, 'grannies' would be provided with beads and taught to make HIV/AIDS lapel pins for which they would be paid. She decided to go to Durban in order to attend these classes. Unfortunately, on the day she visited the organisation and paid the stipulated 'fee', the instructor failed to appear and Simosini was no further forward in her quest to make money. A friend then arranged for her to be taught how to make the beaded lapel pins by another woman who had been making them for some time. Until 2007, Simosini managed to garner a small but fairly regular income based on supplying these pins to an organisation that had recently received a number of large orders for their beadwork. Although she did not remember the name of the organisation, from her general description of it and where it was located in Durban, it is likely to have been Sinikithemba, which was dedicated to the eradication of HIV/AIDS and was based at McCord Hospital on the Durban Berea. At the time the hospital had international funding to run a large HIV/AIDS prevention and treatment programme. Because the hospital authorities took an holistic view towards the prevention of HIV, as well as to the treatment of AIDS, in the years between 2000 and 2007 the hospital ran beadwork classes in order to assist patients and other local women earn money by making and selling beadwork.

During this time Simosini also attended beading workshops organised by the AAC and improved her skills and beadwork repertoire by watching the work of other beaders who often got on with their beading while waiting to sell their completed items of beadwork to the AAC

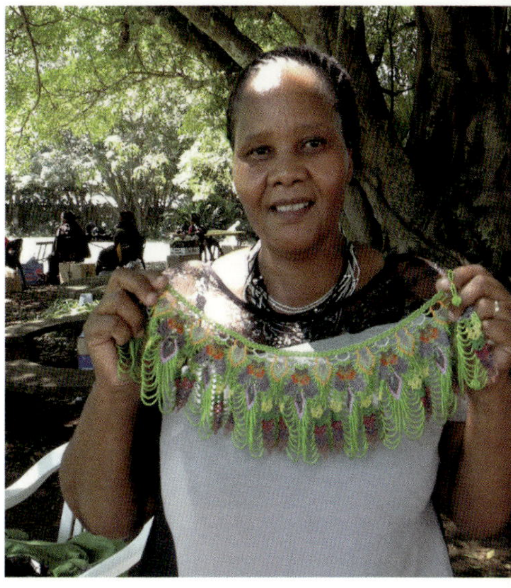

Simosini Mwelase holding a beautiful 'Peacock' necklace, circa 2013. (VG)

buyers. The importance of the bead making circle around the Centre Manager, Jo Thorpe, has already been described. It is important to note the impact the AAC has had on the lives and survival strategies not only of local bead makers, but of those who, like Simosini, were migrants from more distant rural areas.

The origin of the exquisite Peacock necklaces for which Simosini is now well known, dates from this period of her life. She copied the design from a necklace made by a friend who had copied it from one she had seen in a book. In 2010 Simosini entered her rendition of the Peacock necklace in a craft exhibition held in Durban. It was there that a representative of the Vukani Cultural Museum, which was closely associated with the then Vukani Arts Assocation, saw Simosini's work and began to buy necklaces and other beadwork from her. To quote Simosini herself: 'Since then my life has been much better than it used to be...'

In 2011 Simosini represented the Vukani Arts Association at a conference on beadwork and bead making in Malaysia. Speaking about the experience after returning home, she captured the impact of the event:

This was the highlight of my career and my life...I sold over R10 000 worth of beads...I never thought something like this would happen to me...I am so grateful to Vukani for choosing me and giving me the opportunity...I am now registered with DTI [The South African Department of Trade and Industry] *to export my work.* Simosini Doris Mwelase

Bead necklaces made in the peacock design have become extremely popular. While many beaders have tried to copy it, it requires great skill and a long time to bead the intricate pattern. Each Peacock necklace takes Simosini at least a week to complete. Unfortunately it is often not possible to sell these necklaces at a price commensurate with the time and skill that has gone into their creation. She feels, however, well rewarded in terms of the appreciation she receives from the many admirers and buyers of her beadwork.

2. Siyazama

Beginning in the late 1990s much of Sub-Saharan Africa was engulfed by the rapid spread of HIV/AIDS. KwaZulu-Natal was no exception, and together with much of South Africa, was often referred to as the 'AIDS Capital' of the world. Local and international funding became widely available, not only for medical research on HIV/AIDS, but also for intervention projects designed to ameliorate the social impact of the disease at both national and local levels. It was at this time that a number of HIV/AIDS beadwork projects were put in place, one of which was discussed briefly in Chapter 3. At first the mandate of most early HIV/AIDS related beading projects was to design and make small lapel pins fashioned in beadwork that incorporated the inverted red cross to signal the danger of unprotected sex in transmitting the HIV virus. Although these pins were on sale in curio stores throughout the country, they were also provided free of charge as part of many of the HIV/AIDS intervention programmes and were distributed at the many conferences held throughout Africa to report on the state of the epidemic

Lobolile Ximba of Siyazama. (KW)

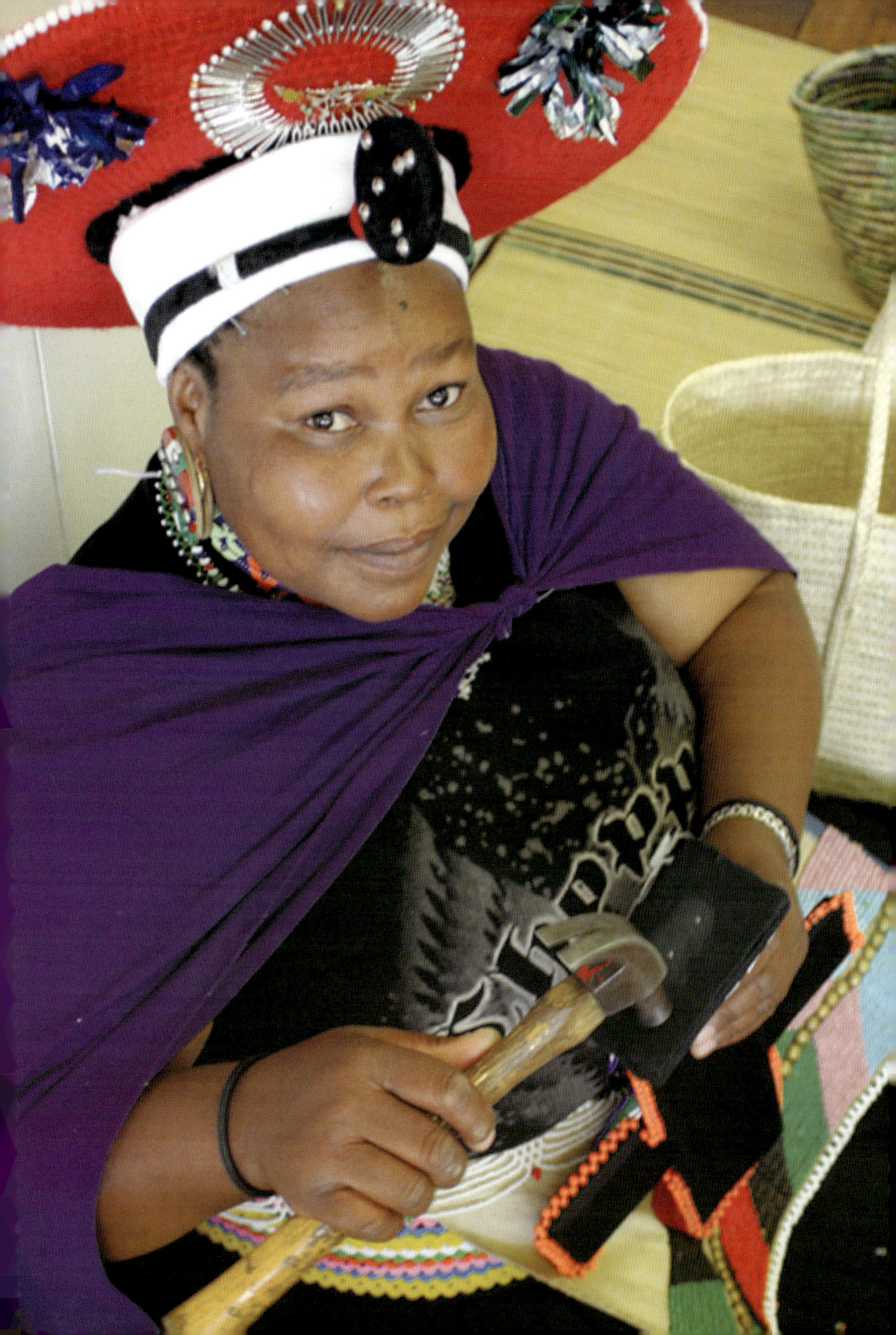

and to discuss new methods of prevention and innovative
intervention strategies. The lapel pins were soon followed by a
proliferation of beaded AIDS dolls, ranging from small to nearly
life-size, bearing the same red inverted cross either on the torso
or skirt. In KwaZulu-Natal most of these dolls were dressed
in beaded costumes based on the traditional dress of Zulu
matrons.

One of the projects devoted to making beaded AIDS dolls was
Siyazama which took its name from the isiZulu for 'we are
trying' and was initiated with international funding in 1998
when the epidemic was fast gaining ground in the rural areas of
KwaZulu-Natal. At this time, because neither protection against
HIV infection nor AIDS amelioration were in place, the infection
constituted a virtual death sentence for those who became
infected. Although treatment for HIV/AIDS is now available,
Siyazama was and continues to be focused on providing
information to women, not only on the dangers of HIV itself,
but on how to protect themselves, their sexual partners and
their families from becoming infected.

The leader and initiator of Siyazama was Kate Wells who was
then a lecturer in Graphic Design at the Durban University
of Technology. A multidisciplinary team made up of local
healthcare workers, medical doctors, traditional healers and a
Medical Anthropologist joined her in this venture. Considerable
thought was given by the design team as to how the beadwork
produced by the project would reach both local and, later,
international markets. As critical, however, was how their
beadwork could be made attractive to prospective buyers
despite the negative connotations carried by the association of
the project with HIV/AIDS. With time and increased experience
of their expanding market, Siyazama proved more than capable
of meeting these challenges.

From the start, the major objective of Siyazama was to serve
the needs of rural women who almost invariably constitute the

poorest and most neglected section of any rural or peri-urban community in KwaZulu-Natal. At first the project focused largely on the expert craftswomen living in The Valley of A Thousand Hills just outside Durban, the beadwork of a number of whom was discussed in a previous chapter. The project soon spread, however, further into the Inanda Valley and to Melmoth, which is a few hours' drive from Durban. Some 12 years later it is still flourishing and successfully keeping up with changes in the beadwork market, as well as in treatment and protection against HIV/AIDS. Siyazama has gone from strength to strength and a small but attractive shop has been established there, from which the beaded dolls, now the hallmark of the project, can be purchased. Alternatively, these can be bought online.

In 2003 Siyazama mounted an exhibition in the United Kingdom which served to increase its international visibility and to remind non-South Africans that although treatment is now available for HIV/AIDS in South Africa, it is neither available to all poor people in the country, nor is it without its potential hazards and complications.

An ongoing collaboration was set up between Siyazama and the Durban University of Technology, to which the project is affiliated, and with the Michigan State University Museum in order to collaborate in disseminating up-to-date information on the progress of the AIDS epidemic and on the latest protective strategies and treatment available to women. Exhibitions of Siyazama's beadwork have been mounted, both in South Africa and internationally, and a number of publications made available in which the research findings and the lessons learned from the project are disseminated. One of the results of this collaboration has been a recent publication by Kate Wells and others, entitled *Siyazama: Art, AIDS and Education in South Africa (2012),* which details not only the history and experiences of the project, but the educational implications of what is referred to as the 'Siyazama Project Model' for the ongoing management of the disease.

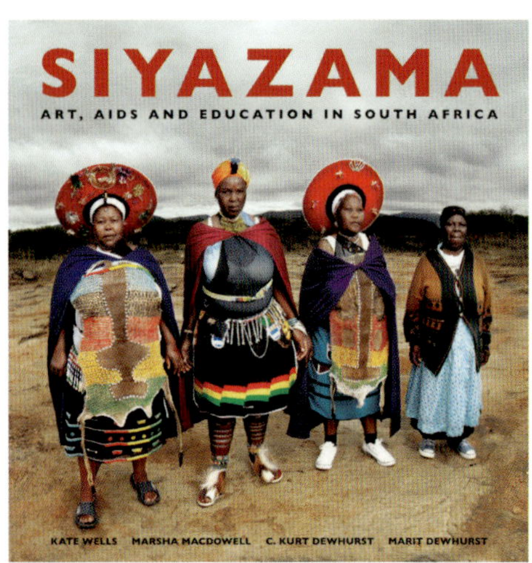

Siyazama: Art, AIDS and Education in South Africa (2012). (KW)

The book is illustrated by photographs of the women participating in the project taken together with, and in some cases proudly holding, examples of their beadwork. The text is based on their life stories and the comments made by a number of the participants in the project on the impact Siyazama had had on their welfare and that of their families and friends. The reactions that are reported are universally positive, and it is clear that the women interviewed benefited in having had the opportunity to make their beadwork in an increasingly stimulating and even challenging educational environment. While most commented on the financial benefits Siyazama had brought them, they also emphasised their personal satisfaction in seeing the pleasure that their beadwork brought to buyers, and of hearing the latter's appreciative comments on individual dolls.

Some of the original beaders who participated in Siyazama lived in the same geographical area as the bead makers who supplied the AAC in Durban. A number were, moreover, regularly supplying the Centre with its beaded dolls and also with beaded tableaux during the period when the AAC was run by Jo Thorpe. In the book Wells *et al* use the term 'soft sculptures' rather than 'bead sculptures' to describe these items, but it is clear that they describe items of the same beadwork genre. They also write of 'narrative' tableaux in relation to those works that include a number of figures and which tell an often complex visual story. Perhaps most striking, is that it is clear that a number of the same women were selling their beadwork to both the AAC and to Siyazama.

The names of Sizakhele Mchunu and her co-wife Celani Nojiyeza, as well as those of Thembi Mchunu and Kulumelaphi

Mlaba, whose work was discussed in Chapter 5 in relation to the AAC, are mentioned by Wells *et al* as being among the beaders supplying Siyazama in the early days of its existence. Written well after the end of apartheid, the books is more politically forthright than was Jo Thorpe, who wrote at an early point in South Africa's repressive political history. Wells *et al* comment specifically on the fact that some of the works brought to the AAC for sale in the late 1960s 'provided glimpses into the racial and economic divisions that still linger in South Africa'. In support of a political interpretation, the authors cite the bead sculptures of a black woman pushing a stroller, and of a white woman playing tennis. The intriguing question is, of course, whether bead sculptures of this nature were merely simple reflections of what their makers saw, or whether they were as Sue Williams (1989) has argued, clear evidence of subtle, but astute political commentary on the part of their makers.

Siyazama beadmakers' Stories

The personal stories of a number of the beaders working under the auspices of Siyazama have been selected from *Siyazama: Art, AIDS and Education in South Africa,* in order to illustrate both the variety of the beadwork produced by the organisation, as well as some of the benefits that have accrued to the makers from their association with Siyazama.

Celani Mchunu Nojiyeza reflected at some length on the way in which she was able to tell stories through her beadwork.

Roughly translated, these were her words:
> *I think of the story I'm going to tell first, which is very important. So it's always important to tell different stories in my work. It's always a true story.*

She continued:
> *The dolls do not normally tell stories but the AIDS ribbon is always on them, embedding them with messages that help*

*me and my people know more about AIDS...it makes people
not afraid of telling about such issues and nothing is really
sensitive these days.*

Celani learned beading from a member of her family when
she was young. The staff of both the AAC and Siyazama
encouraged her to expand her beading repertoire and this led
to the construction of beaded tableaux like those made by her
sister, Sizakhele Mchunu, whose work, as we have seen, was
gaining local and even international recognition. In turn Celani
taught her daughter, Princess, as well as other women in her
extended family, to do beadwork. Through her connection with
Siyazama, her work has been shown around the world, and in
1999 she travelled to the United States in order to participate in
a Folklife festival held in Washington DC.

Lobolile Ximba

In contrast to Celani, Lobolile Ximba was born in the inland
rural area of Msinga in1953. The area is very much a stronghold
of Zulu tradition with a fair number of its inhabitants still
making and wearing traditional beadwork, not only on
ceremonial occasions, but in the course of their everyday lives.
She learned her beading skills, and particularly how to make
traditional beaded dolls, from her mother who made them in
order to sell and so make money to feed and clothe her large
family. In turn Lobolile taught her six daughters, and other
members of the local community, to make these dolls. She was
one of the early participants in Siyazama and won a gold medal
in 2002 in a prestigious set of craft awards sponsored by a local
bank. In 2004 she won another award for a beaded crucifix
representing a woman crucified to AIDS.

The dolls which Lobolile makes are typically tall standing
figures mounted on a firm wooded base. They are clothed
in the traditional dress and beadwork of the Msinga area.
Lobolile explained the history and current use of her dolls in the
following terms:

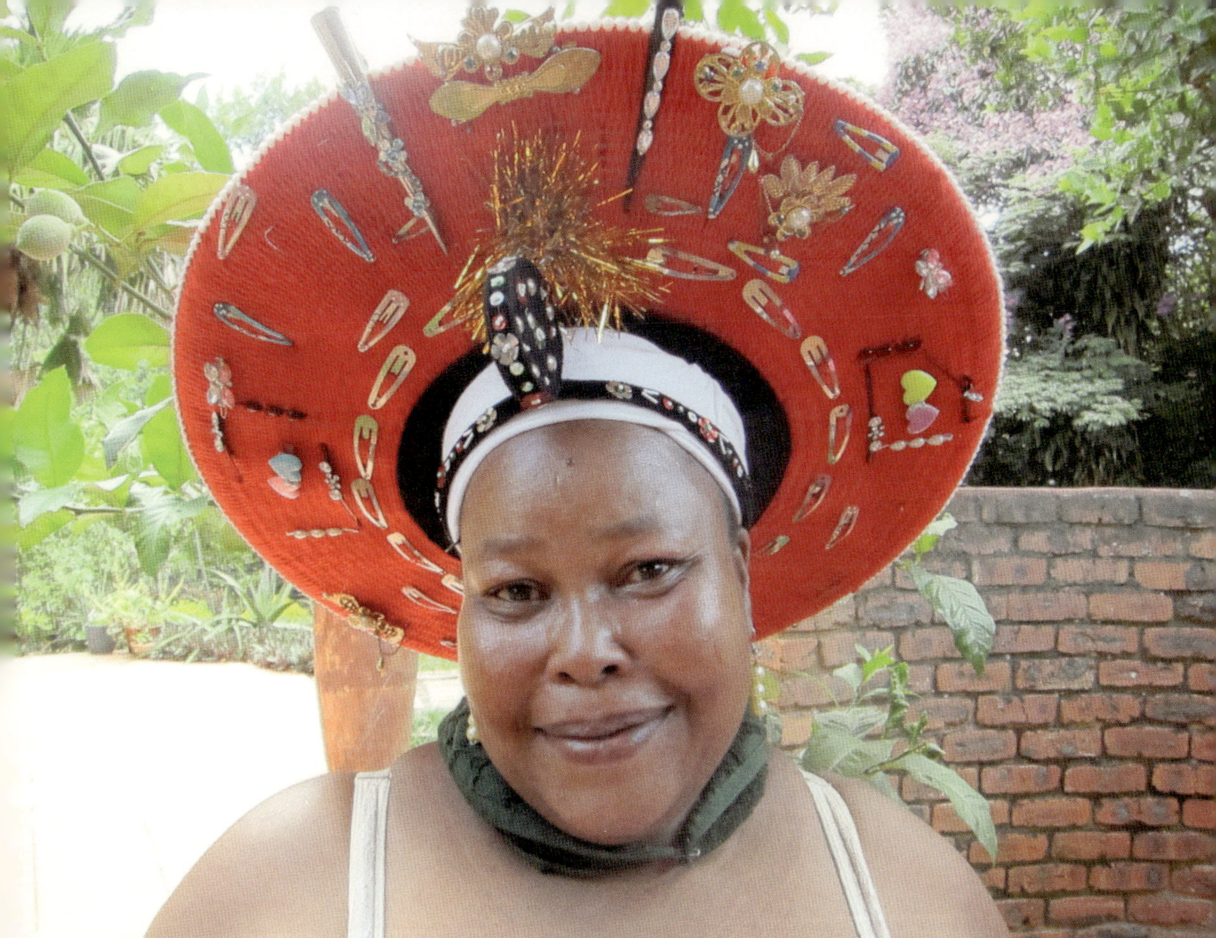

We used to give them to our boyfriends as gifts. We didn't keep them for long as soon as it is done we'll then give it to the boyfriends. They used to keep them in their rooms like real babies and sometimes you'll ask your boyfriend to bring that doll back to you just to visit you.

Modernity has impacted the accessorising of the *makoti* red hat worn by Lobolile Ximba. (2013) (KW)

Commenting on the meaning of the motif of the red AIDS ribbon which she often incorporated in her designs, Lobolile explained that it was a reminder of the various ways in which HIV/AIDS affected, or as she put it, 'touched' her community.

Fokosile Ngema

In contrast to many of the bead makers described above, Fokosile Ngema is now an elderly woman. She was born in 1938 into a Christian home and began beading fairly late in life. Speaking of her family she explained as follows:

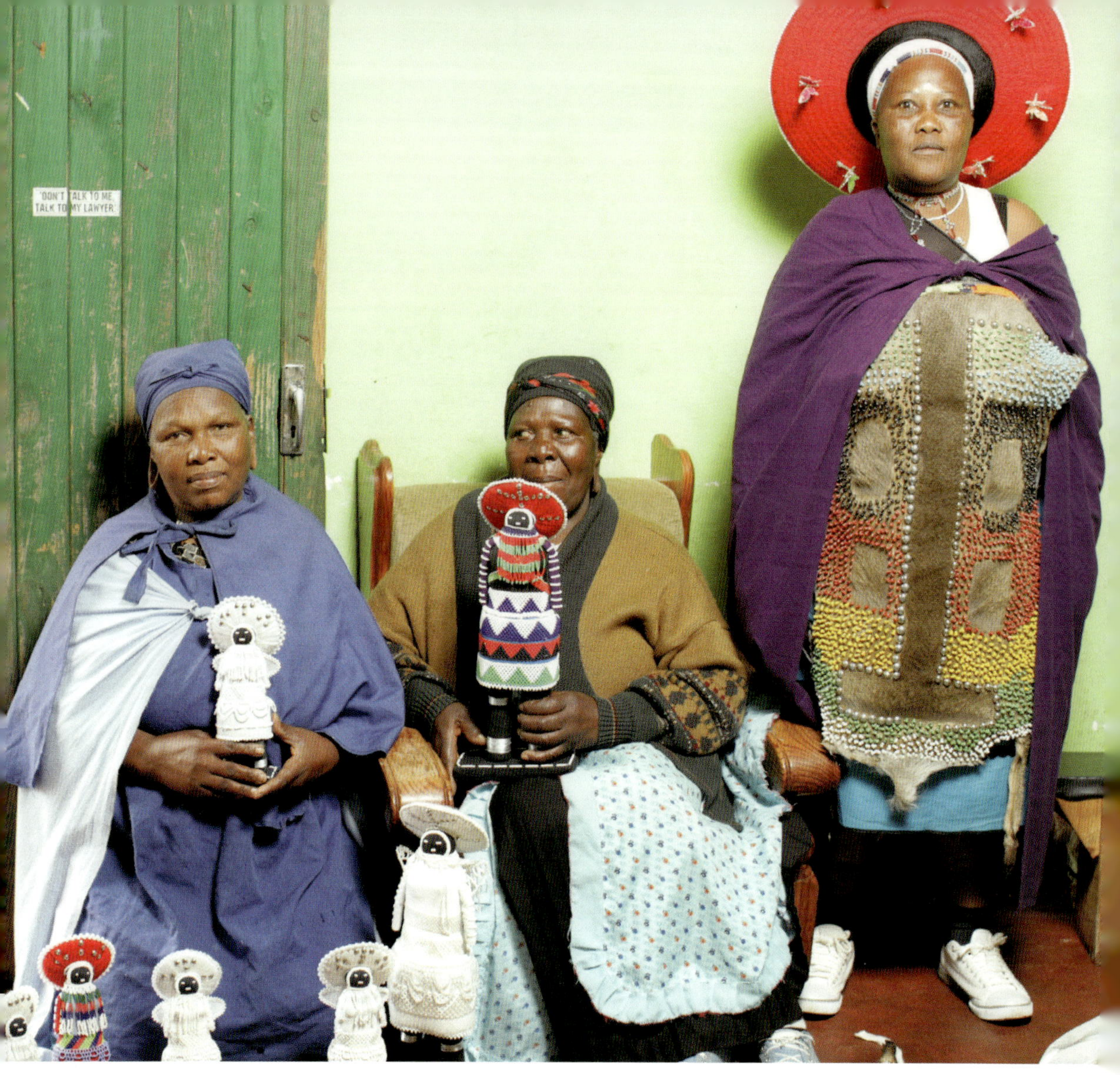

A group of doll makers at the Ximba residence in Muden, Msinga.
Left to right: Fokosile Ngema, Tholiwe Sitole and the late Kishwepi Sitole.
(KW)

I am part of the first generation to make dolls and the tradition has been started because we have taught younger people who will be left after we have passed on... There has been a lot of positive transformation because now we've learned a lot of design. We can actually do anything and everything with beads.

Fokosile Ngema learned bead making from Lobolile Ngema, who was her neighbour in the late 1980s. She spends most of her free time bead making, and often works up to 15 hours a day on designing and dressing her easily recognisable dolls and believes that her beading and design skills improve with every one she makes. She is meticulous in the attention she pays to the clothes in which her dolls are dressed and in most cases these are based on the traditional dress of the women living around her. Describing the results of this she exclaimed, 'It's like we put a breath of life in them', and then added that although she had not had any formal education, the dolls were the most practical way to teach the people living around her about the dangers of HIV/AIDS.

Tholiwe Sithole

The convivial atmosphere in which beadwork is often taught by instructors from Siyazama to groups of young girls and women was vividly described by Tholiwe Sithole in the following terms:

We were taught in a group so it was easy 'cause if you didn't catch what the person teaching was saying, then you'll just ask your fellow mate.

Initially Tholiwe simply wore the beadwork she had learned to make, or gave it to her boyfriend. Later, however, she was able to sell it to a number of Durban shops and galleries. After participating in the discussions and workshops held by Siyazama on HIV/AIDS and, in particular, those on anti-retro viral treatment, she began to weave designs in which images of small pills were specifically incorporated in order to send messages about AIDS to all who saw or wore that item of beadwork.

It is important to note that one of the unexpected consequences of the Siyazama project format was that combining bead making and the giving of information about the dangers of HIV/AIDS served to expose the dangers experienced almost daily by many of the beaders in their relations with men. Some of these put the women at high risk of contracting HIV and later succumbing to AIDS. This led to a number of graphic bead sculptures of the negative relationships with which the women lived, including not only death from

AIDS, but child abuse, domestic violence and rape. These sculptures did not enter the market place, but were noted by the project leaders for further attention and work-shopping on the topic by the Siyazama project leaders. What these tableaux did do, however, was indicate the potential power of at least one Zulu beadwork project to pinpoint social and cultural problems and point a possible way to their amelioration.

The benefits of networking: beadwork projects in Durban

Over the last 15 years a number of predominantly Durban based beadwork projects have emerged, which work together regularly and which form a loose cooperative grouping. Their members interact with and, where possible, assist each other in developing their beading skills. As important, they help each other in finding and opening up new markets for their beadwork. At the time of writing these include among others, the Hillcrest AIDS Centre, the eThekwini Community Foundation, as well as the Melmoth based Siyazama discussed above. Apart from producing its own beadwork, Umcebo Design acts as an umbrella organisation which assists the other projects to network widely in order to advertise and market their work.

In all cases these Durban based projects take care to give public recognition to beaders and other crafters, not only by making their names known to prospective buyers, but by encouraging their members to participate in project design, rather than merely working from the designs of other artists. The eThekwini Community Foundation assists the other projects to secure local and international funding for their ongoing work, and recently, for the development of a number of ambitious multimedia public art projects in which beadwork plays an important role. In this sense it acts as a modern day 'culture broker' in that it performs much the same role as did Jo Thorpe and the AAC in the 1960s and 1970s.

Variety and experimentation are the keynotes and driving forces behind the work of the constituent projects of the Durban grouping. Most have come to fill a specialty niche market which allows them not only to experiment but also extend the scope and existing boundaries of their craft. At the same time, the close ties that the projects have with each other provide the opportunity for members to collaborate on large scale beading enterprises that would have been beyond the scope of the individual projects. It has also brought them into contact with a wide range of artists and craftspeople working in mediums as diverse as wirework, decoupage, crochet as well as beadwork itself, and some have begun to experiment with using these techniques in their own work. These craft and design groups make up a loose 'collective' and, when working together on joint ventures, they refer to themselves as the eThekwini Craft Consortium. Each group of crafters adds its particular skills to the mix of diverse handwork talent represented in the grouping as a whole, with often spectacular results. In attempting to capture the variety of this association, we begin by describing one of the oldest and widely known projects that is now part of it.

3. Woza Moya
(also known as the Hillcrest AIDS Centre)

The Hillcrest HIV/AIDS Centre, or Woza Moya, was one of the earliest HIV/AIDS oriented beadwork projects to be developed in KwaZulu-Natal. It was, and still is, situated just outside Durban on the way to the Valley of a Thousand Hills, from where it draws many of its beaders. The original mandate of the project was to raise awareness of HIV/AIDS through the making and distribution of modern beadwork, much of which bore the inverted red HIV/AIDS cross. Its early repertoire also included the beaded lapel pins that had, by then, come to symbolise the fight against the epidemic. A noteworthy recent 'ambassador' for the Hillcrest AIDS Centre are their lapel pin-size dolls called 'little travellers'. A popular Tourist item these now carry the message of the centre worldwide.

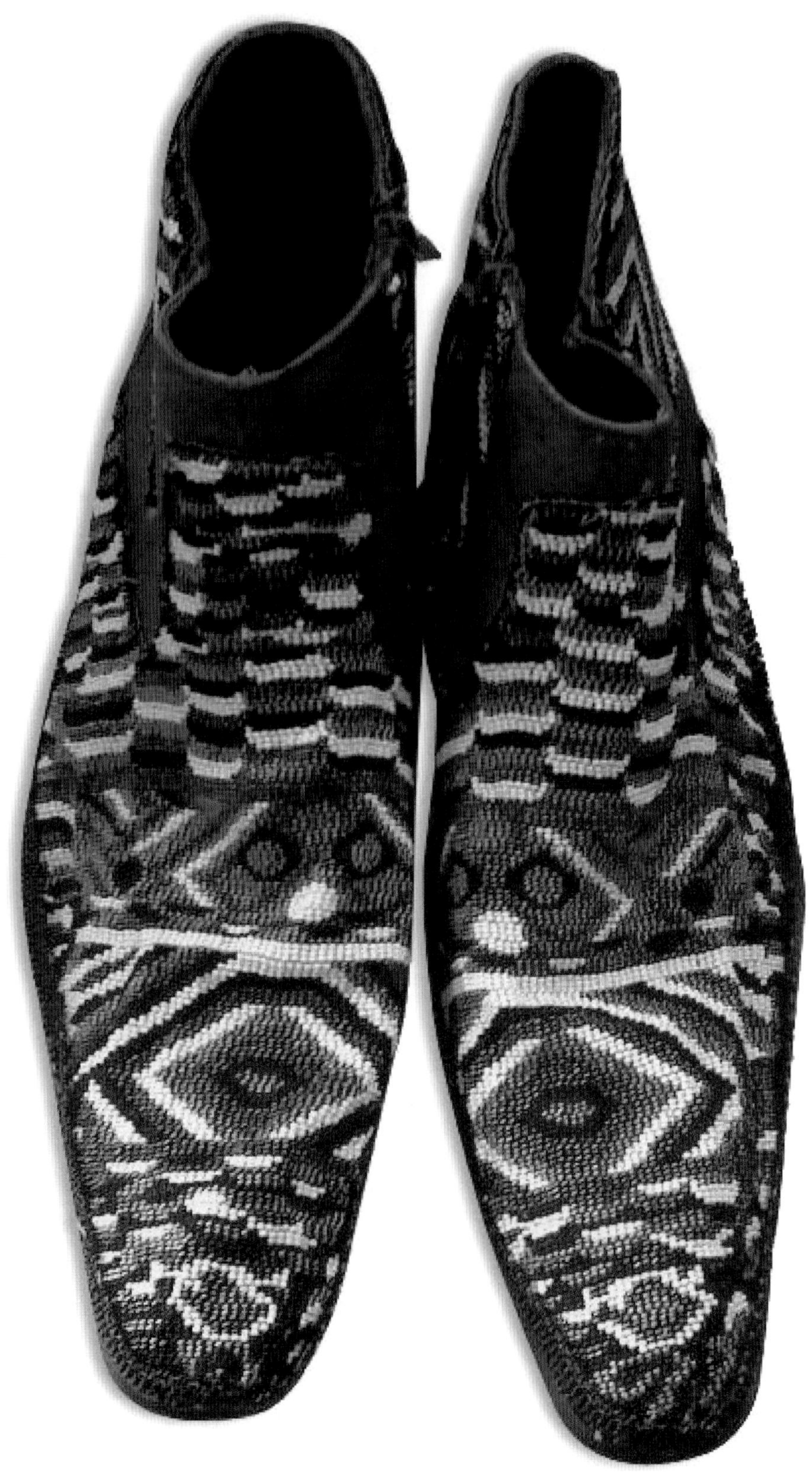

As advances in the treatment of AIDS began to ameliorate the impact of the disease in the province, the Hillcrest AIDS Centre expanded the range of its beadwork. High quality glittering costume jewellery made from shiny beads similar to those that characterised the beadwork produced by a number of the rural projects discussed in Chapters 3 and 4 were added to their beadwork repertoire. The project also developed new and highly innovative beading styles, designs and colour combinations which make use of beads sourced from Durban wholesalers and a number of specialist bead shops that have recently opened in the city in response to the growing use of beadwork, not only as a fashion item but as a hobby. If this trend continues beadwork may, in time, come to rival the popularity of embroidery and knitting. Indeed, the latter is already being replaced by the purchase of relatively inexpensive machine-made knitwear.

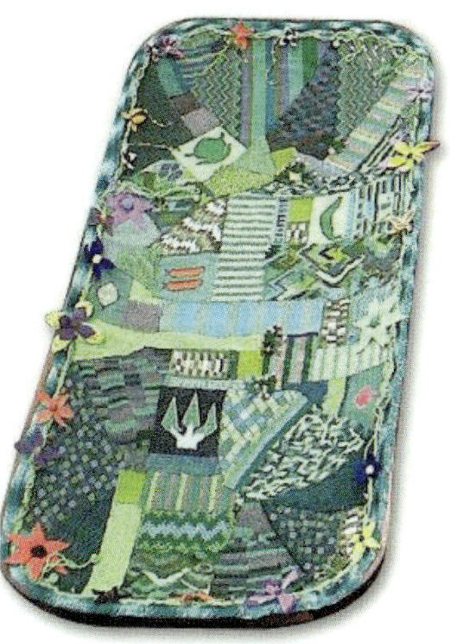
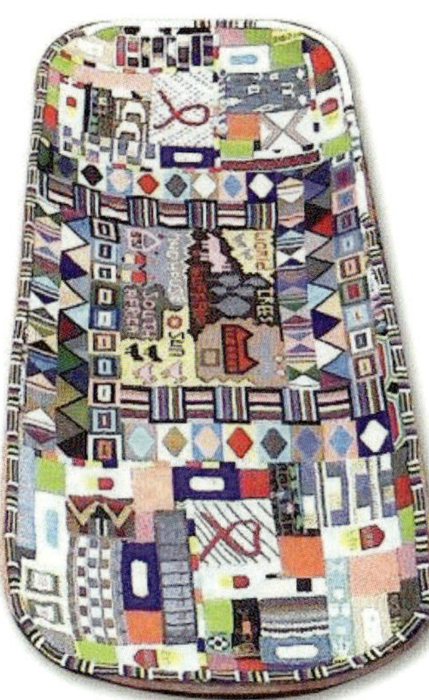

Beaded trays made by the crafters at Woza Moya (The Hillcrest AIDS Centre). (HAC)

In search of new markets, The Hillcrest AIDS Centre has branched out into the design of beaded clothing and also beaded furniture, wall hangings and other items of interior décor.

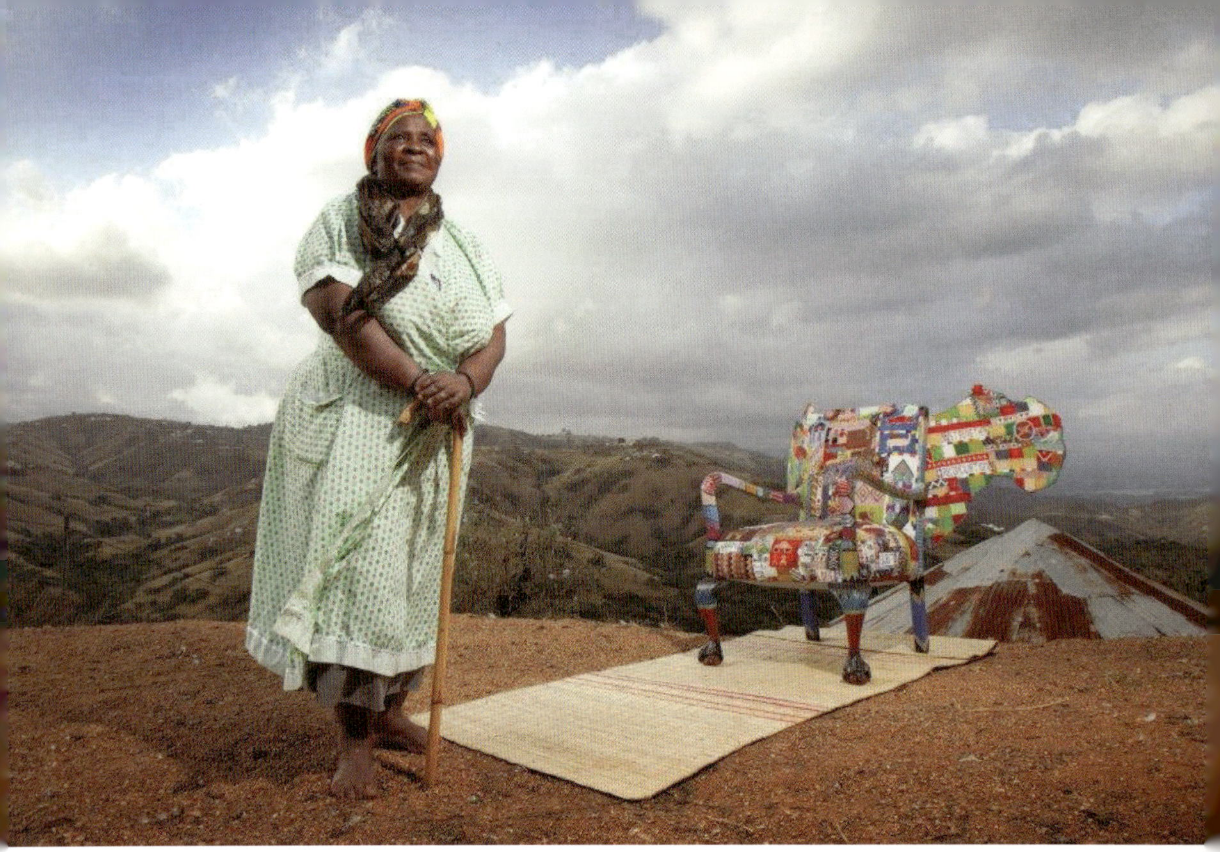

Above: Gogo Zondikile
with the Africa Chair, chair
upholstered with beaded
fabric.

Below: Attractive and highly
saleable embroidered and
beaded items from Woza
Moya.

Right: Beaded evening
gown worn by
Princess Charlene,
of Monaco – a
former South African
Olympic swimmer
– wife of Prince
Albert II,
of Monaco. (HAC)

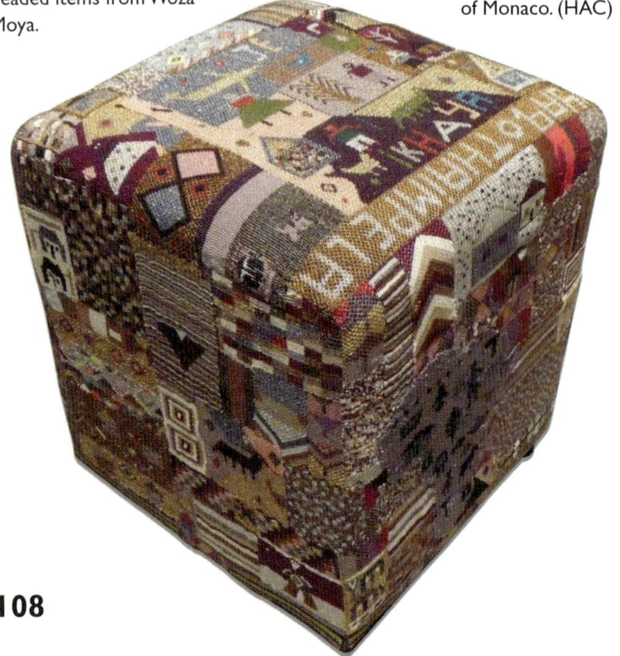

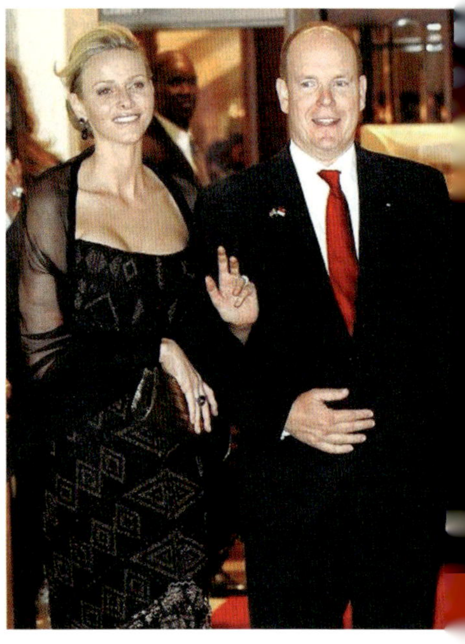

4. Umcebo Design

Umcebo Design is a business that emerged from Robin Opperman's long-standing interest in community-based art and craft. He established a viable income-generating business model to provide unemployed and marginalised people with a means of using their creativity and beading skills to earn a regular income.

In 2011 Umcebo moved to a studio in Bulwer Road, Glenwood, Durban, where he and his collaborating partner, Jackie Sewpersad, work closely with a network of home-based artists, crafters, partner organisations and educational institutions.

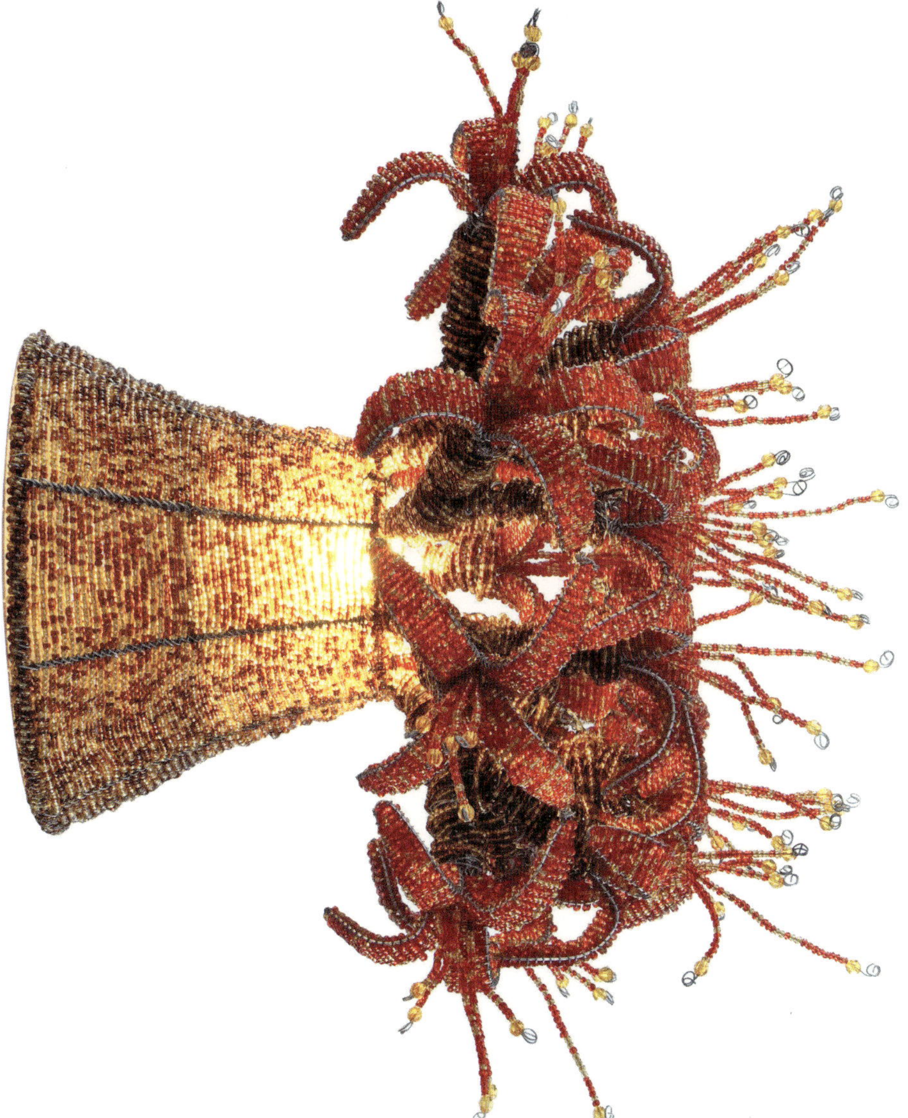

A beaded wall sconce lamp, Umcebo Design, circa 2011-12. (RO)

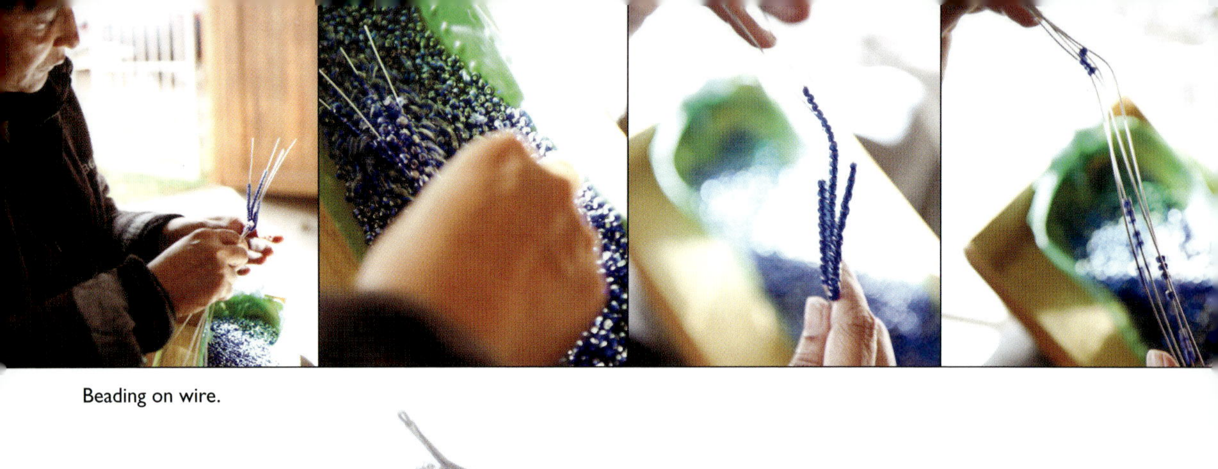

Beading on wire.

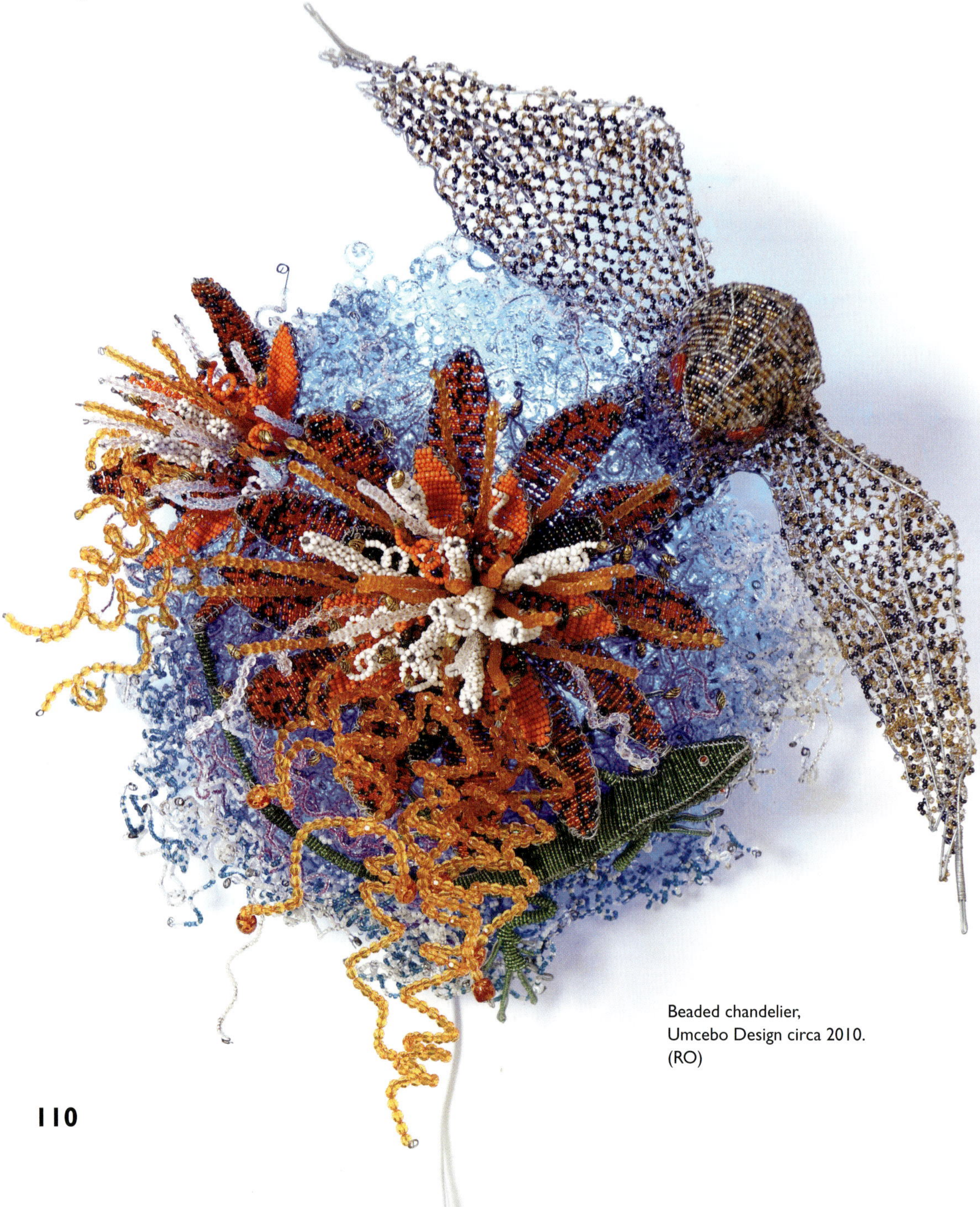

Beaded chandelier,
Umcebo Design circa 2010.
(RO)

The Umcebo Design team work on commission and create, among other items, spectacular beaded chandeliers. In addition they offer training for emerging community craft projects. It is in this capacity that Robin and Jackie provided design expertise and management for the Yenza and Nkanyezi rhino projects. They have also worked extensively with info4africa and Ubunye Craft helping to create a set of beaded 'hotpots' and establish them as up and coming community crafters and designers in KwaZulu-Natal.

5. Ubunye Craft Co-Operative

The Ubunye Craft Co-Operative is largely made up of women and young people living in the Mzimela District of KwaZulu-Natal. It was started with funding from the South African Development Agency and was the brainchild of **Patricia Zungu,** who was born in the small Zululand town of Mtunzini and now lives just outside Eshowe. She left school after completing Grade Nine and for a while was employed as a domestic worker. She dreamed, however, of 'doing something' with her life that would allow her to make a positive contribution to her community and, as she put it, 'would bring hope into people's lives'. The Ubunye Co-Operative was, as she puts it 'born of this vision'. When asked about her objectives in starting the organisation she explained:

In many rural places across South Africa youth leave school and are left without the opportunity to study further or gain proper employment. In light of this, youth often turn to crime as a means to create an income. Our Co-Operative

Ubunye Craft Co-Operative Hot Pots (small beaded plants in tin mugs of various sizes. Now also available in traditional clay pots).

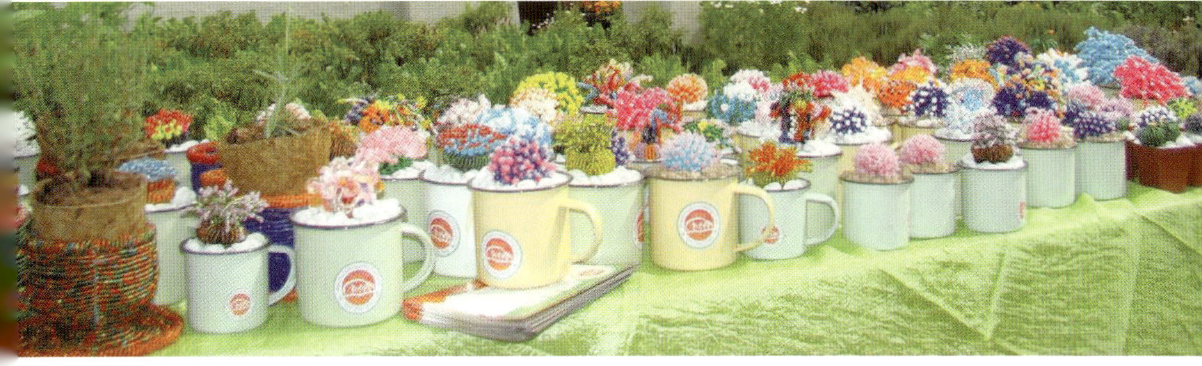

works to prevent youth from viewing crime as an option.
By providing skills training, opportunities and broadening
people's horizons, we've found that youth and adults
are able to create a future for themselves. Our name,
Ubunye Ba'Mzimela, *signifies 'community'… it is through*
standing together that we are able to improve our lives,
create beautiful things and be proud of our heritage. Our
eco-tourism and traditional dance, storytelling and craft
programmes let tourists explore our way of life – it's the
authentic Zululand experience.

Ubunye has worked with an umbrella funding agency that not
only raised the funding for the project, but provided ongoing
guidance and mentorship for members of the Co-Operative.
Describing the importance of the latter, Patricia commented:

As a result, what was once a dream is now a reality and
we see the positive effects in our community. Being part
of the Co-Operative is hard work but our members are
committed and try very hard to learn new skills…we have
been part of amazing community projects such as the
eThekwini Community Foundation Rhino Projects. Yenza
and Nkanyezi are something we can be proud of. These
rhino projects gave us an opportunity to work with several
other craft and design groups. That was a very good
experience for us. We beaded all of the sections of Nkanyezi
and helped with the development of the design. This was a
privilege and steep learning curve for us…Umcebo Design
[has] shown us that we need to create our own designs and
our 'hotpot' range is a good example of this…We make
small pots with little beaded cacti and plants that remind
us of Zululand, but also become beautiful decorations for
visitors' homes all over South Africa and the world.

Other projects made by the co-operative include a richly
beaded tapestry that reflects Mzimela and its people. This
tapestry formed part of an exhibition of KwaZulu-Natal craft
held at a well known art gallery in Durban in late 2012. Patricia
described the scene as follows:

6. Co-operative craft ventures: Two rhinoceros 'bead sculptures'

A fitting climax to this chapter is provided by images of the two large beaded rhinoceroses made recently by the members of the Durban based eThekweni Craft Collective. Based on the well known 'cow parades' held in other parts of the world during the 1960s and early 1970s, the objective of the members of the Collective has been to draw attention to the threat posed by the increase in rhinoceros poaching in KwaZulu-Natal game parks in order to obtain their horns for medicinal purposes. The beaded rhinos were constructed on a cladding base to which swathes of multi-coloured beadwork were attached. The beading of the separate beadwork panels was undertaken by beaders drawn from the Collective and took some months to make.

Beaders adding panels of beadwork to a beaded rhino called Yenza – 'Just do it'. (DH)

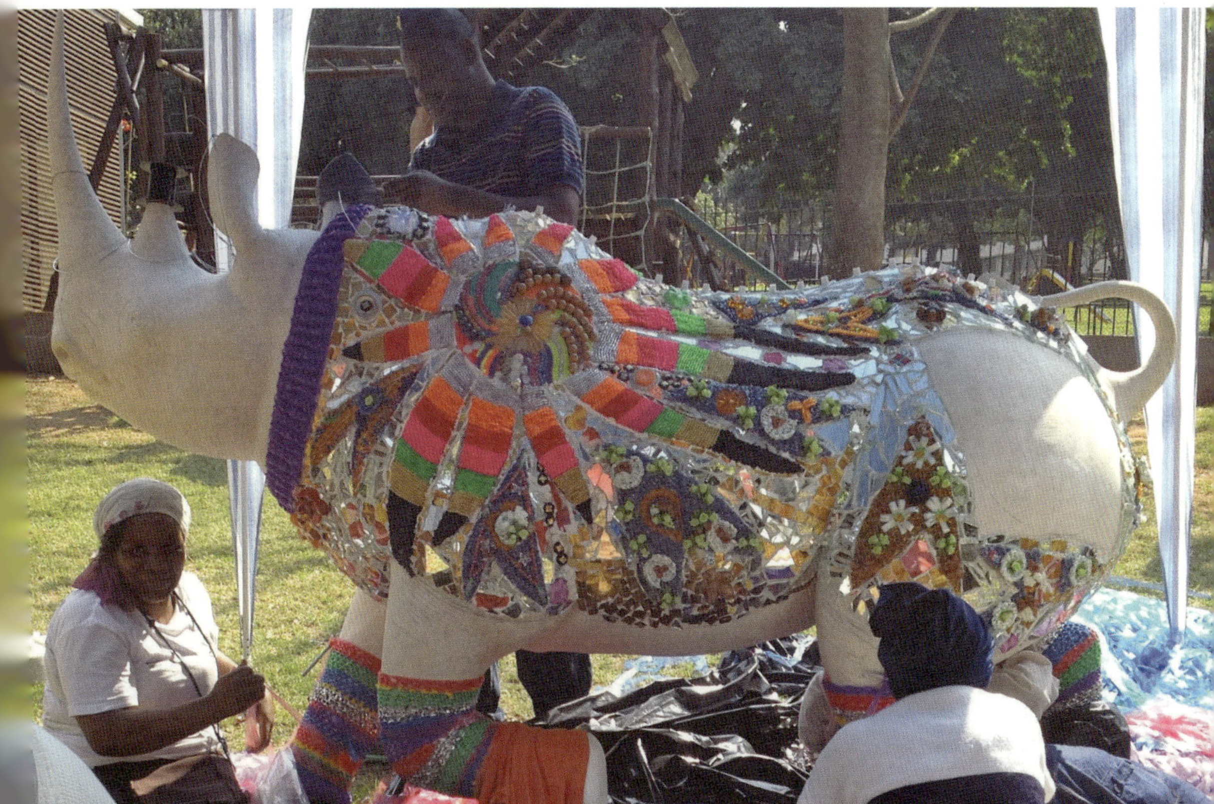

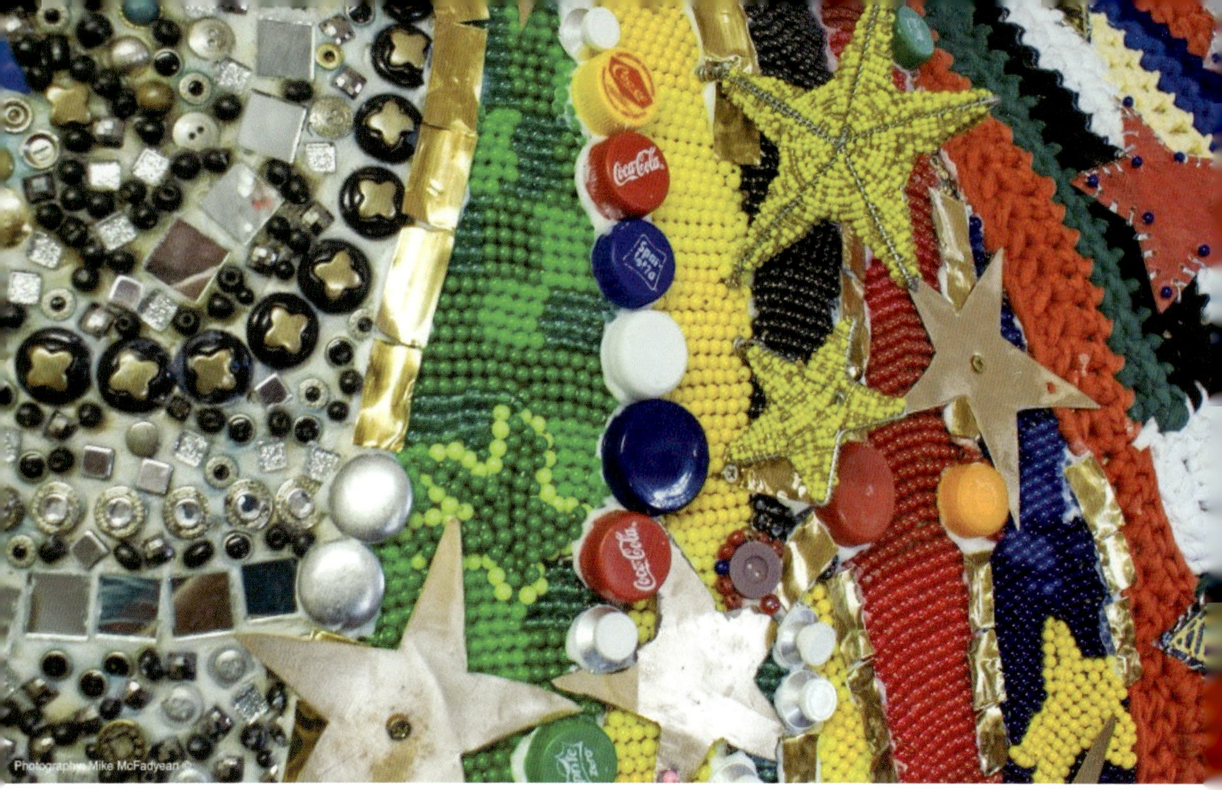

Above: Detail of a beaded panel for one of the beaded Rhinos. (MF)

Below: Detail of the rhino beaded panels. (MF)

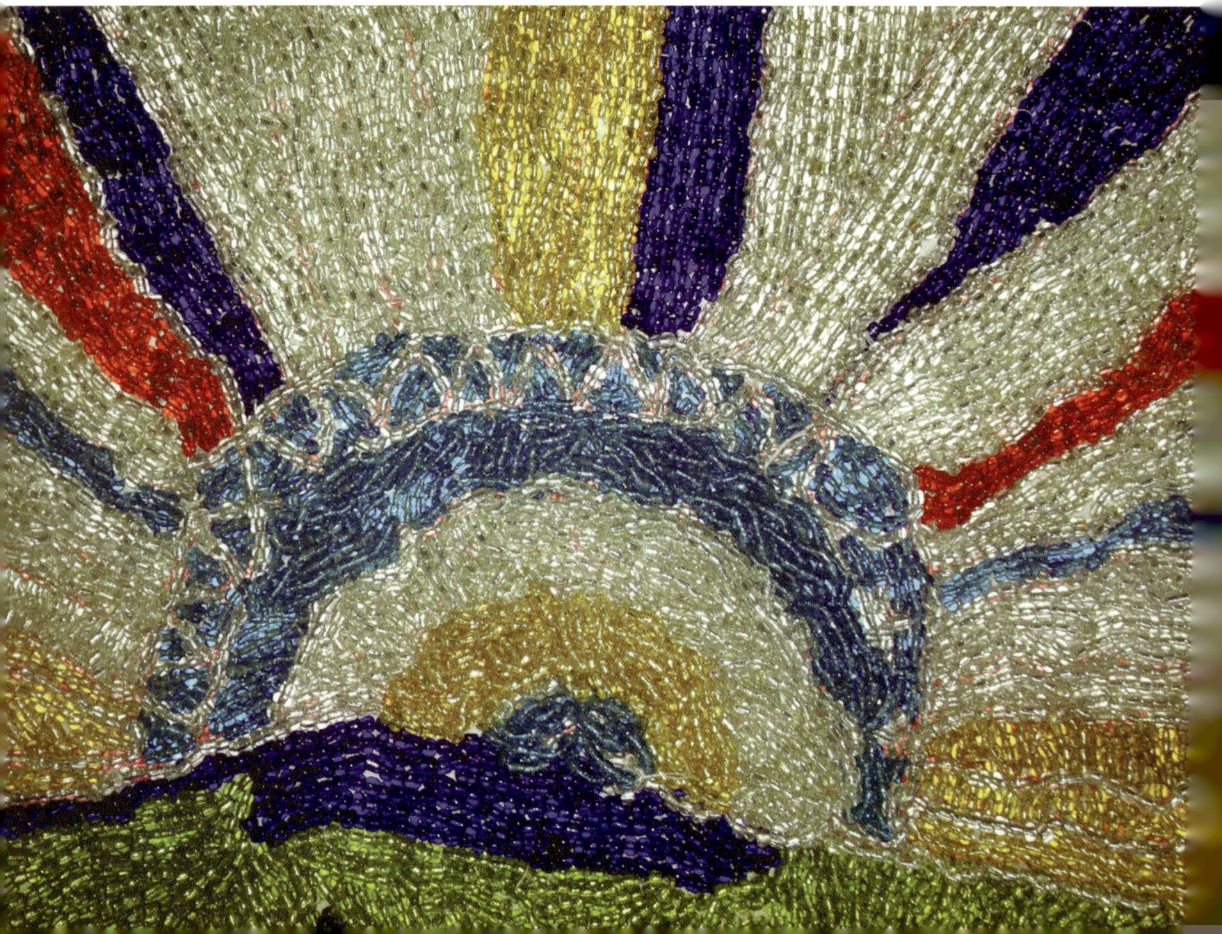

The two rhinoceros sculptures have been named
Yenza (just do it) and Nkanyezi (shining star). Both
were on display for several months at the Durban
Art Gallery. Later Yenza welcomed travellers at the
Domestic arrivals terminal of King Shaka International
Airport. Both endangered species are used by the
South African Wildlife Trust to raise funds in order
to track poachers and promote the conservation
of South African wildlife. Plans are being made to raise funds
to take the Rhinos to Cape Town in 2014 where they will be
part of displays highlighting the current pillage of the species
by hunters. These unusually large beadwork figures have been
followed by the development of several smaller limited editions.

In the next and concluding chapter of this book we move from
the description of Zulu beadwork made largely for sale on the
commercial market to examine the beadwork worn by the
participants in the annual *Umhlanga* or Reed Dance.

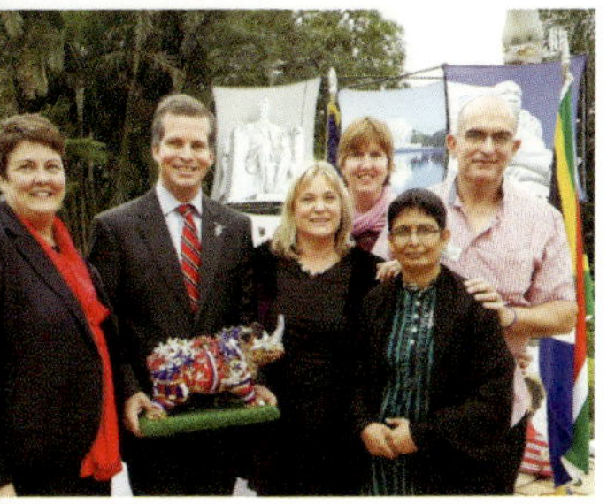

The design team
with a small replica
of the large Nkanyezi
Rhino. It was created
to thank the US
Mission to South
Africa for their
support of craft
development and
Rhino Conservation
in the country.

A completed beaded
rhino called *Nkanyezi*
– 'Shining star'. (MF)

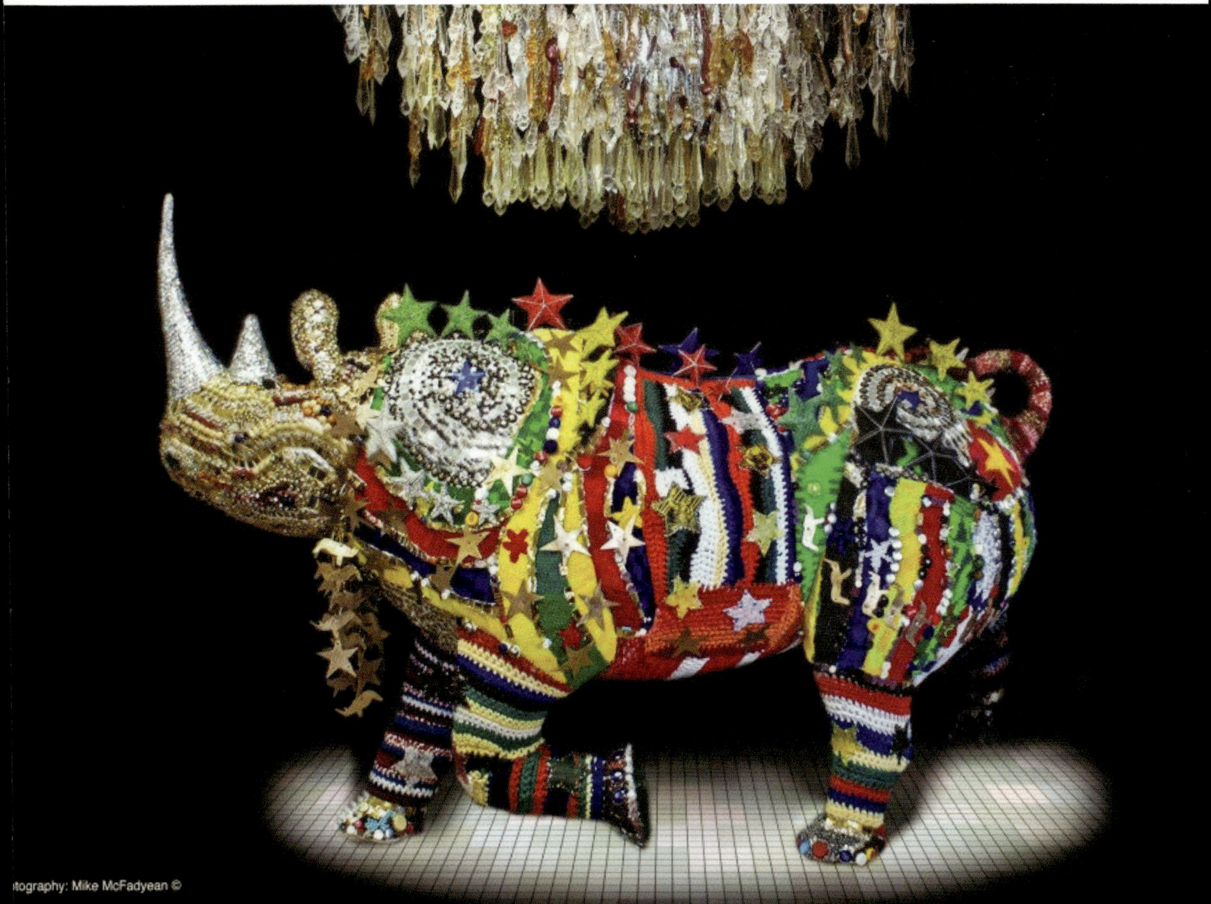

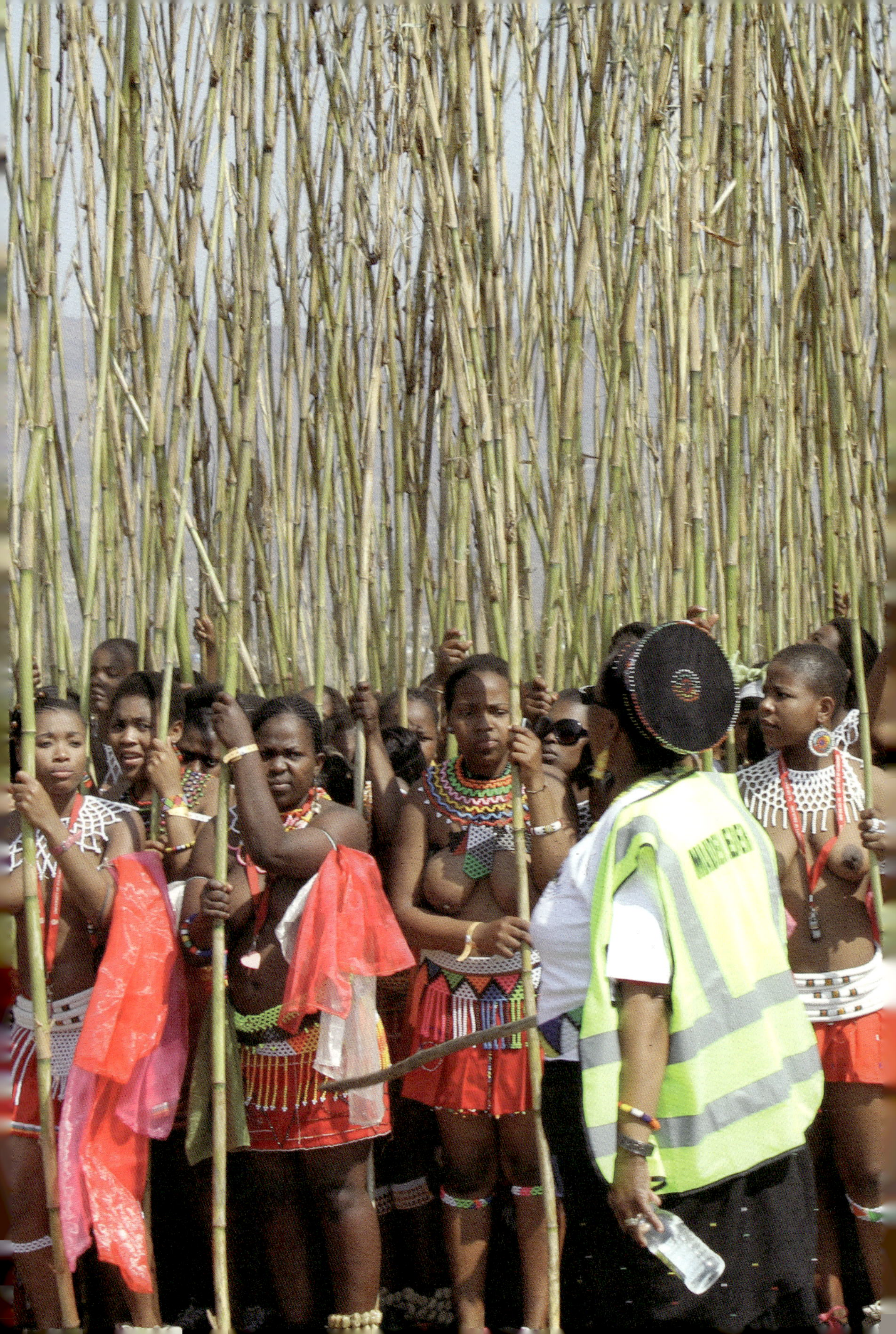

7

speaking of Zulu and national South African identity

In *Speaking with Beads,* Jean Morris and Eleanor Preston-Whyte comment that:

> *...Contemporary beadwork 'speaks' not only of personal adornment and money-making, but on appropriate occasions, of nationalism and ethnic identity. (Morris and Preston-Whyte, 1994: 89).*

The *Umhlanga* or Reed Dance is held every year in early spring to mark the cutting of the first reeds of the year by groups of young women and girls drawn from across Zululand, and sometimes from even further afield. The reeds harvested during the ceremony are used for renewing the thatched roofs of the various royal residences, together with the fences that surround each residence, particularly in the Zulu capital of Nongoma where the ceremony takes place. The ceremonial role played by traditional Zulu beadwork in the costumes of the participants in the *Umhlanga* make this event one of the most spectacular, popular and well-attended ceremonies of the Zulu royal calendar.

The harvesting of the reeds is followed by massed Zulu dancing in which the young women who have brought the reeds to the capital join with other groups of dancers made up of mature and older women and by men and youths. The dancers wear the Zulu traditional dancing regalia appropriate to their age and social status. It is a scene that has, in terms of its essentials, remained largely unchanged and might well have greeted Henry Francis Fynn when he visited the court of the great King Shaka on his travels through early Zululand.

What follows is a general outline of the main events that characterise the *Umhlanga.* It is based on observations made by the author, or other outside observers, of a number of the ceremonies held between 1992 and 2012. In order to convey the colour and drama, much of the description is written in the present tense. Most of the accompanying photographs were taken by professional photographers intent on capturing the grandeur and the political importance of the event. Among these were Jean Morris (Morris and Pretson-Whyte, 1994) and, more recently, Bruce Hopwood to whom the author is indebted for his recent photographs. Woven into the general description are comments made to the author by other spectators in 1992 and in 2005. These capture not only the general atmosphere of the occasion, but the positive reactions of onlookers who followed each stage of the ceremony with appreciation and enthusiasm.

Although by no means all of the large crowd of spectators who have gathered to watch the dancing are in traditional dress, most of the women have combined bead necklaces or bracelets with their normal Western attire. Many of the men and youths carry fighting sticks and, in some cases, a Zulu shield and a Zulu spear or *assegai.* Beadwork predominates in the dancing costumes of the women spectators who will later take their turn to dance in the public arena and it may feature also in the men's dancing regalia.

The maidens return to the capital with reeds they have gathered at the riverside. (BH)

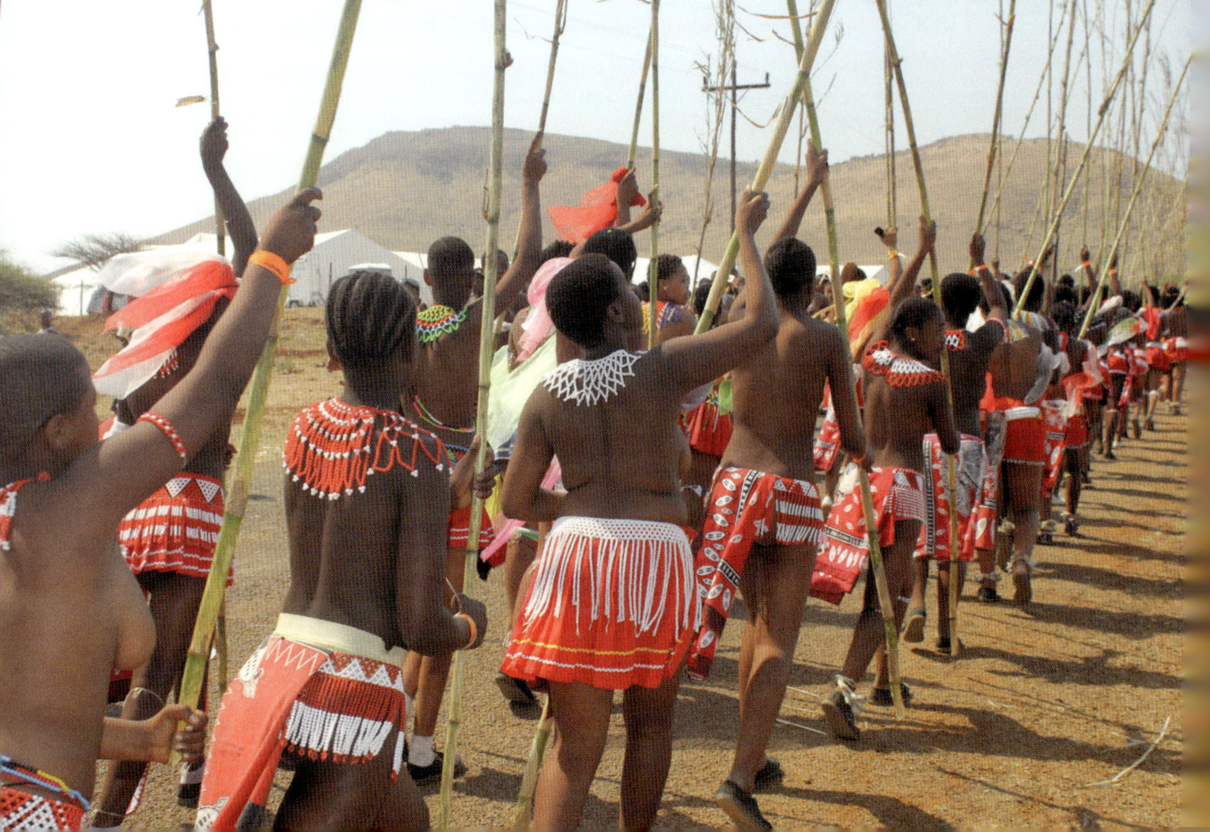

The latter is, however, made largely from animal skins with a headdress which is decorated by long and often colourful feathers.

The Reed Dance is the most public and well-known traditional Zulu ceremony and, besides the participants, it draws thousands of spectators and, increasingly, local and international tourists. It has, indeed, become a major tourist attraction and it is possible for non-Zulu speakers to book a place on a tour bus that includes the services of a knowledgeable local guide who explains not only the ceremony itself, but often the 'meaning' of the beadwork worn by the participants in the ceremony.

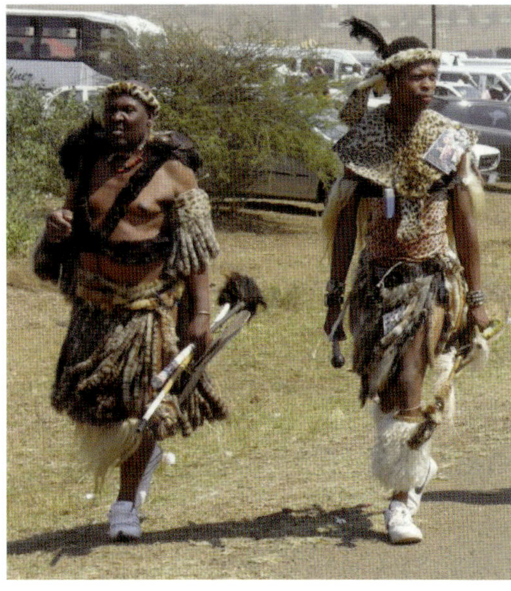

Two men in full Zulu ceremonial regalia as befits the occasion. (BH)

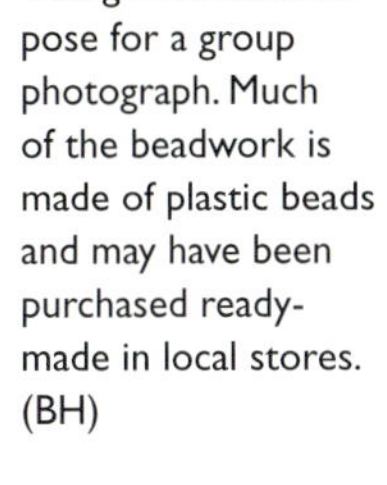

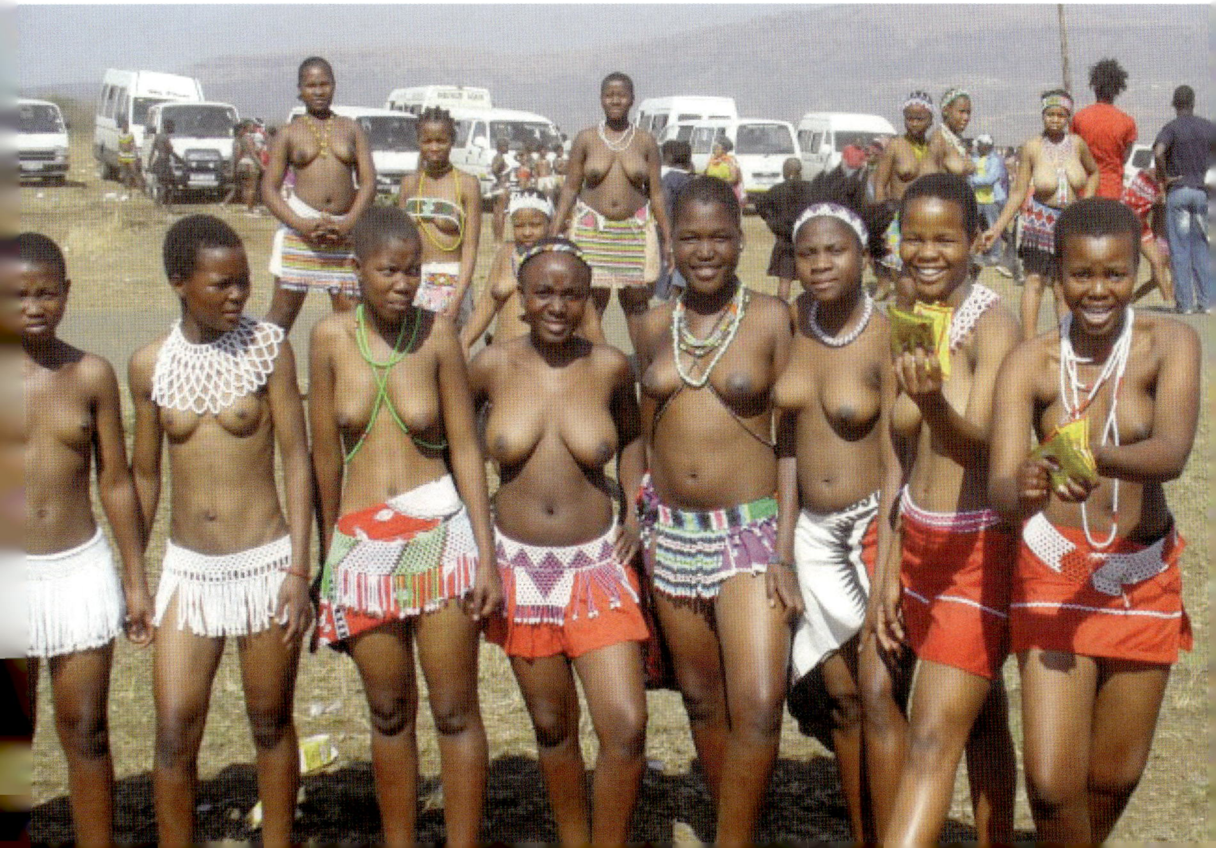

Young Zulu maidens pose for a group photograph. Much of the beadwork is made of plastic beads and may have been purchased ready-made in local stores. (BH)

Zulu beadwork, Zulu tradition and Zulu ethnic identity

The ambiance of the *Umhlanga* and of the massed dancing
is that of Zulu tradition and of the continuity between past
and present. Although the wearing of beadwork was once
eschewed by large sections of the Zulu community, it was kept
alive in areas where Christianity and education had not fully
penetrated. The same was true of many of the domestic and
family celebrations that marked important social transitions in
the life of the individual such as the attainment of marriageable
age by young women, and of marriage itself. A number of
other great festivals of the past, including the ceremony which
celebrates the harvesting of the first fruits of the new season,
also continue to be held, albeit often in an attenuated form, in
areas dominated by traditionalists.

Through the years these ceremonies have provided Zulu
women from traditional homes with regular opportunities to
put their bead making skills to use, not merely for beading
everyday wear, but also for public occasions that call for

Similar elaborate
bead necklaces
made with fairly
large beads. These
necklaces may have
been bought at the
local store. (BH)

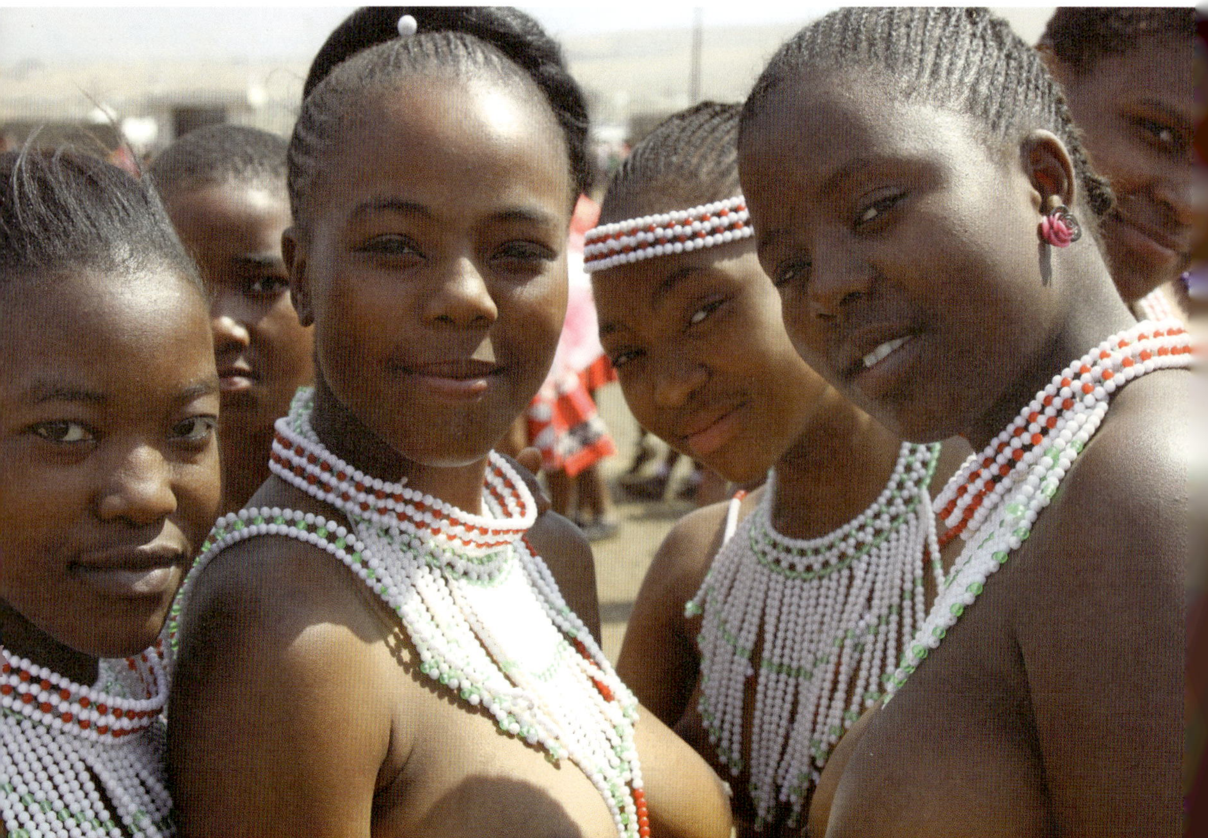

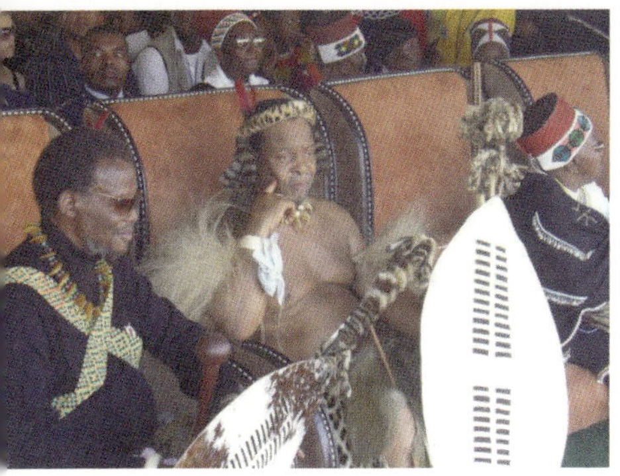

His Majesty, King Goodwill Zwelithini, surrounded by invited guests including Dr Mangosuthu Buthelezi (left) and a member of the Nazareth Baptist Church (right) who is identifiable by her characteristic beaded headdress. (BH)

elaborate and particularly striking beaded costumes. In this way beadwork skills and local beadwork styles are not only preserved, but over the years they have flourished and diversified. With the democratisation of South Africa came a renewed interest in the past on the part of black South Africans. This enthusiasm prompted a revival of a number of the ceremonies that had all but died out in many areas of KwaZulu-Natal. Among these was the *Umhlanga*, which, although it had once been one of the major events of the Zulu agricultural and ceremonial calendar, does not appear to have been celebrated in its entirety since it lapsed following the dismantling of the Zulu kingdom by the British during the reign of King Mpande. The ceremony was revived by His Majesty King Goodwill Zwelithini in the mid 1950s and it is often used by him as an occasion on which to speak directly to the youth of the nation. For instance, at the height of the HIV/AIDS epidemic the King took the opportunity to warn the

Married women are identified by their flared headdresses decorated with beads. (BH)

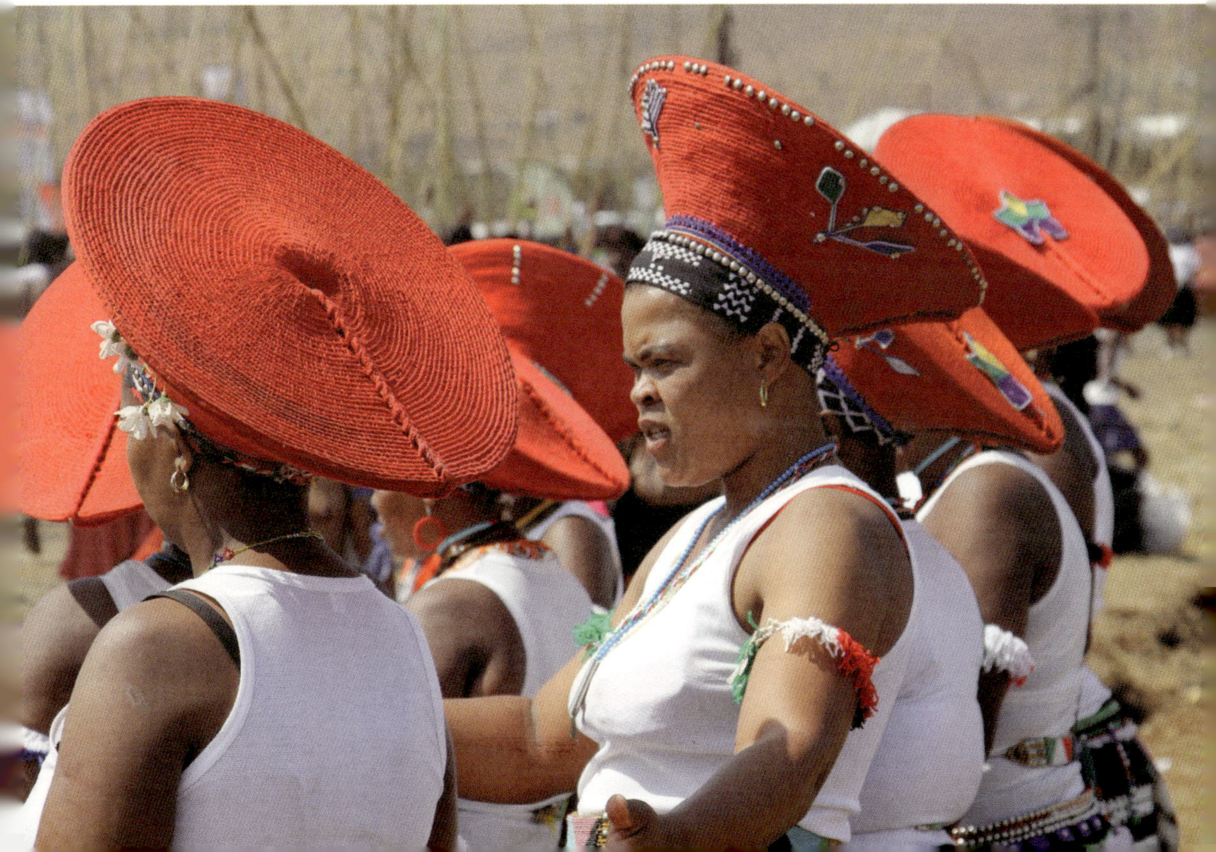

nation about the dangers of unprotected sex, going so far as to champion male circumcision, which was not then widely practised by Zulu-speaking people, as a protection against HIV infection.

The *Umhlanga* has important and potentially far-reaching political connotations, for among the invited guests seated on the stage alongside the King are often leaders of other African nations or their diplomatic and consular representatives. They too may wear the traditional dress of their countries and this adds to the colour and diversity of the occasion. In few cases, however, is beadwork a dominant feature of the costumes worn by non-South Africans, and if it is, there is little doubt that it pales into insignificance beside the profusion and variety of the Zulu beadwork worn, not only by the important members of the Zulu community who are among the invited guests on the stage, but by the row upon row of Zulu dancers who take their turn to dance in the central arena below the stage. Certainly there is little doubt in the minds of the Zulu-speakers present, which beadwork is the superior.

A Zulu maidens poses against a cloth decorated with a photograph of the Zulu Monarch, King Goodwill Zwelithini. (BH)

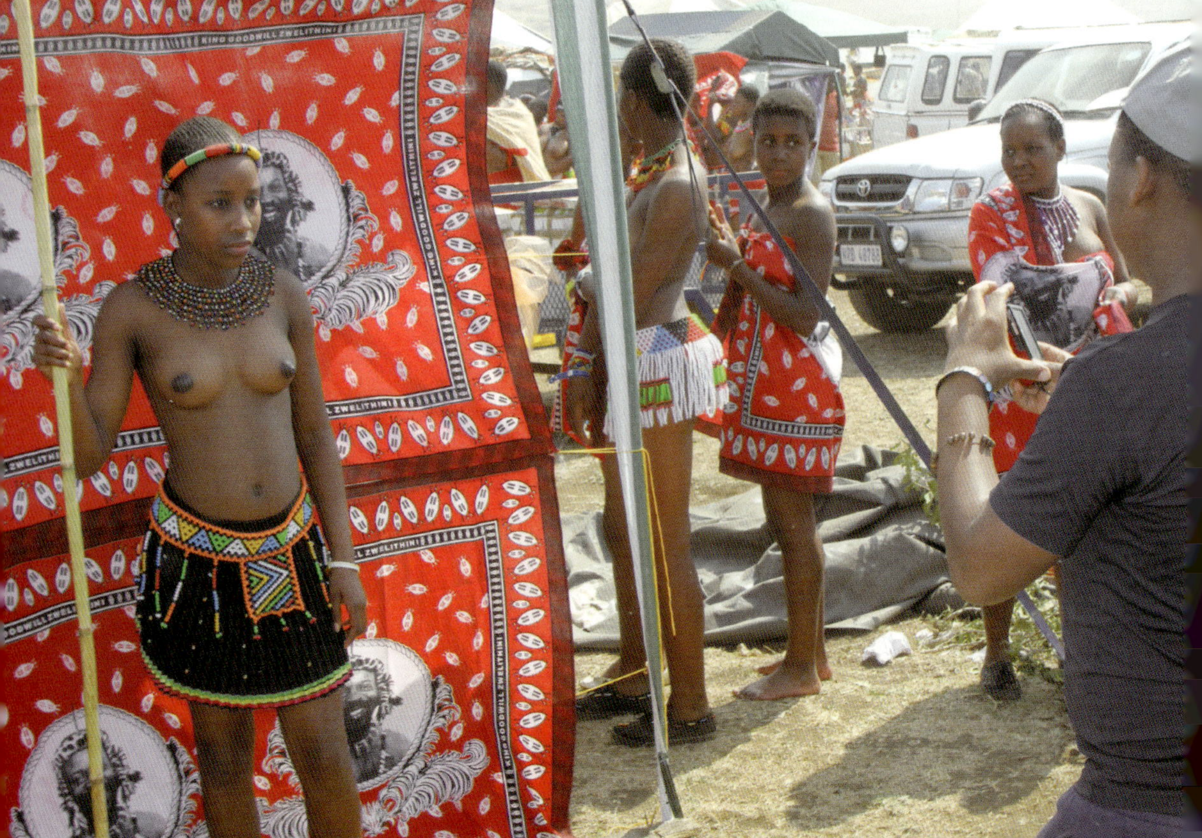

Beadwork, symbols and meaning

The *Umhlanga* has been likened to the harvest festivals once held in many parts of the world and echoed today by the taking of agricultural produce to be blessed in a number of Christian churches in early spring. It has, however, another and more important connotation. This is summed up in the term used to describe the girls and young women who are the focus of the ceremony and who are referred to throughout as 'maidens'. This is indicative not only of their unmarried status, but of the value placed in this context on virginity before marriage. In a recent television documentary made of the *Umhlanga* ceremony held in 2013, this point was made strongly, both by the presenter of the programme and by the young women participating in the ceremony, a number of whom were interviewed on camera.

As befits Zulu maidens, the young women are bare breasted. They wear broad bead necklaces in a lacy design, which decorate their shoulders and the upper part of their breasts. Bands of magnificent multi-coloured beadwork encircle

Young warriors hasten to join the dancing. (BH)

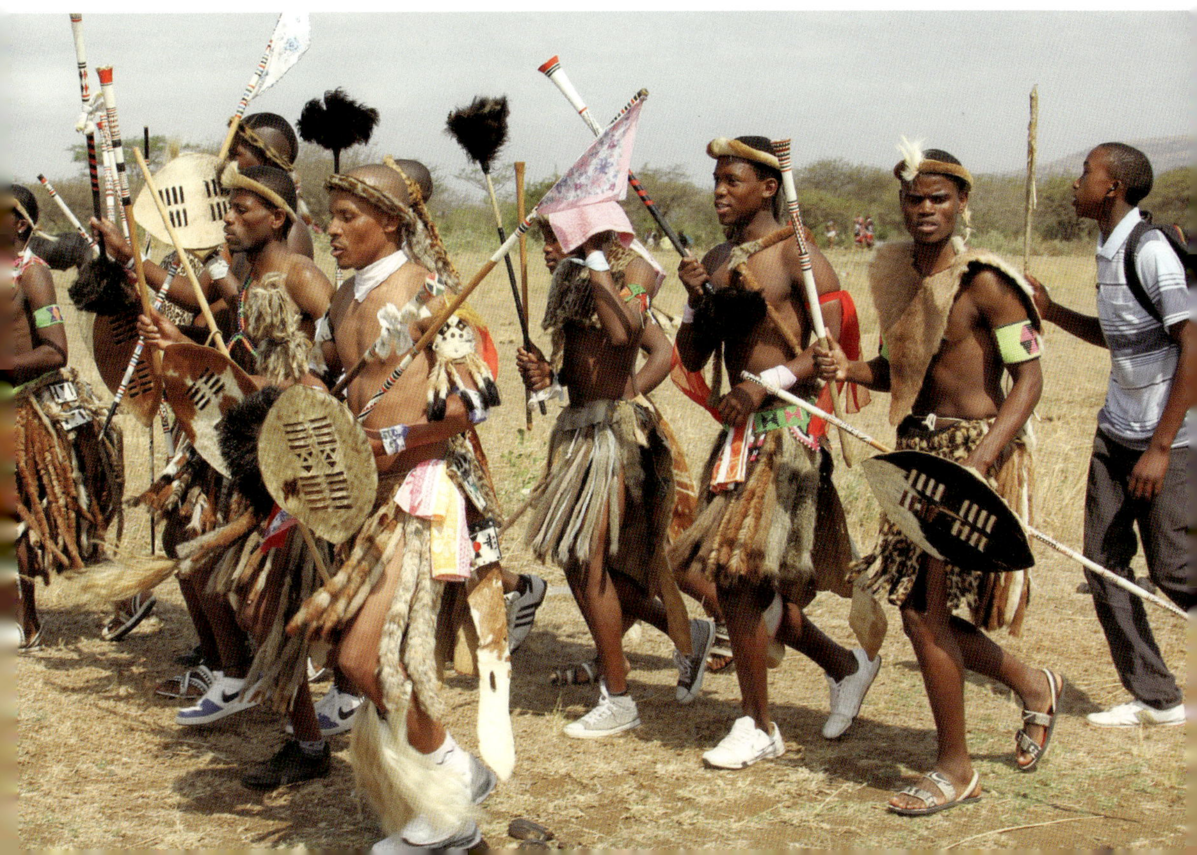

their waists and hips above short dancing skirts, to which
a profusion of beaded bands in contrasting colours and
patterns are attached. In many of these the colours and
patterns that predominate are those characteristic of the
area from which the members of the dancing teams come.
Although in the past the dancing costumes worn by the
maidens may have been made largely, if not entirely, with
glass beads, today plastic beads or a mixture of both glass
and plastic beads is now common. While they are not as
brilliant in colour as glass beads, plastic beads are on the
whole cheaper and come in a variety of sizes and 'modern'
colours. It is also now possible to purchase in local stores
ready-made dancing skirts made with fairly large plastic beads
along with strings of matching beads.

The girls participating in the ceremony are divided into two
categories based on age. The younger girls wear miniscule
skirts made of rolled bands of beadwork with fringed loin
coverings, while the older girls wear short pleated cloth
skirts, the tops of which are virtually hidden by roll upon roll.

A beaded girdle
typical of the
Nongoma area. (BH)

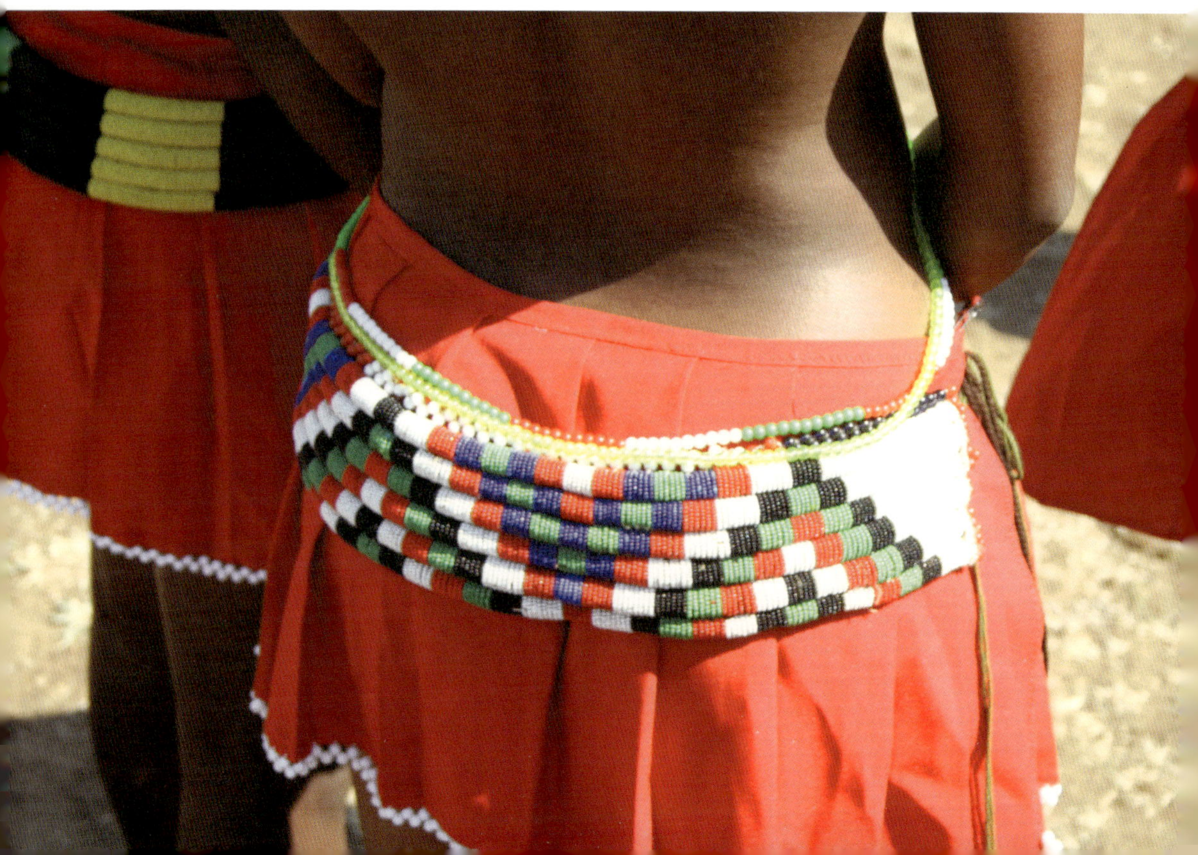

of multi-coloured beadwork. Slight decorative changes tend to be introduced into the costume details each year as local fashions change and new materials and even new bead colours become available. In 1972, for instance, some of the younger group of maidens wore long green woollen sashes decorated with red and white pom-poms around their hips, together with decorative beaded headbands. In 2007 the woollen sashes had been replaced by long scarves of white tulle which fluttered in the wind as the young women moved and danced. The maidens are always barefooted, but their ankles may be decorated with beaded or leather anklets. Dancers from the Nazareth Baptist Church stand out by virtue of their characteristic beadwork in which geometric designs are built upon a pure white background.

The young women sing what are described as 'traditional' songs appropriate to the occasion which they have been practising in the weeks leading up to ceremony. These songs can be heard as the young women go to the river and when they return to the capital carrying the reeds they have

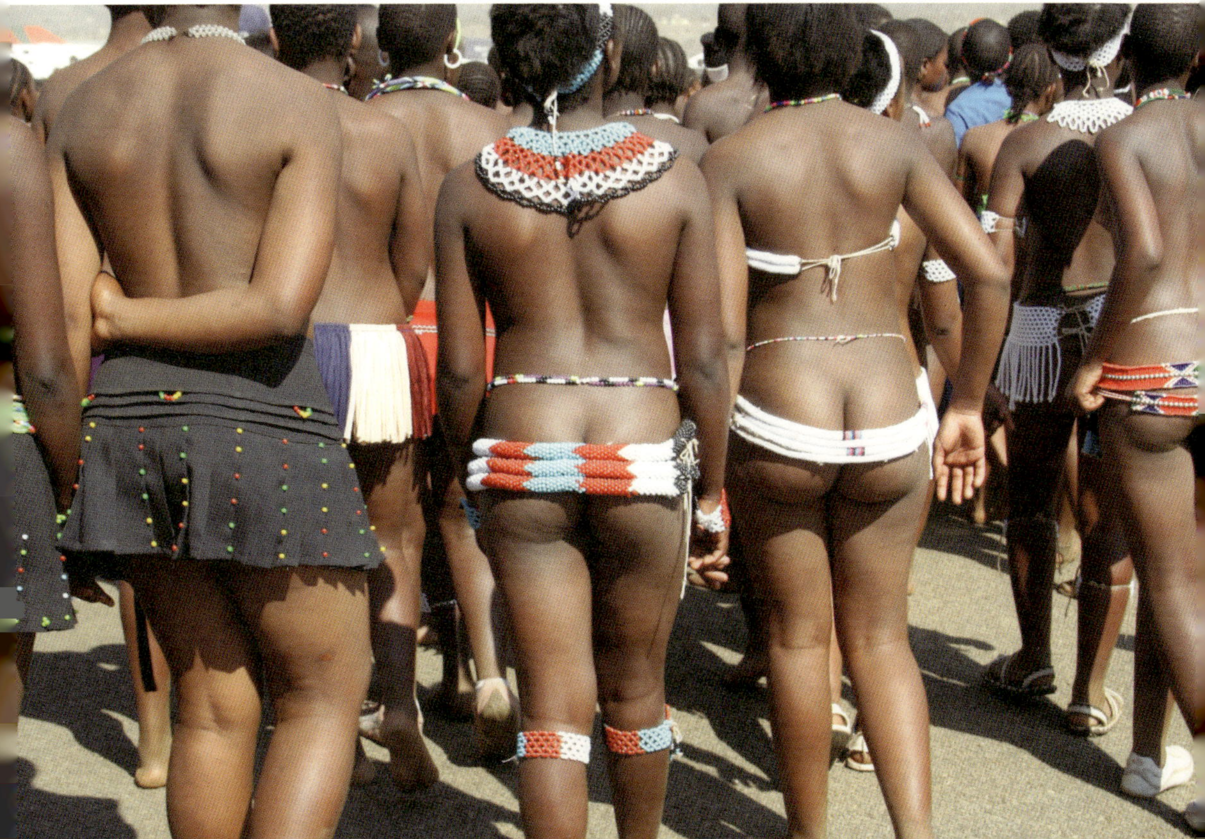

Maidens wearing a range of different skirts and loin coverings. (BH)

harvested. New songs may also be composed especially for the ceremony, but in both cases there is an element of secrecy about the words, and particularly about their exact meaning. Indeed, it is knowledge of these songs that distinguishes the girls and young women who have participated as maidens in *Umhlanga* ceremonies from those who have not. As they grow older and marry, most will attend future Reed Dances, and may eventually come to be leading figures in the organisation of these ceremonies and in the preparation and training of new generations of Zulu maidens.

The other active participants in the ceremony are the older women, or as they are often referred to in the press, the 'matrons', who wear the appropriate costume and beadwork for their age and marital status. They are the girls' mentors, and it is they who have played a major role in organising the ceremony and who direct proceedings throughout the day and orchestrate the massed dancing which follows the return of the maidens from river bank bearing the all-important thatching reeds. When it is their turn to dance, the matrons

Maidens holding the reeds awaiting instructions. (BH)

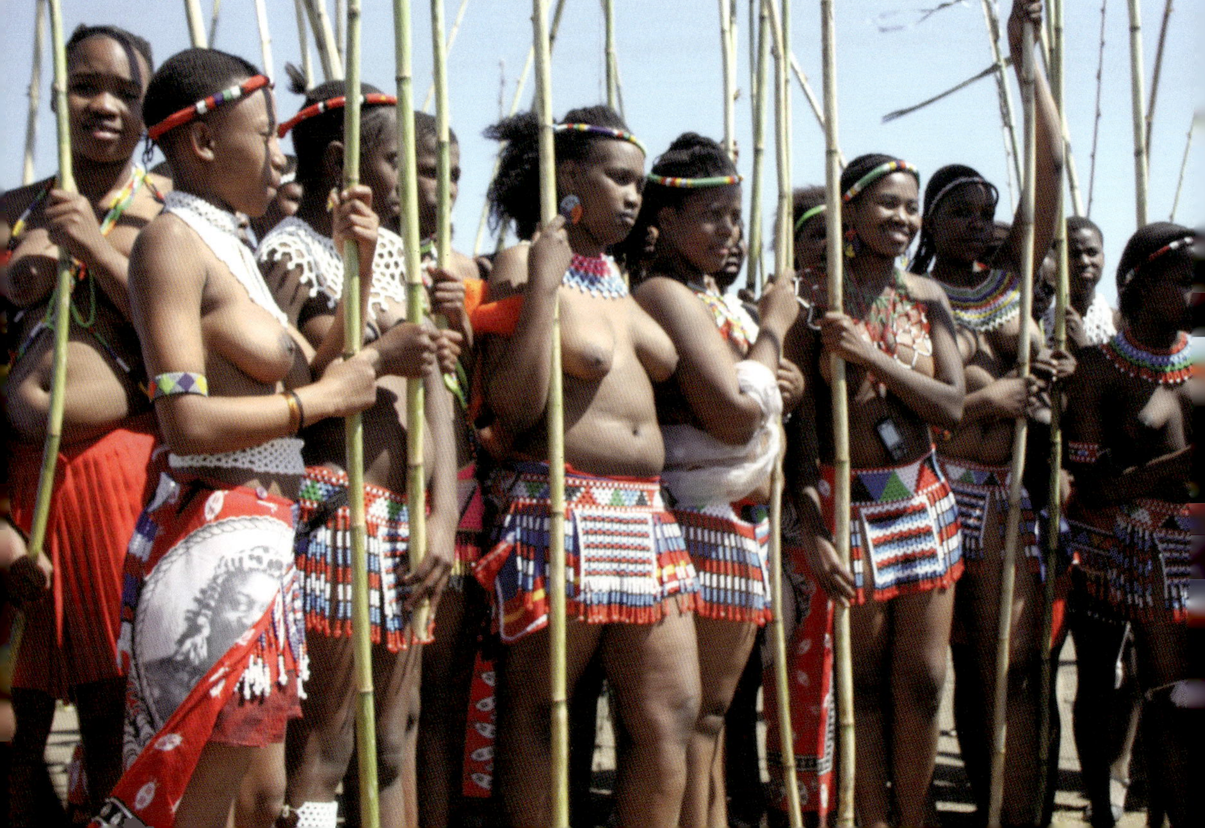

do so with gravity and the skill honed by years of practice. Their tall headdresses and leather skirts are decorated with magnificent beadwork panels, many of which indicate the area from which they come, while in others, the bead maker may introduce new and often novel motifs and colour combinations. Here again the interplay of continuity and change that is characteristic of contemporary Zulu beadwork is clearly demonstrated.

As the dancing proceeds and the excitement of the onlookers increases, it often happens that an elderly woman amongst the crowd gathered to watch the massed dancing, runs into the midst of the dancers singing and praising loudly. Her gesture is made to honour the dancers and their dancing skill and above all to celebrate what is often referred to as the 'coming of age' of the maidens who have now reached or are reaching the age when they can marry. Although the woman who is praising loudly may be dressed in ordinary western garb, her gesture is a traditional one, and is much appreciated and lauded both by the dancers, and by the watching crowd.

Participants and onlookers move towards the central dancing arena. (BH)

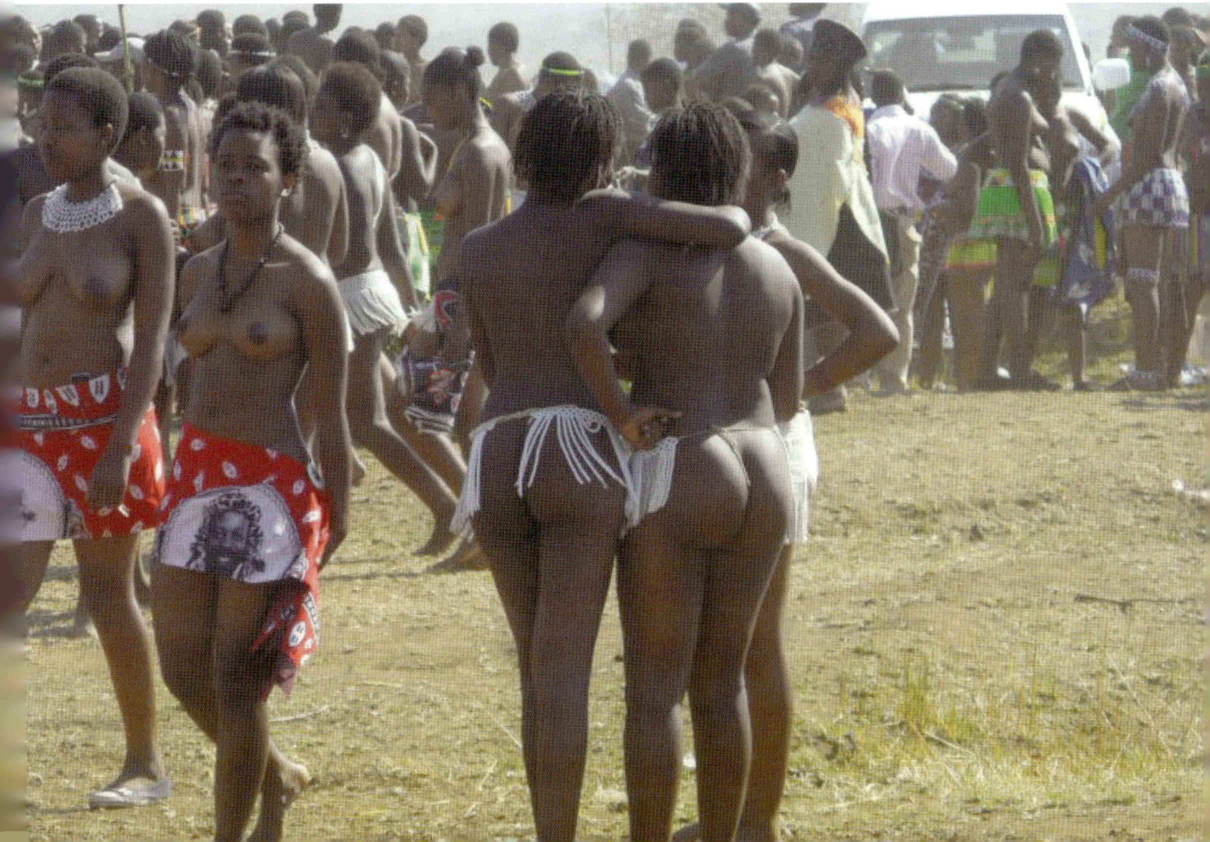

One after another the teams of dancing maidens and of senior men and women come and go in the arena and with each new team so the general excitement begins to reach fever pitch. Cameras click incessantly as both professional and amateur photographers seek to record the scene. Camera teams from local and even international television networks record the dancing and seek interviews with the main players in the ceremony and also with members of the excited crowd of onlookers. The King's address to the Zulu people is recorded, and if he is willing, he or one of his senior counsellors may comment further on the content and purpose of his message to the assembled crowd. Many members of the crowd also wear traditional Zulu dress, and if they do not themselves own a complete traditional outfit, many of the women, in particular, wear at least one of the beaded Zulu headdresses that can be bought at a number of urban curio stores and even in local small supermarkets and trading stores in rural areas.

In the *Umhlanga* of 1972 many of the senior men attending the ceremony wore large bead panels in the style and colours of the Nongoma area, which echoed the beadwork of the women from the same area who sat nearby waiting their turn to dance. On the stage the King and his *imbongi* or praise singer formed the focal point of the ceremony. The former wore the feathered and beaded ceremonial dress of a senior Zulu warrior. In contrast the *imbongi,* whose role it is to recite the traditional praises of the monarch before he speaks, had chosen to wear an intricate knee length beaded necklace of traditional design but made in modern bead colours, and the stylish patterned trousers of a fashionable man about town.

On the stage behind the king and the *imbongi* sat important and honoured guests, amongst whom was a contingent of older women from the Nazareth Baptist Church who were easily identified by their characteristic headdresses decorated with bands of brightly coloured beads in geometric designs set against a white beaded background. Predominant also were members of the royal family, many of whom were wearing the beadwork of the Nongoma area. As row upon row of dancers came and went on the dancing floor below the King and his invited guests, each group was easily identified by the pattern and design of their beadwork and this added a competitive edge to the dancing, and with it, to the day's excitement.

It was clear that spectators had flocked from near and far to attend the ceremony, wearing whatever beadwork they owned, or could borrow for the occasion. For those who did not own beadwork themselves there were a number of small stalls set up by hawkers offering strings of beadwork and even complete traditional outfits that could be purchased along with the more usual snacks and cool drinks. Long before the King and his invited guests were due to arrive and the event was due to begin, the excitement was palpable. Onlookers cheered the arrival of the young women bringing the reeds they had cut by the riverside and the appearance of teams of their male supporters and dancers in traditional regalia.

The *Umhlanga* is invariably a long ceremony and in 1972 it did not get underway much before midday because many of the spectators and even some of the participants had made long journeys to reach Nongoma. From early morning coach after coach packed with excited participants and spectators had been arriving from surrounding areas and even as far afield as Durban. Crowds of local spectators had also been gathering since early morning, many hoping to secure a good vantage point from which to view the arrival both of the rival dancing teams and also of the invited guests who were accommodated on the central grandstand overlooking the dancing arena. This was shaded from the elements by a large open marquee the bright colours of which contrasted with, and in some cases, echoed, those of the costumes of the dancers.

Tourism and the Reed Dance

Among the crowd were a number of spectators made up both
of South Africans and of international tourists who had joined
one of the escorted tours mentioned earlier. The latter clustered
around their guide who, besides explaining the main elements
of the ceremony to them, organised opportunities for those
with cameras to take photographs or to video the proceedings.
One guide, indeed, seemed to know many of the participants
in the ceremony who laughingly posed for photographs, either
in groups or, upon request, with the tourists themselves.

In a number of other countries, colourful local customs and
'traditional' ceremonies have become the focus of tourist
interest. Just as in the case of the Zulu Reed Dance organised
tours can be taken to watch these events and, in some cases
what the tourist watches is not the real event itself, but a
staged performance based on the 'real' ceremony which is both
shorter and less taxing for the audience than attending 'the real
thing'. The attraction for tourists visiting the Zulu Reed Dance
is, to quote one of the international 'guests', that they were not
only witnessing 'a real ceremony', but had had the opportunity
to see important local leaders and particularly the Zulu King
'in the flesh'. For them the colour and excitement of the Reed
Dance was, to quote another of the tourists, 'an experience of a
lifetime'. One elderly woman remarked as she was boarding the
bus in order to return to her Durban hotel after the ceremony
held in 2012:

> Whoever would have thought that I would be present at a
> real Zulu Ceremony … and after all these years of reading
> and seeing films about the wars of colonial times…It is just
> wonderful that all this has survived … and I am so glad that
> all this wonderful beadwork is still made … Look, I have bought
> this beautiful necklace from one of the stalls over there. It will
> remind me of my visit to South Africa every time I wear it.

Mingling with the excited crowds it was a simple matter for
the author to exchange pleasantries with bystanders and to

gauge the reactions of the growing number of enthusiastic
onlookers to the ceremony, and, in particular to the profusion
of beadwork that many of the spectators had donned for the
occasion. The general feeling was summed up in the words of a
young black man who had come all the way from Durban with
his wife and children, and who was dressed in a smart business
suit adorned by a long bead necklace:

> *These traditional ceremonies are great…even though I am
> a committed Christian I would not miss one for the world…
> I have ordered a full traditional outfit from the lady over
> there who sells them so that I can be properly attired next
> time… My wife has already bought a beadwork necklace
> and I think she will be buying some more before the day is
> out… she even wants a Zulu headdress and says she knows
> a shop that stocks them quite near our home.*

Overhearing our conversation the man standing next to him
observed: 'Yes! Traditional dress identifies me as a good South
African.' Both men admired the beaded skirt that I had worn to
the ceremony. As one commented 'I like to see a white person
wearing beads…it shows that you are one of us.'

These spontaneous comments made by two members of the
excited crowd that had gathered to watch the Reed Dance in
1972 illustrate an important point made in the introduction to
this book: over time Zulu beadwork has carried very different
meanings and messages, both for its viewers and for those
who have chosen to wear and make it. In many cases these
meanings are held simultaneously and, although the observer
may be completely unaware of it, herein lies much of the
continued fascination that contemporary Zulu beadwork holds
for those who view and wear it. In short, patterns woven in
multi-coloured beads mean different things to different people.
More important, Zulu beadwork often means different things to
the same person in different situations.

Beadwork in the wider South African context

Many countries have what are referred to as national or sometimes 'traditional' costumes, which are worn either for dancing on days of national importance, or when competing with other nations in the international sports arena. These often feature either distinctive local fauna or flora or distinctive styles of local weaving or embroidery. Although beadwork may not yet be a feature of national dress in this country, it was reported by Carey (1998) that at a meeting held by older women in two Sotho-speaking communities to discuss a suitable form of 'traditional dress' that would indicate their senior position in society, beadwork was specifically mentioned as being an appropriate possibility. Carey also reminds us that traditional dress was used on one historic South African occasion to transmit what was then a subversive political message. Although not Zulu in origin, it should be remembered that when Nelson Mandela was on trial for treason he chose to appear in court wearing a spectacular Thembu beaded collar. Photographs of this defiant action were not released until after the liberation struggle had been won and Nelson Mandela was President of South Africa.

Beaded necklaces, a headdress, beaded sticks and a Zulu 'love letter' for sale on the sidelines of the dancing arena. (BH)

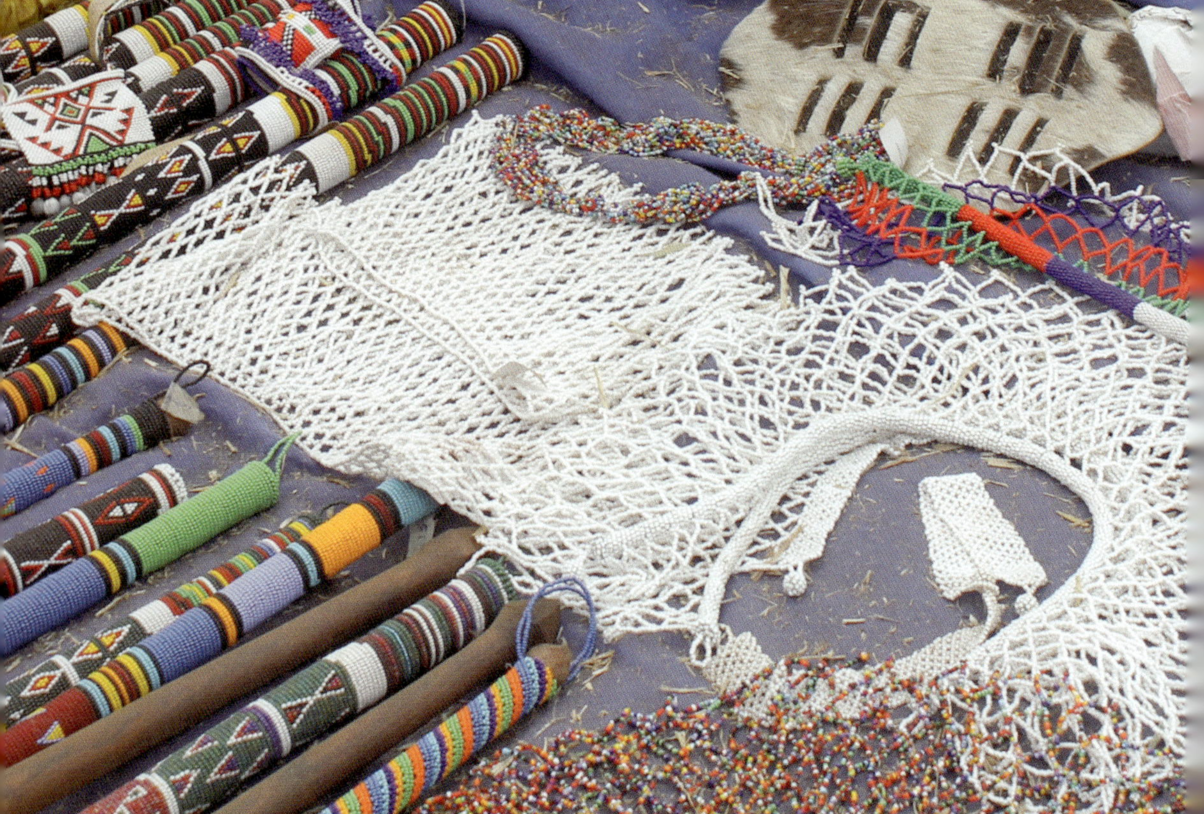

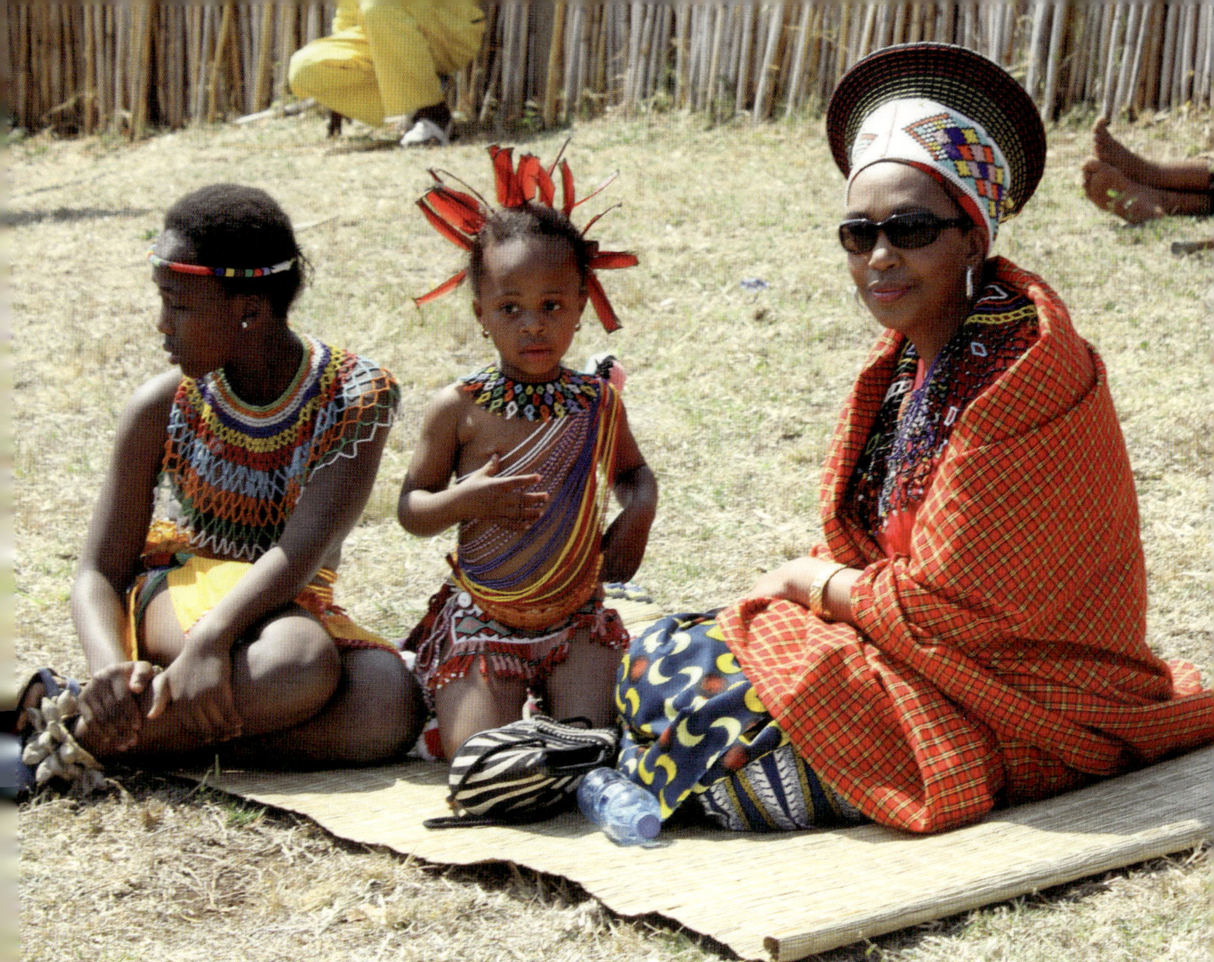

Since the fieldwork was undertaken upon which much of this book has drawn, the popularity of not only Zulu beadwork, but also that made in other areas of South Africa has continued to grow. Evidence of this is to be found in curio stores and on the shelves of fashionable boutiques and department stores. Although by no means all of this beadwork is locally made and some, indeed, is imported from other countries, the general use of beadwork as an item of fashion is assured, at least in the short term. In addition, beadwork has now expanded beyond the domain of fashion, and is a well established element in both interior design and in contemporary public art. Clear evidence of the value placed on beadwork in this country has been demonstrated by the issue of a set of South African stamps which have beaded animals and birds as their motif.

Taking a break during the ceremony. Note the broad beaded collar and headband worn by the older girl and the beaded headband of the mother's headdress which is reminiscent of the beadwork of the Nazareth Baptist Church. (BH)

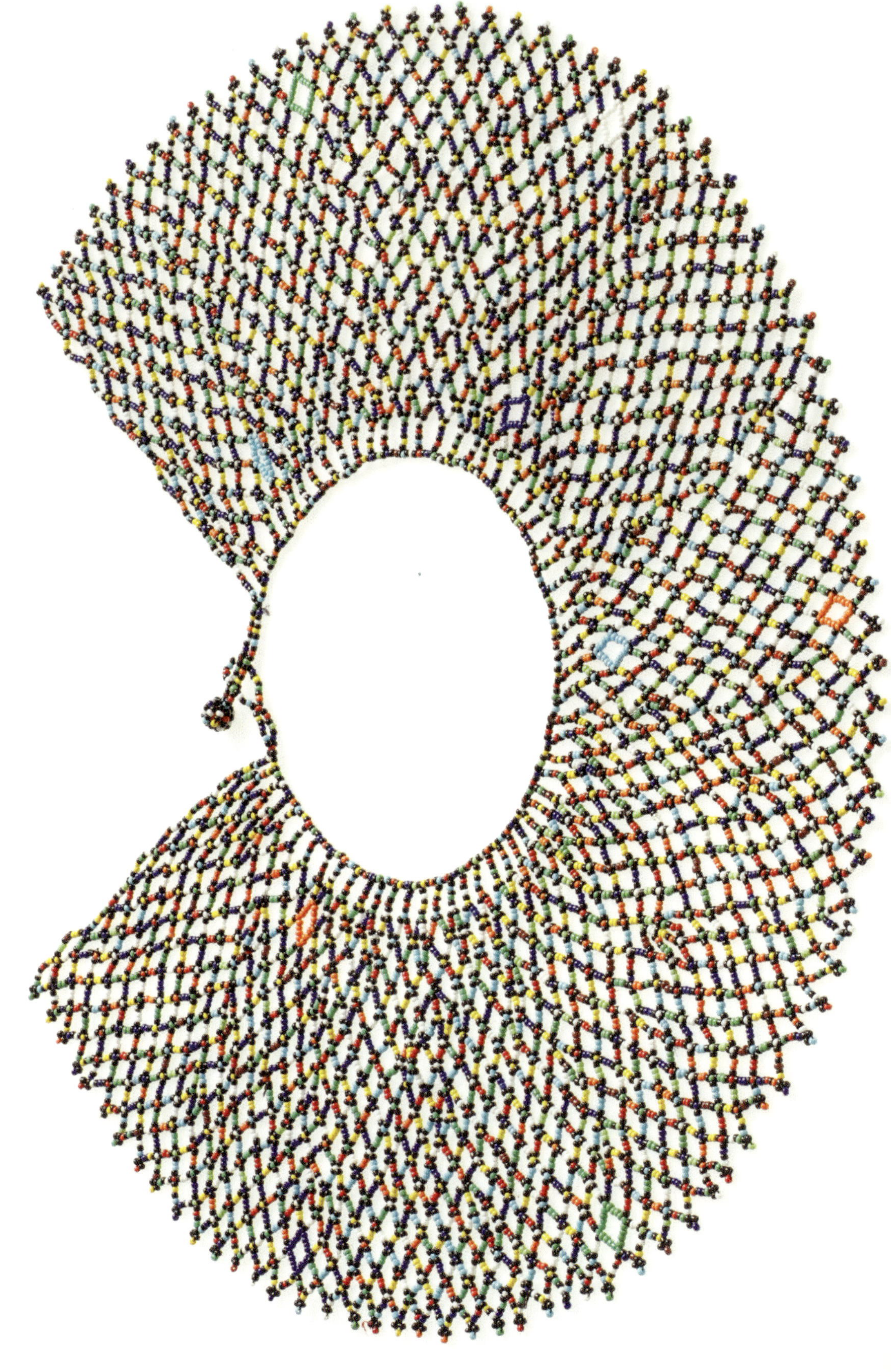

museums and galleries with significant holdings of Zulu beadwork

A beaded necklace which formed an integral part of the beaded dancing costume of the McCord Hospital choir and dancing team between 2000 and 2007.

DURBAN

THE CAMPBELL COLLECTIONS

The Mashu Museum of Ethnology and, in particular, the Jo Thorpe Collection of Zulu Beadwork is housed in the Muckleneuk Building of the University of KwaZulu-Natal. The Museum is situated off the main Durban campus at 220 Gladys Mazibuko Road, Durban. Zulu beadwork ranging from traditional to modern items are either on display or available for research purposes. The museum's holdings of early African Art Centre 'Bead Sculptures' discussed in Chapter 5 are particularly fine and varied. Also in the Collections are prints of, and original studies, by Barbara Tyrrell of Zulu and other South African beadwork.

Viewing is by appointment only. Contact Vusi Buthelezi on 031 260 0723
Email: campbellcollections@ukzn.co.za
http://campbell.ukzn.ac.za

THE DURBAN ART GALLERY

This is situated in the center of the city in the Durban City Hall. It is the current home of one of the beaded rhinoceroses discussed in Chapter 6 which is currently on display in the foyer of the building. On occasions this rhinoceros is lent to other institutions and, in order to avoid disappointment, visitors wishing to view it should check its whereabouts before visiting the Durban Art Gallery. Other interesting Zulu beadwork is on display in a number of the galleries.

Tel: +27(0)31 311 2229/8
http://www.durban-history.co.za/

KWA MUHLE MUSEUM
This museum is devoted to recording the history of colonial and
Apartheid Durban, but includes some fine early traditional Zulu
beadwork.
130 Bram Fisher Rd
Durban 4001
Telephone: 031 311 2237

PHANSI MUSEUM
This is a private museum run by the Phansi Museum Trust. It is
located in a large and historically interesting Victorian building
which is situated in the suburb of Glenwood on the Durban
Berea. The beadwork holdings of the Museum are varied and,
because it is associated with the Phansi Publishing Company, it
produces books and calendars featuring among other subjects,
traditional Zulu art and craft.
Tel:+27 (0) 31 206 2889
Email: info@phansi.com
http//www.phansi.com

PIETERMARITZSBURG

TATHAM ART GALLERY
Holdings include both traditional and modern Zulu beadwork
and attire.
Chief Albert Luthuli Road (opposite City Hall)
Phone +27(033) 392 2800/1
Fax +27 (9033) 394 9831

JOHANNESBURG

WITZ ART MUSEUM
(situated in Johannesburg)
Corner Jan Smuts Avenue and Jorisson Street, Braamfontein.
This is an excellent and extensive collection, particularly of
traditional Zulu beadwork. The research value of the collection
has been considerably increased as a result of recent work,
both by local and international beadwork experts and by senior
students working towards higher degrees.
https://www.facebook.com/Witz Art Museum

ESHOWE

VUKANI MUSEUM
(situated in Eshowe)
Although the major focus of attention is placed on Zulu
basketry, the Vukani Museum houses a small collection of Zulu
beadwork and, in particular, of Shembe beadwork. A well
stocked shop now sells the distinctive local Zulu beadwork for
which Vukani is becoming increasingly well known and which
is discussed in Chapter 6. A project to digitalise all Museum
holdings is under way, but at the time of writing, is not yet
available to the public.
Tel: +27 (0)35 474 5274
Email: vukanimuseum@lantic.net

9

Where to purchase Zulu beadwork

CRAFTERS

eTHEKWINI COMMUNITY FOUNDATION
Kathryn Kure
Director
031 764 5094
083 252 0992
femkathryn@gmail.com
www.ecft.org.za
PO Box 4855, Durban 4000

HILLCREST AIDS CENTRE TRUST
Paula Thomson
Woza Moya Manager and Craft Co-Ordinator
031 765 5866
wozamoya@hillaids.org.za
www.hillaids.org.za
PO Box 2474, Hillcrest 3650

BRUCE HOPWOOD
Photographer and Web Designer
035 340 7013
083 301 2958
bruhop@mweb.co.za
www.toadtree.co.za

INFO4AFRICA
Debbie Heustice
Director
031 260 2975
082 909 7886
heusticed@info4africa.org.za
www.info4africa.org.za
info4africa, Hut 10, Howard College Campus,
University of KwaZulu-Natal, Durban 4041

SIYAZAMA PROJECT
Linda Rethman
Siyazama Marketing and Sales
082 806 5949
linda@goldenrays.co.za

UBUNYE CO-OPERATIVE
Patricia Zungu
Chairperson
031 260 2975
071 922 0015
theubunyecoop@gmail.com
www.theubunyecoop.wordpress.com
Ubunye Co-Operative, Mzimela Outreach Centre,
Ngoye Forest Road, Kwapelisilwane Sub-Ward,
Mzimela Tribal Authority, Mtunzini 3867
c/o PO Box 1963, Mtunzini 3867

UKHAMBA CRAFT
Wendy Chatterton
Facilitator and Designer
031 765 3494
082 431 3617
ukhambacraft@telkomsa.net
www.ukhambacraft.co.za
Ukhamba Craft, Department of Education Grounds,
Buthulezi Road, Hammarsdale 3670
PO Box 428, Hillcrest 3650

UMCEBO DESIGN
   Robin Opperman
   Creative Designer
   031 301 6723
   083 793 3408
   robin@umcebodesign.co.za
   www.umcebodesign.co.za
   Umcebo Design, C/O Birthright, 171 Bulwer Road,
   Glenwood, Durban
   PO Box 10073, Marine Parade, Durban 4056

VUKANI, FORT NONGQAYI MUSEUM VILLAGE
   Vivienne Garside
   Craft Facilitators
   By appointment
   035 474 5274 OR 035 474 2281
   vukanimuseum@lantic.net OR zhm@umlalazi.org.za
   www.eshowemuseums.org.za
   Vukani, Fort Nongqayi Museum Village, 7 Nongqayi Road,
   Eshowe 3815
   PO Box 38001, Emlalazi 3894

ZULU BEADWORK PROJECT
   Janet Shaw
   Designer
   082 497 5977
   jayshaw@mweb.co.za

RETAILERS

AFRICA!IGNITE
    Craft Marketing & Supply
    Wilna Botha
    031 303 5482
    082 8284994
    wilna@Africaignite.co.za
    www.africaignite.co.za
    59 Henwood Road, Berea 4001

AFRICAN ART CENTRE
    Sharon Crampton
    Director
    031 312 3804/5
    africanartcentre@afri-art.co.za
    www.afriart.org.za
    African Art Centre, 94 Florida Road, Morningside,
    Durban 4001

HILLCREST AIDS CENTRE TRUST
    Paula Thomson
    Woza Moya Manager and Craft Co-Ordinator
    031 765 5866
    wozamoya@hillaids.org.za
    www.hillaids.org.za
    26 Old Main Road, Hillcrest
    PO Box 2474, Hillcrest 3650

KWAZULU-NATAL SOCIETY FOR THE ARTS
    KZNSA Gallery and Shop
    Curator
    031 277 1705
    083 673 4569
    curator@kznsagallery.co.za
    www.kznsagallery.co.za
    166 Bulwer Road, Glenwood, Durban 4001
    Postnet Suite 150, Private Bag X04, Dalbridge 4014

PHANSI MUSEUM AND SHOP
    Paul Mikula
    Director
    031 206 2889
    083 450 3270
    info@phansi.com
    www.phansi.com
    500 Esther Roberts Road, Glenwood, Durban 4001
    PO Box 17181, Congella 4013

WOZA MOYA SHOP, WINDERMERE CENTRE
    Paula Thompson
    Woza Moya Manager and Craft Co-ordinator
    031 765 5866
    wozamoya@hillaids.org.za
    www.hillaids.org.za
    Windermere Centre, Morningside, Durban 4001
    PO Box 2474, Hillcrest 3650

VUKANI, FORT NONGQAYI MUSEUM VILLAGE
    Vivienne Garside
    Craft Facilitators
    By appointment
    035 474 5274
    035 474 2281
    vukanimuseum@lantic.net OR zhm@umlalazi.org.za
    www.eshowemuseums.org.za
    Vukani, Fort Nongqayi Museum Village, 7 Nongqayi Road,
    Eshowe 3815
    PO Box 38001, Emlalazi 3894

GUIDED TOURS
    For organised guided tours to attend selected local
    ceremonies at which beadwork is worn – Bruce Hopwood
    035 340 7013
    083 301 2958
    Email: bruhop@mweb.co.za
    www.toadtree.co.za

recommendations for further reading

THE FOLLOWING annotated list provides suggestions for further reading on Zulu Beadwork. The majority of these readings have been referenced in the text and appear in the full bibliography. In what follows, however, some guidance is provided on a number of issues which may be of interest to readers who wish to undertake a more in-depth study of the topic than is provided in this book, and those whose interests cover African craft in general, as opposed to beadwork alone. Highlighted also are texts documenting the impact of tourism and other growing commercial markets for African craft on the diversity and quality of much contemporary Zulu beadwork.

Grossert, J.W. *Zulu Craft.* Pietermaritzburg: Shuter & Shooter, 1978.

> This slim volume was based on extensive local research undertaken by the author in Natal and Zululand from as early as the 1940s in order to inform the teaching of local craft in black schools. At the time craft skills appeared to be dying out, particularly in areas dominated by Christian families from which the local scholars were largely drawn. In addition to writing this book, the author compiled a teaching manual on the topic and presented his research findings in a doctoral dissertation submitted to the University of Stellenbosch in 1978. The book provides a detailed description of indigenous Zulu crafts, with line drawings to assist in the teaching and preservation of these skills. It is still regarded as one of the basic and most authoritative texts on the subject.

Jolles, Frank. *African Dolls Afrikanische Puppen:the Dulger-Collection.* Arnoldsche: 2012.

> This book presents a fascinating and exhaustive review of a unique collection of beaded dolls made by related women living in the impoverished Msinga district of KwaZulu-Natal, which now make up the Dulger Collection in Munich. The book is informative and liberally illustrated and indicates clearly the development and impact of an outside market on the design and making of dolls originally used in courting as a means of communicating the interest felt by girls and young women in the young men of their choice.

Jules-Rosette, B. *The Messages of Tourist Art: an African Semiotic System in Comparative Perspective.* New York: Plenum Press, 1984

> Although first published nearly three decades ago, this volume which documents the impact and repercussions of the growth of so-called tourist art in Africa, provides a useful introduction to the broader topic of how local crafts are modified and often simplified to meet the relatively undemanding and uninformed trade in tourist memorabilia. The book is instructive and thought provoking and, besides providing a useful introduction to the topic of tourist art, outlines a suggestive theoretical model which has wide applicability in similar situations, both in Africa and elsewhere in the world.

Morris, Jean, and Eleanor Preston-Whyte. *Speaking With Beads: Zulu Arts from Southern Africa.* London: Thames and Hudson,1994.

> Published in 1994, this was one of the first exhaustive full-colour photographic records made of Zulu Beadwork. The photographs were taken by Jean Morris as she travelled around South Africa and were arranged for publication with the assistance of anthropologist Eleanor Preston-Whyte, who provided the associated text and explanation

of the contexts in which the beadwork was made
and worn. The impact of the growing tourist trade in
KwaZulu-Natal and the increasing demand for curio and
fashion beadwork as opposed to that made for personal
wear, is examined in some detail. The book concludes
with a detailed discussion of the combination of the so-
called 'traditional' and 'modern' Zulu beadwork worn in
the context of the annual Zulu Reed Dance celebrated at
the Zulu capital of Nongoma.

Nettleton, Anitra and David Hammond -Tooke(eds). *African Art
in Southern Africa/From Tradition to Township*. Johannesburg: AD
Donker,1989.

At the time when this collection of essays was put
together, there were few books that spanned the
transition from black rural art, or as it was then somewhat
scathingly referred to 'craft', to the art emerging in
the South African black urban areas or 'townships'.
The editors threw their net widely but judiciously and
creatively, and their different scholarly backgrounds
allowed them to draw upon the skills and knowledge of a
wide range of contributors. Re-reading the papers some
twenty years after the book first appeared, one is struck
not only by the variety of subject matter, but by the wide
ranging backgrounds and interests of the contributors,
many of whom have subsequently became well known
in African art circles. Although it is invidious to draw
attention to some chapters rather than others, today's
readers will find those by Sack and Koloane, the one on
early 'Street Art', and the other describing the Polly Street
'art scene', both instructive and thought provoking.

Preston-Whyte, Eleanor. "Zulu Bead Sculptors" in *African Arts*
vol. XX1 (Number 1) 1991.

The focus of this paper is on the makers of Zulu bead
sculptures rather than on the beadwork itself. A number
of family groups are identified and the homes and home

circumstances from which they came are illustrated
and described in order to provide an insight into the
environment from which the bead makers came, and
what influenced their choice of subject matter. The paper
adds depth to the analysis presented in chapter 9 of this
book, particularly in respect to the value of the theoretical
constructs of Jules-Rosette (1984) in understanding the
progression of, and changes in, Zulu beadwork as bead
makers responded to the lucrative tourists market that
developed in KwaZulu-Natal from the 1960s onwards.

Sciama, L.D. and Eicher, J.B. *Beads and Bead makers: Gender,
Material Culture and Meaning.* New York: Berg, 1998.
   Although little concerned with Zulu, or, indeed, South
   African beadwork, this collection provides a useful point
   of departure for comparisons of local South African
   beadwork and the characteristics of beadwork, not only of
   the African continent, but of elsewhere in the world and,
   indeed, of different historical periods. The emphasis on
   gender issues is a welcome one.

Thorpe, Jo. *It's Never too Early: African Art and Craft in KwaZulu-
Natal 1960-1969.*Durban: Indicator Press, 1994.
   This charming and informative book recounts the story
   of the pivotal role played by Jo Thorpe in the foundation
   and early days of the African Art Centre in Durban. One of
   her objectives was to provide a source of income for black
   women from the rural areas surrounding Durban, who
   were unable to obtain local employment, but who were
   skilled in a wide range of local crafts then still made in
   deep rural areas. Among these was traditional beadwork
   and, in time, the African Art Centre became the first port
   of call, not only for the more discerning tourist, but for
   local art lovers seeking high quality local craft and also the
   work of black artists whose artistic aspirations the staff of
   the Centre encouraged and supported.

Tyrrell, Barbara. *Tribal Peoples of Southern Africa*. Cape Town:
Books of Africa, 1968.

> Barbara Tyrrell's meticulous drawings of Southern African
> traditional dress are world renowned and evoke both
> vividly and in minute detail a past era that is increasingly
> valued and, increasingly used as a model for current
> African ceremonial dress. Exquisite line drawings which
> are enhanced by delicate colour washes are the hallmark
> of Tyrrell's art, which was recently celebrated by a
> retrospective of her work held in Cape Town.

Sellschop,Susan, Goldblatt, Wendy and Doreen Hemp (eds).
Craft South Africa/Traditional/Transitional/Contemporary,
Johannesburg: Pan Macmillan SA, *2002.*

> This is a beautiful and informative collection of illustrated
> essays on South African craft, including two contributions
> in which Zulu beadwork is shown and briefly discussed.
> One of these features Siyazama beaded dolls discussed
> in this book. For those interested largely in Zulu
> beadwork, the value of the collection lies in that it allows
> comparisons to be made between Zulu Beadwork and
> other South African beadwork traditions, such as Ndebele
> and Pedi beadwork. It also indicates how beading may be
> used to enhance other craft mediums, as is illustrated by
> Perrill in a previous publication in this series (2012:9).

Wells, Kate, a Macdonald, Marsha, Dewhurst, C. Kurt and
Dewhurst, M. (eds). *SIYAZAMA:Art, AIDS and Education in South
Africa*. Pietermaritzburg: University of KwaZulu-Natal Press,
2012.

> This collection of essays is devoted to exploring the
> impact of a long standing HIV/AIDS intervention project
> focused on Zulu beadwork which was undertaken
> by members of the staff of the Durban University of
> Technology and Michigan State University Museum. It
> examines the underlying motivation for the project and its
> theoretical underpinnings, followed by an assessment of

its impact and degree of success. The latter is presented
through the personal stories of a number of the local
participants in the project, whose profiles, together with
exerpts from their discussions on the value of the project
to them and their families, are quoted in some detail.
The main product of the project was, and continues to
be, distinctive beaded AIDS Dolls which are sold locally
and in some cases internationally. Within KwaZulu-Natal,
Siyazama has links with a number of other related bead
projects, including *Umsebo* which is also discussed in this
book.

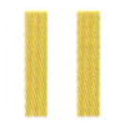

bibliography

Angas, G.F. *The Kaffirs Illustrated* – 1849 Facsimile. Cape Town: A Balkema, 1974.

Berglund, Axel-Iver. *Zulu Thought-Patterns and Symbolism.* Cape Town: David Philip, 1976.

Brottem, Bronwen,V. and Lang, Anne. "Zulu Beadwork" in *African Arts VI (3) 8-13,* 1973.

Bryant, Alfred, T. *Olden Times in Zululand and Natal.* London: Longmans, 1929.

Carey, Margret. "Gender in African Beadwork", in Sciama, Lidia, D and Eicher, Joanne,B. (eds). *Beads and Bead Makers: Gender, Material Culture and Meaning.* Oxford and New York: Berg, 1998.

Fynn, Henry Francis. *The Diary of Henry Francis Fynn.* Pietermaritzburg: Shuter and Shooter, 1990.

Jules-Rosette, B. *The Messages of Tourist Art: An African Semiotic System in Comparative Perspective.,* New York: Plem Press, 1984.

Graburn, Nelson. *Ethnic and Tourist Art.* Los Angeles: University of California Press, 1976.

Grossert, J. W. *Zulu Crafts.* Pietermaritzburg: Shuter and Shooter, 1978.

Klopper, Sandra. "The Art of Traditionalists in Zululand – Natal" in. Hammond-Tooke, D. Nettleton, A. J. (eds.) of catalogue, *Ten Years of Collecting (1979-1989.* Johannesburg: Johannesburg Art Galleries Collection: 32- 38, University of the Witwatersrand, 1989.

Jolles, Frank. "Interfaces between Oral and Literate societies: Contracts, runes and bead work" in Sienaert, E.R; Bell, A.N. and Lewis, M. (eds). *Oral Tradition: New Wine in Old Bottles?* Durban: Natal University Oral Documentation Research Centre, 1991.

Jolles, Frank. *African Dolls: The Dulger-Collection*, Germany: Arnoldsche, 2010.

Krige, Eileen Jensen. *The Social System of The Zulus*, (esp. Appendix 11). Pietermaritzburg: Shuter and Shooter, 1936.

Levinsohn,R *Symbolic Significance of Traditional Beadwork*, Black Art, 3(4): 29-45, 1979.

Morris, Jean. and Levitas, B. *South African Tribal Ornamentation, Beadwork and Clothing.* Kaapstad: College Press, 1987.

Morris, Jean. and Preston-Whyte, Eleanor. *Speaking with Beads.* London: Thames and Hudson, 1994.

Mthethwa, B.N. "Decoding Zulu Beadwork" in Sienart, E. and Bell N. (eds). *Catching Winged Words: Oral Traditions and Education.* Pietermaritzburg: Natal University Oral Documentation Centre, 1988.

Nason, J.D. "Tourism, Handicrafts, and Ethnic Identity in Micronesia", *Annals of Tourist Research,* 11: 421-449, 1984.

Ngubane, Harriet. *Body and Mind in Zulu Medicine.* London: Academic Press, 1977.

Perrill, Elizabeth. *Zulu Pottery.* Cape Town: Print Matters, 2012.

Preston-Whyte, E. "Zulu Bead Sculptures" in *African Arts xxiv, 1,* 1991.

Preston-Whyte, Eleanor, M. "Contexts of Vulnerability: sex, secrecy and HIV/AIDS" in *AJAR 2(2) 89-94,* 2003.

Preston-Whyte, Eleanor, and Thorpe, Jo. "Ways of Seeing, Ways of Buying: Images of Tourist Art and Culture Expression in Contemporary Beadwork" in Hammond-Tooke, D and Nettleton, A. (eds). *African Art in Southern Africa : From Tradition to Township.* Johannesburg: AB Donker, 1989.

Sciama, Lidia, D. and Eicher, Joanne, B. (eds). *Beads and Beadmakers: Gender, Material Culture and Meaning.* Oxford and New York: Berg, 1998.

Sundkler, B. *Bantu Prophets in South Africa* (Second Edition).
London: Oxford University Press, 1961.

Thorpe, Jo. *It's Never Too Early: African Art and Craft in KwaZulu-
Natal, 1960-1990*. Durban: Indicator Press, Centre for Social
and Development Studies, University of Natal, 1994.

Twala, R.G. "Beads as regulating the social life of the Zulu and
Swazi" in *African Studies 10, 3, 113-123*, 1958.

Tyrrell, Barbara. *Tribal Peoples of Southern Africa*. Cape Town:
Books of Africa, 1968.

Sellschop, Susan; Goldblatt, Wendy, and Hemp, Doreen. *Craft
South Africa:Traditional / Contemporary*. Johannesburg: Pan
Macmillan SA, 2002.

Schoeman, H. S. "A Preliminary Report on Traditional Beadwork
in the Mkhwanzi Area of the Maputuland District Zululand"
(Part One), *African Studies, 2, 57-81*, 1968a.

Van Heerden, Jannie. *Zulu Basketry*. Cape Town: Print Matters,
2009.

Vilakazi, Absolom. *Zulu Transformations*. Pietermaritzburg:
University of Natal Press, 1957.

Wells, Kate; MacDowell, Marsha; Dewhurst, C. Kurt and
Dewhurst, Marit (eds). *Siyazama, Art, AIDS and Education in
South Africa*. Pietermaritzburg: University of KwaZulu-Natal
Press, 2012.

Williamson, Sue. *Resistance Art in South Africa*. Cape Town.
David Philip,1989.